THE

NORTON SCORES

An Anthology for Listening

Fourth Edition · Standard

THE

NORTON SCORES

An Anthology for Listening

FOURTH EDITION • STANDARD

EDITED BY

ROGER KAMIEN

ASSOCIATE PROFESSOR OF MUSIC, QUEENS COLLEGE
OF THE CITY UNIVERSITY OF NEW YORK

W · W · NORTON & COMPANY

New York · London

Acknowledgments

The text translations for items 2 and 7 are by Dr. Yvette Louria.

The texts for items 23 and 30 are from *The Ring of Words* by Philip L. Miller. Reprinted by permission of Doubleday & Company, Inc., and Philip L. Miller.

The text translation for item 33 is taken from *Seven Verdi Librettos* by William Weaver. Copyright © 1963 by William Weaver. Reprinted by permission of Doubleday & Company, Inc.

The text translation for item 48 is reprinted through the courtesy of London Records, a Division of PolyGram Classics, Inc.

The text for item 53 is from Federico García Lorca, *Selected Poems.* Copyright 1955 by New Directions Publishing Corporation. Reprinted by permission of New Directions Publishing Corporation.

Page makeup and highlighting by Roberta Flechner.

Published simultaneously in Canada by
Penguin Books Canada Ltd,
2801 John Street, Markham, Ontario L3R 1B4.

PRINTED IN THE UNITED STATES OF AMERICA.
Library of Congress Cataloging in Publication Data
Main entry under title:
The Norton scores.
    Includes index.
    Contents: v. 1. Gregorian chant to Beethoven—v. 2. Schubert to Glass.
    1. Music appreciation—Music collections.   I. Kamien, Roger.
MT6.5.N7   1984   83-19427

ISBN 0-393-95302-5

W. W. Norton & Company, Inc., 500 Fifth Avenue, New York, N. Y. 10110
W. W. Norton & Company Ltd., 37 Great Russell Street, London WC1B 3NU
    3 4 5 6 7 8 9 0

Contents

Preface

This anthology is designed for use in introductory music courses, where the ability to read music is not a prerequisite. The unique system of highlighting employed in this book enables students to follow full orchestral scores after about one hour of instruction. This system also has the advantage of permitting students who *can* read music to perceive every aspect of the score. It is felt that our system of highlighting will be of greater pedagogical value than artificially condensed scores, which restrict the student's vision to pre-selected elements of the music. The use of scores in introductory courses makes the student's listening experience more intense and meaningful, and permits the instructor to discuss music in greater depth.

The works included in this Fourth Edition have been chosen from among those most frequently studied in introductory courses. The selections range from Gregorian chant to the present day, and represent a wide variety of forms, genres, and performing media. To make this Fourth Edition reflect today's concert repertory more closely, increased emphasis has been placed on instrumental and secular music of earlier periods and on music of the present century. A majority of the pieces are given in their entirety, while the others are represented by complete movements or sections particularly suitable for classroom study. Scenes from operas and some choral works are presented in vocal score, while all others are reprinted in their full original form. This anthology may be used independently, or along with any introductory text. The publishers have prepared a set of recordings to accompany *The Norton Scores*.

A few words about the highlighting system employed in the full scores: Each system of score is covered with a light gray screen, and the most prominent line in the music at any given point is spotlighted by a white band (see No. 1 in sample on page *x*). In cases where two or more simultaneous lines are equally prominent, they are each highlighted. When a musical line continues from one system or page to the next, the white highlighting band ends with a wedge shape at the right-hand margin, and its continuation begins with a reverse wedge shape (see No. 2 in sample). By following these white bands in sequence through the score, the listener will perceive the notes corresponding to the most audible lines. Naturally, the highlighting will not *always* correspond with the most prominent instruments in a specific recording, for performances differ in their emphasis of particular lines. In such cases, we have highlighted those parts that, in our opinion, *should* emerge most clearly. (There are occasional passages in complex twentieth-century works where no single line represents the musical continuity. In such passages we have drawn the listener's attention to the most audible musical events while endeavoring to keep the highlighting as simple as possible.) To facilitate the following of highlighted scores, a narrow white band running the full width of the page has been placed between systems when there is more than one on a page.

It must be emphasized that we do not seek here to *analyze* melodic structure, contrapuntal texture, or any other aspect of the music. The highlighting may break off before the end of a phrase when the entrance of another part is more audible, and during long-held notes the attention will usually be drawn to more rhythmically active parts. The highlighting technique has been used primarily for instrumental music; in vocal works, the text printed under the music provides a firm guideline for the novice score-reader.

A few suggestions for the use of this anthology may be found useful:

1. The rudiments of musical notation should be introduced with a view to preparing the student to associate audible melodic contours with their written equivalents. It is more important for beginning students to recognize rising and falling lines, and long and short notes, than to identify specific pitches or rhythms. It is helpful to explain the function of a tie, and the layout of a full score.

2. Before listening to a work, it is best for students to familiarize themselves with the names and abbreviations for instruments used in that particular score (a glossary of instrumental names and abbreviations will be found at the conclusion of the book). We have retained the Italian, German, French, and English names used in the scores reproduced in this· anthology. This exposure to a wide range of terminology will prepare students for later encounters with scores.

3. Students should be careful to notice whether there is more than one system on a page of score. They should be alerted for tempo changes, repeat signs, and *da capo* indications. Since performances often differ, it is helpful for the instructor to forewarn the class about the specific repeats made or not made in the recordings used for listening.

4. When a piece is very fast or difficult, it is helpful to listen once without a score.

5. It is best to begin with music that is relatively simple to follow: e.g. (in approximate order of difficulty) Handel, *Comfort ye* from *Messiah;* the first and third movements of Mozart's *Eine kleine Nachtmusik;* the Air from Bach's *Suite No. 3 in D major;* and the second movement of Haydn's *Symphony No. 104 in D major* (*London*).

6. Important thematic material and passages that are difficult to follow should be pointed out in advance and played either on the recording or at the piano. (We have found that rapid sections featuring two simultaneously highlighted instruments sometimes present difficulties for the students—e.g. Beethoven, *Symphony No. 5*, first movement, m. 65 ff.)

We have attempted to keep the highlighted bands simple in shape while showing as much of the essential slurs and dynamic indication as possible. Occasionally, because of the layout of the original score, stray stems and slurs will intrude upon the white area and instrumental directions will be excluded from the highlighting. (Naturally, the beginning of a highlighted area will not always carry a dynamic or similar indica⁺ tion, as the indication may have occurred measures earlier when the instrument in question was not the most prominent.) As students become more experienced in following the scores, they can be encouraged to direct their attention outside the highlighted areas, and with practice should eventually develop the skill to read conventional scores.

I should like to record here my great debt to the late Nathan Broder, who originated the system of highlighting employed here and whose advice and counsel were invaluable. My thanks go also to Mr. David Hamilton, and to Claire Brook and Kathleen Wilson Spillane of W. W. Norton, for many helpful suggestions. I am most grateful to my wife, Anita, who worked with me on every aspect of the book. She is truly the co-editor of this anthology.

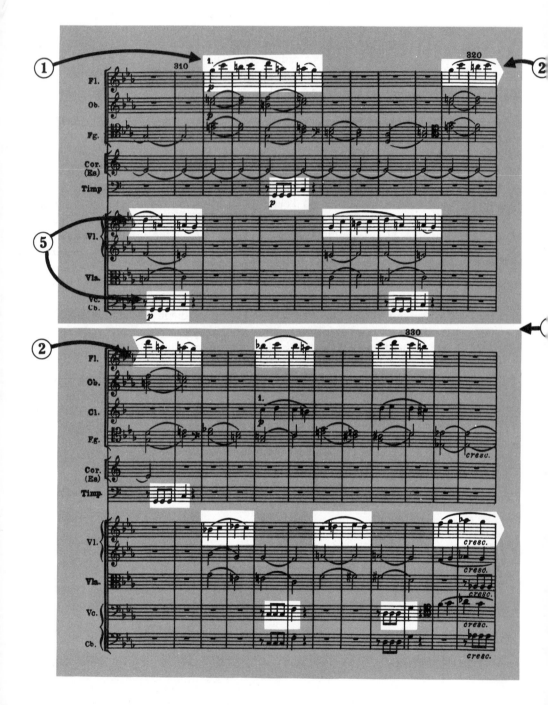

How to Follow the Highlighted Scores

1. The most prominent line in the music at any given time is highlighted by a white band.

2. When a musical line continues from one system (group of staffs) or page to the next, the white highlighted band ends with a wedge shape, and its continuation begins with a reverse wedge shape.

3. By following the highlighted bands in sequence through the score, the listener will perceive the notes corresponding to the most audible lines.

4. A narrow white band running the full width of the page separates one system from another when there is more than one on a page. It is very important to be alert for these separating bands.

5. When two or more lines are equally prominent, they are each highlighted. When encountering such passages for the first time, it is sometimes best to focus on only one of the lines.

A Note on Performance Practice

In performances and recordings of earlier music, certain variations from the printed scores will frequently be observed. These are not arbitrary alterations of the music, but are based upon current knowledge concerning the performance practice of the period. In earlier times, the written notes often represented a kind of shorthand, an outline for performers, rather than a set of rigid instructions. The following specific practices may be noted:

1. Ornaments are frequently added to melodic lines, particularly at cadences and in repetitions of musical material.

2. During the Middle Ages and Renaissance, performers were often expected to supply sharps, flats, and naturals that were not written in the music. Some modern editors indicate these accidentals above the notes,

while others do not. Moreover, modern editors and performers often differ in their interpretation of the conventions governing the use of accidentals in early music.

3. In many early sources, the placement of words in relation to notes is not clearly indicated, or shown only in part; thus, modern editions and performances may differ.

4. In music before about 1600, the choice of voices or instruments and the choice of specific instruments was a matter of some freedom. Thus, in performance, some parts of a piece may be played rather than sung, or alternate between voices and instruments.

5. Since, at certain times and places in the past, pitch was higher or lower than it is today, modern performers sometimes transpose music to a key lower or higher than written, in order to avoid performance difficulties.

6. In Baroque music, the figured bass part, consisting of a bass line and numbers indicating harmonies, will be "realized" in different ways by different performers. In some editions included here (e.g. Monteverdi, *L'Orfeo*), a suggested realization is included by the modern editor—but it is only a suggestion, and will not necessarily be followed in a given performance.

THE

NORTON SCORES

An Anthology for Listening

Fourth Edition · Standard

In chant notation

In modern notation

Translation

Gaudeamus omnes in Domino,	Let us all rejoice in the Lord,
diem festum celebrantes sub honore Mariae Virginis:	Celebrating a feast-day in honor of the Blessed Virgin Mary,
de cujus Assumptione gaudent Angeli,	For whose Assumption the angels rejoice
et collaudant Filium Dei.	And give praise to the Son of God.

2. GUIRAUT DE BORNELH (c. 1140-1200), *Reis glorios*

Reis glo - ri - os, ve - rais lums e clar - tarz,
Deus po - de - ros, Sen - her, si a vos platz, Al meu com - panh si - atz fi - zels a - ju - da;

Qu'eu no lo vi, pos la nochs fo ven - gu - da; Et a - des se - ra l'al - ba!

Translation

Reis glorios, verais lums e clartatz,	Glorious King, light of truth and splendor
Deus poderos, Senher, si a vos platz,	Almighty God, Lord, if it please you,
Al meu companh siatz fizels a juda;	Give faithful aid to my friend.
Qu'eu no lo vi, pos la nochs fo venguda;	I have not seen him since night fell;
Et ades sera l'alba!	And soon it will be dawn!
Bel companho, si dormetz o veillatz?	Dear friend, are you asleep or awake?
Non dormatz plus, suau vos ressidatz,	Sleep no more, now you must rise,
Qu'en orien vei l'estela creguda	For in the east the star grows bright
Qu'amean-l jorn, qu'eu l'ai ben coneguda:	That heralds the day. I know it well:
Et ades sera l'alba!	And soon it will be dawn!
Bel companho, en chantan vos apel:	Dear friend, my song is calling you.
Non dormatz plus, qu'eu aug chantar l'auzel,	Sleep no more, I hear a bird singing,
Que vai queren la jorn per lo bocsatge;	He goes seeking daylight through the woods;
Et ai paor que-l gilos vos assatge;	I fear the jealous husband will catch you;
Et ades sera l'alba!	And soon it will be dawn!

The friend replies:

Bel dous companh, tan soi en ric sojorn	My dear sweet friend, I am so happy where I am
Qu'eu no volgra mais fos alba ni jorn.	That I wish for neither dawn nor day.
Car la gensor que anc nasques de naire,	For the loveliest woman that ever was born
Tenc e abras, per qu'en non prezi gaire	I hold in my arms. So I'm not going to worry
Lo fol gelos ni l'alba.	About the jealous fool or the dawn.

Adapted from Friedrich Gennrich's transcription in *Der Musikalische Nachlass der Troubadours*.

3. GUILLAUME DE MACHAUT (c. 1300-1377), *Hareu! hareu!—Helas! ou sera pris confors—Obediens usque ad mortem*

Adapted from Leo Schrade's transcription in *Polyphonic Music of the Fourteenth Century: Guillaume de Machaut.* © Editions de l'Oiseau-Lyre, Les Remparts, Monaco.

Translation

TRIPLUM

Hareu! hareu! le feu, le feu, le feu	Help! Help! Fire! Fire! Fire!
D'ardant desir, qu'einc si ardant ne fu,	My heart is on fire with burning desire
Qu'en mon cuer a espris et soustenu	Such as was never seen before.
Amours, et s'a la joie retenu	Love, having started it, fans the flames,
D'espoir qui doit attemprer telle ardure.	Withholding all hope of joy which might put out such a blaze.
Las! se le feu qui ensement l'art dure,	Alas, if this fire keeps on burning,
Mes cuers sera tous bruis et esteins,	My heart, already blackened and shriveled,
Qui de ce feu est ja nercis et teins,	Will be burnt to ashes.
Pour ce qu'il est fins, loyaus et certeins;	For it is true, loyal, and sincere.
Si que j'espoir que deviez yert, eins	I expect I shall be mad with grief
Que bonne Amour de merci l'asseure	Before gentle Love consoles it
Par la vertu d'esperance seure.	With sound hope.

Car pour li seul, qui endure mal meint;
Pitié deffaut, ou toute biauté meint;
Durtés y regne et Dangiers y remeint,

Desdeins y vit et Loyautez s'i feint

Et Amours n'a de li ne de moy cure.
Joie le het, ma dame li est dure.

Et, pour croistre mes dolereus meschiés,
Met dedens moy Amours, qui est mes chiés,
Un desespoir qui si mal entechiés,
Est que tous biens a de moy esrachiés,
Et en tous cas mon corps si desnature
Qu'il me convient morir malgré Nature.

It alone, suffering much Hardship,
Is devoid of Pity, abode of all beauty.
Instead, Harshness rules over it and
    Haughtiness flourishes.
Disdain dwells there, while Loyalty is a rare
    visitor
And Love pays no heed to it or to me.
Joy hates it, and my lady is cruel to it.

To complete my sad misfortune,
Love, my sovereign lord,
Fills me with such bitter despair
That I am left penniless,
And so wasted in body
That I shall surely die before my time.

DUPLUM

Helas! ou sera pris confors
Pour moy qui ne vail nés que mors?
Quant riens garentir ne me puet
Fors ma dame chiere qui wet
Qu'en desespoir muire, sans plus,
Pour ce que je l'aim plus que nulz,
Et Souvenir pour enasprir
L'ardour de mon triste desir
Me moustre adés sa grant bonté

Alas, where can I find consolation
Who am as good as dead?
When my one salvation
Is my dear lady,
Who gladly lets me die in despair,
Simply because I love her as no other could,
And Memory, in order to keep
My unhappy desire alive,
Reminds me all the while of her great goodness

Et sa fine vraie biauté
Qui doublement me fait ardoir.
Einssi sans cuer et sans espoir,
Ne puis pas vivre longuement,
N'en feu cuers humeins nullement
Ne puet longue duree avoir.

And her delicate beauty,
Thereby making me want her all the more.
Deprived thus of heart and hope
I cannot live for long.
No man's heart can long survive
When once aflame.

TENOR

Obediens usque ad mortem

Obedient unto death

4. GUILLAUME DUFAY (c. 1400-1474),
Alma redemptoris mater (c. 1495)

The chant *Alma redemptoris mater*, on which the top voice is based

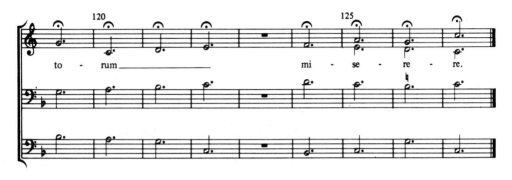

to - rum _____ mi - se - re - re.

Translation

Alma redemptoris mater,
quae pervia caeli porta manes,
Et stella maris, succurre cadenti,
surgere qui curat populo.

Tu quae genuisti, natura mirante,
tuum sanctum Genitorem,
Virgo prius ac posterius,
Gabrielis ab ore sumens illud Ave,
peccatorum miserere.

Gracious mother of the Redeemer,
Abiding at the doors of Heaven,
Star of the sea, aid the falling,
Rescue the people who struggle.

Thou who, astonishing nature,
Has borne thy holy Creator,
Virgin before and after,
Who heard the Ave from the mouth of Gabriel,
Be merciful to sinners.

5. ANONYMOUS, *Saltarello*

Adapted from transcription in *Archiv für Musikwissenschaft.*

6. JOSQUIN DES PREZ (c. 1450-1521), Agnus Dei from *Missa L'Homme armé (sexti toni)* (PUBL. 1502)

The tune *L'homme armé*

In the Recordings for *The Norton Scores*, this is sung a tone higher.

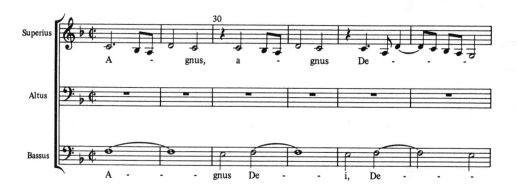

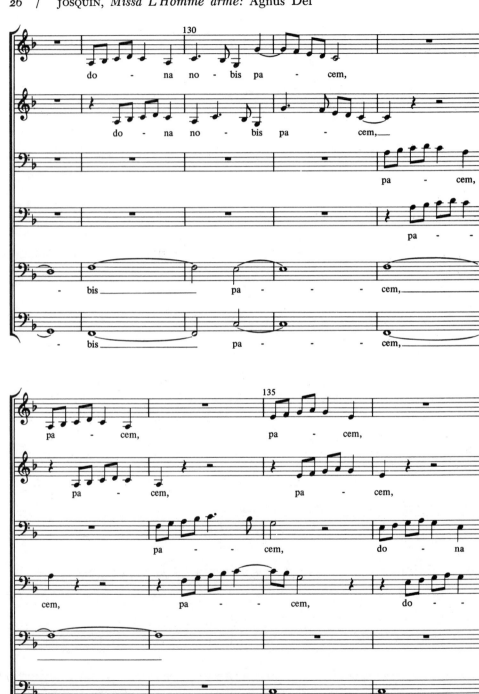

Translation

Agnus Dei,
qui tollis peccata mundi,
miserere nobis,
dona nobis pacem.

Lamb of God,
Who takest away the sins of the world,
Have mercy upon us,
Grant us peace

7. CLÉMENT JANEQUIN (c. 1485-1558), *Les Cris de Paris* (1529)

Vou - lez ou - yr   vou -

Vou - lez ou - yr   vou -

Vou - lez ou - yr   vou -

Vou - lez ou - yr   vou -

- lez ou - yr,

lez ou - yr

vou - lez ou - yr

lez ou - yr

vou-lez ou - yr,   vou-lez ou -

vou - lez ou - yr

Je les don - ne,

niers,

a   six   de -

Tar - - te - let - tes   fri - an - -

Cas - se mu - seaux tous chaulx

je les vendz, je les don - ne, je les vendz.

niers.   Et   est   a l'en - sei - gne du ber -

des   a la bel - le   gauf - fre, a la bel - le

je   don - ne, je   les   vendz, je   les

sa   a boy - re, sa,   sa   a boy - re, ca.

seau   qui est en la   ru - e de la Har - pe.

gauf - fre, a la bel - le   gauf - fre.

vendz, je les don - ne pour ung pe - tit blanc.

Ai - gre, vin .ai - gre,   ai - gre, vin ai - gre.

Ha - renc de la nuyt, ha - renc de la nuyt,   ha - renc

Fault   il   point   de   sault - -

Mou - star - - - -

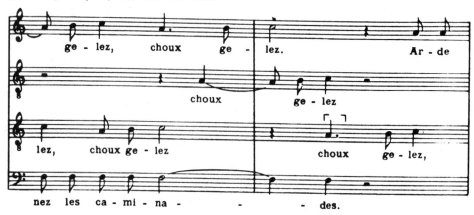

ge - lez, choux ge - lez. Ar - de

choux ge - lez

lez, choux ge - lez choux ge - lez,

nez les ca - mi - na - - - des.

bu - che, bu - - che. Qui veult

choux ge - lez, ge - lez.

choux ge - lez, choux ge - lez. Qui

Choux ge - lez, choux ge - lez.

du laict, qui veult du laict? Poys vers, poys

Qui veult du laict qui veult du

veult du laict? Poys vers, poys vers, poys vert.

C'est moy, c'est moy, Je meurs de froit.

pi - gnes vui-dez. Char-lo -
pi - gnes vui-dez. Char-lo - te m'a -
pi - gnes vui-dez, pi - gnes vui-dez.
pi - gnes vui-dez, pi - gnes vui-dez. Char-lo - te m'a
110
te m'a - my - e. A - pe - tit, a - pe - tit nou-veau, a - pe -
my - e, Char-lo - te m'a - my - e. A - pe - tit nou-veau, a - pe -
Char-lo - te m'a - my - e. A - pe - tit nou-veau, a - pe -
my - e A - pe - tit nou-veau, a - pe -
tit nou-veau pe - tit, a - pe - tit nou-veau, a - pe - tit nou -
tit nou-veau pe - tit, a - pe - tit nou-veau, a - pe - tit nou -
tit nou-veau pe - tiz, a - pe - tit nou-veau.
tit nou-veau pe - tit, a - pe - tit nou-veau.
115
veau. A - men-dez vous da - mes, a - men -
veau. A - men-dez vous da - mes, a - men -
A - men-dez vous da - mes, a - men - dez,
A - men-dez vous da - mes, a - men - dez,

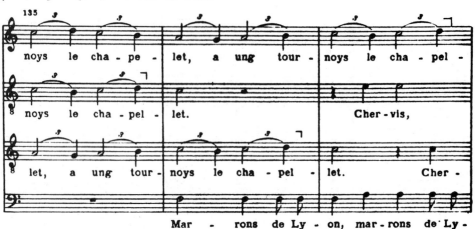

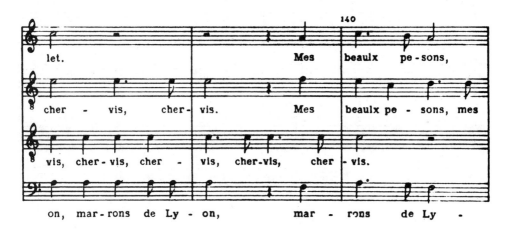

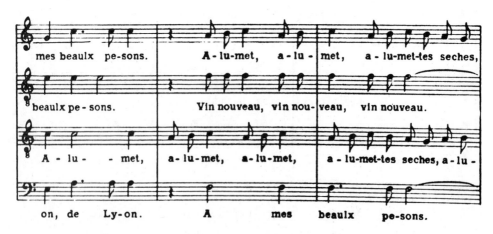

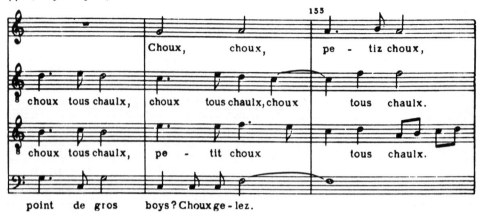

Choux, choux, pe - tiz choux,

choux tous chaulx, choux tous chaulx, choux tous chaulx.

choux tous chaulx, pe - tit choux tous chaulx.

point de gros boys? Choux ge - lez.

pe - tiz choux.

Et qui l'au-ra le

Et qui l'au-ra le mou-le de gros boys

Et qui l'au-ra le

Et qui l'au-ra le mou-le de gros boys

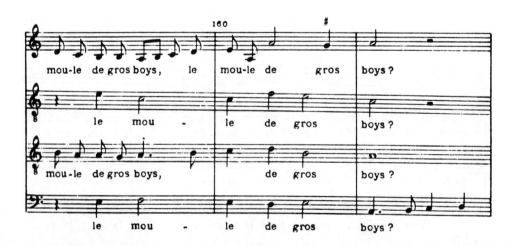

mou-le de gros boys, le mou-le de gros boys?

le mou - le de gros boys?

mou-le de gros boys, de gros boys?

le mou - le de gros boys?

185
fa - lour - - de.
- - lour - de.
Fa - lourde, fa - lourde fa - lourde, fa - -
de, fa - lour - de fa - lourde, fa - lourde, fa -
190
A Pa - ris sur pe - - tit pont
A Pa - ris sur pe - tit
- - - lour - de.
- - lour - de.
ge - li - - ne de feur - - re.
pont ge - li - ne de feur - re.
A
A Pa - ris sur pe - tit
195
. Pa - ris sur pe - tit pont ge - li - - ne de
pont, a Pa - ris sur pe - tit pont ge - li - ne de

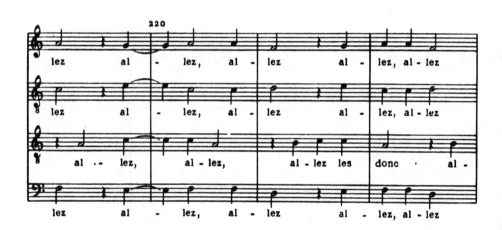

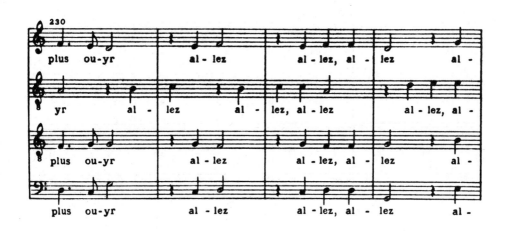

Translation

Voulez ouyr les cris de Paris?	Would you like to hear the cries of Paris?
Où sont ilz ces petiz pions?	Where's the crowd?
Pastez tres tous chaulx, qui l'aira?	The patés are very hot, who will buy them?
Vin blanc, vin cleret, vin vermeil, à six deniers.	White and red wine, claret at six sous.
Casse museaux tous chaulx,	Come and get your hot pies,
Je le vendz, je les donne pour ung petit blanc.	I sell them, I give them for a five-spot.
Tartelettes, friandes à la belle gauffre!	Delicious tarts like waffles,
Et est à l'enseigne du berseau	Fresh from the Sign of the Cradle
Qui est en la rue de la Harpe.	Which is on the Rue de la Harpe.
Sa à boyre, ça!	Who wants a tasty drink?
Aigre, vin aigre!	Vinegar, good and sharp!
Faut il point de saultce vert?	Anybody want green sauce?
Moustarde, moustarde fine!	Mustard, excellent mustard!
Harenc blanc, harenc de la nuyt!	White herring, delicious at night!
Cotrez secz, cotrez! souliers vieux!	Cheap doublets! Old shoes!
Arde buche! Choux gelez!	Chewing tobacco! Cold cabbage!
Hault et bas rammonez les caminades!	Who needs a chimney sweep?
Qui veult du laict?	Anybody want milk?
C'est moy, c'est moy, je meurs de froit.	It's me, it's me, I'm dying of cold!
Poys vers! Mes belles lestues, mes beaulx cibotz!	Green peas! My beautiful lettuce! Onions!
Guigne, doulce guigne!	Cherries, sweet cherries!
Fault il point de sablon? Voire joly!	Anybody need soap? What a beauty!
Argent m'y duit, argent m'y fault.	I have money coming to me! I need it!
Gaigne petit! Lye! Alumet! Houseaux vieux!	Small earnings! Lye! Old boots!
Pruneaux de Saint Julien!	Prunes from St. Julien!
Febves de Maretz, febves! Je fais le coqu, moy!	Beans from Maretz! I make husbands jealous!
Ma belle porée, mon beau persin,	My beautiful leeks, lovely parsley!
Ma belle oseille, mes beaulx espinards!	Beautiful sorrel and spinach!
Peches de Corbeil! Orenge! Pignes vuidez!	Peaches from Corbeil! Oranges! Look at these combs!
Charlote m'amye! Apetit nouveau petit!	Charlotte, my darling! Makes your mouth water!
Amendez vous dames, amendez! Allemande nouvelle!	Make yourselves pretty, ladies! Something new from Germany!
Navetz! Mes beaux balais! Rave doulce, rave!	Turnips! My beautiful barley! Sweet radishes!
Feure, feure Brie! A ung tournoys le chapellet!	Wonderful Brie! Prayer beads, very cheap!
Marons de Lyon! Chervis! Mes beaulx pesons!	Chestnuts from Lyon! Limes! A pair of scales, the best!
Alumet, alumet, alumette seches! Vin nouveau!	Dry tinder wood! New wine!
Fault il point de grois? Choux, petit choux tous chaulx!	Anybody need lard? Sweet hotcakes!

Fault il point de gros boys? Choux gelez!
Et qui l'aura le moule de gros boys?
Eschaudez chaux! Seche bouree!
Serceau beau serseau! Arde chandelle!
    Palourde!
A Paris sur petit point geline de feurre!

Si vous en voulez plus ouyr, allez les donc
    querre!

Anyone for tinder wood? Cold cabbage!
Anybody need a hamper for wood?
Plaster you can heat! Dry firewood!
Hoops, lovely hoops! A candle that burns!
    Cockles!
In Paris they scatter straw over the little
    bridge!
If you want to hear more, go ask them about it!

8. GIOVANNI PIERLUIGI DA PALESTRINA (c. 1525-1594),
Sanctus from *Missa Ascendo ad Patrem* (PUBL. 1601)

Benedictus

Translation

Sanctus, sanctus, sanctus,	Holy, holy, holy,
Dominus Deus Sabaoth.	Lord God of hosts.
Pleni sunt coeli et terra gloria tua;	Heavens and earth are full of thy glory;
Hosanna in excelsis.	Hosanna in the highest.
Benedictus qui venit in nomine Domini;	Blessed is he that cometh in the name of the Lord;
Hosanna in excelsis.	Hosanna in the highest.

9. CLAUDIO MONTEVERDI (1567-1643),
Scene from *L'Orfeo* (1ST PERF. 1607)

e in - te-ne - ri - to il cor___ del re de l'om - bre, me-co trar-rot - ti

a ri - ve-der le stel - le, o se ciò ne-ghe-ram-mi em - pio de-sti - no,

ri-mar-rò te - co, in com-pa-gnia di mor - te. Ad - dio ter - ra,

ad - dio cie - lo, e so - le, ad - di - - - o.

Translation

ORFEO

Tu se' morta, se' morta, mia vita,
ed io respiro; tu se' da me partita,
se' da me partita per mai più,
mai più non tornare, ed io rimango—
no, no, che se i versi alcuna cosa ponno
n'andrò sicuro al più profondi abissi,
e intenerito il cor del re dell'ombre,

meco trarotti a riveder le stelle,
o se ciò negherammi empio destino,
rimarrò teco in compagnia di morte!
Addio terra, addio cielo, e sole, addio.

CORO DI NINFE E PASTORI

Ahi, caso acerbo, ahi, fat'empio e crudele,
ahi, stelle ingiuriose, ahi, cielo avaro.
Non si fidi uom mortale di ben caduco e frale,

che tosto fugge, e spesso a gran salita il
precipizio è presso.

You are dead, dead, my darling,
And I live; you have left me,
Left me forevermore,
Never to return, yet I remain—
No, no, if verses have any power,
I shall go boldly to the deepest abysses,
And having softened the heart of the king of
shadows,
Will take you with me to see again the stars,
Or if cruel fate will deny me this,
I will remain with you in the presence of death!
Farewell earth, farewell sky, and sun, farewell.

CHORUS OF NYMPHS AND SHEPHERDS

Ah, bitter chance, ah, fate wicked and cruel,
Ah, stars of ill omen, ah, heaven avaricious.
Let not mortal man trust good, short-lived and
frail,
Which soon disappears, for often to a bold
ascent the precipice is near.

10. THOMAS WEELKES (c. 1575-1623),
As Vesta Was Descending (PUBL. 1601)

Long live fair O - ri - a - - - na.

-a - na, Long live fair O - ri - a - na.

live fair O - ri - a - na, fair O - ri - a - na.

-na, _____ fair O - ri - a - na.

-na, Long live fair O - ri - a - - na.

O - - - ri - a - - na.

11. HENRY PURCELL (c. 1659-1695),
Dido's Lament from *Dido and Aeneas* (1ST PERF. 1689)

DIDO

Thy hand, Bel - in - da! dark - - - ness shades me, On thy

bos - om let me rest, More I would, but death— in -

vades me Death is now— a wel - come guest!

When I am laid,— am laid_____ in

12. HANDEL, Excerpts from *Messiah* (1741)

No. 1: Overture

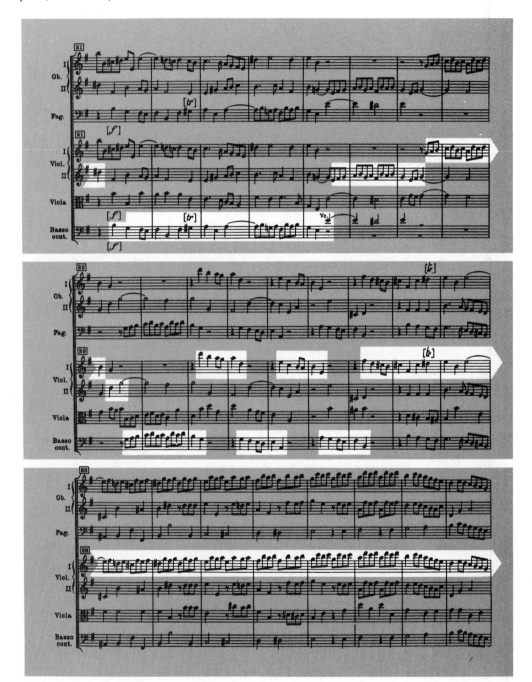

No. 2: *Comfort ye*

i - qui-ty is par-don'd, that her in - i - qui-ty is par -

don'd.

The voice of him that crieth in the wilderness, Pre-pare ye the way of the

Lord, make straight in the desert a high-way for our God.

No. 3: *Ev'ry valley*

No. 12: *For unto us a Child is born*

The might-y God,   The ev-er-last-ing Fa-ther,   The Prince of Peace,   The

The might-y God,   The ev-er-last-ing Fa-ther,   The Prince of Peace,   The

The might-y God,   The ev-er-last-ing Fa-ther,   The Prince of Peace,   The

The might-y God,   The ev-er-last-ing Fa-ther,   The Prince of Peace,   The

ev-er-last-ing Fa-ther, The Prince of Peace.

ev-er-last-ing Fa-ther, The Prince of Peace.

ev-er-last-ing Fa-ther, The Prince of Peace.

ev-er-last-ing Fa-ther, The Prince of Peace.

No. 44: *Hallelujah*

No. 45: *I know that my Redeemer liveth*

*) This appoggiatura is not in Händel's score

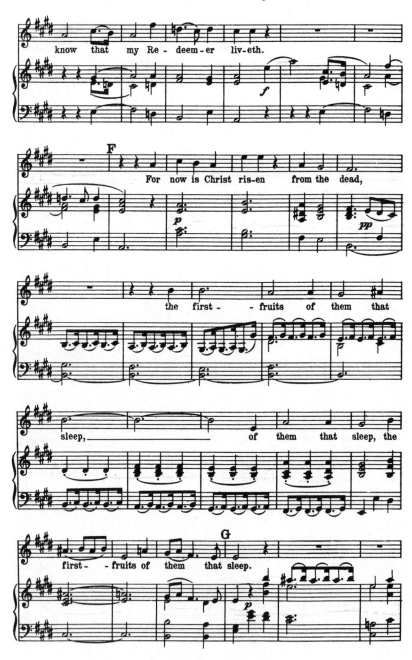

13. JOHANN SEBASTIAN BACH (1685-1750),
Organ Fugue in G minor (Little) (1709?)

14. BACH, *Brandenburg Concerto No. 2 in F major* (1721?)

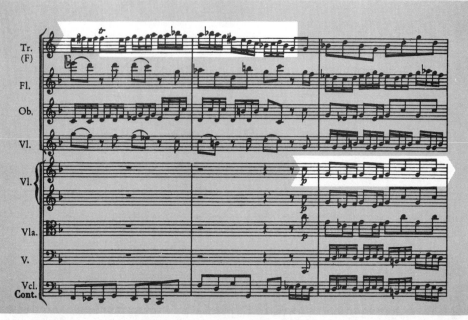

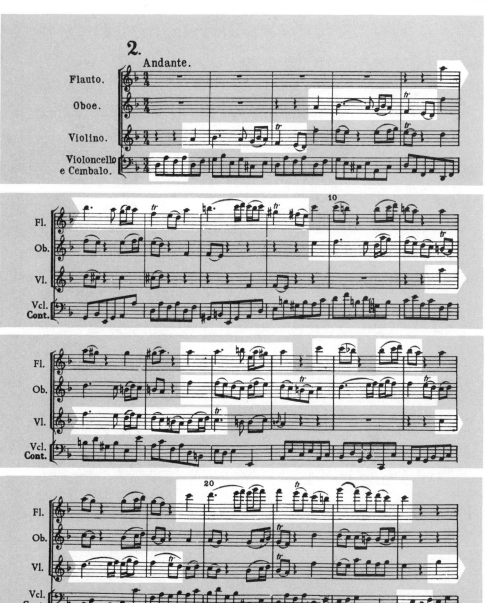

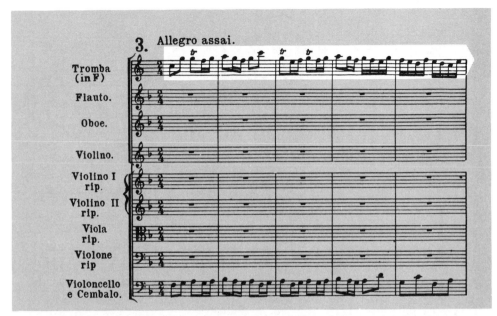

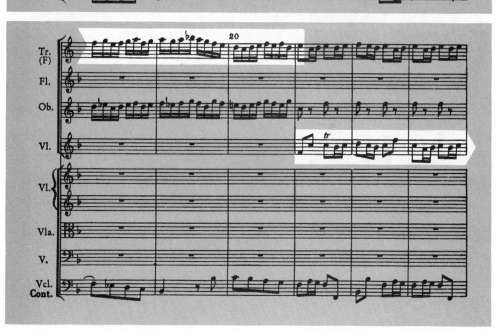

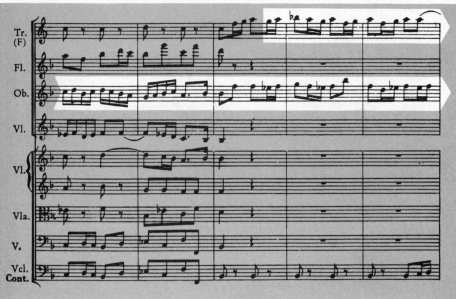

15. BACH, Air and Gigue from *Suite No. 3 in D major* (1723?)

I

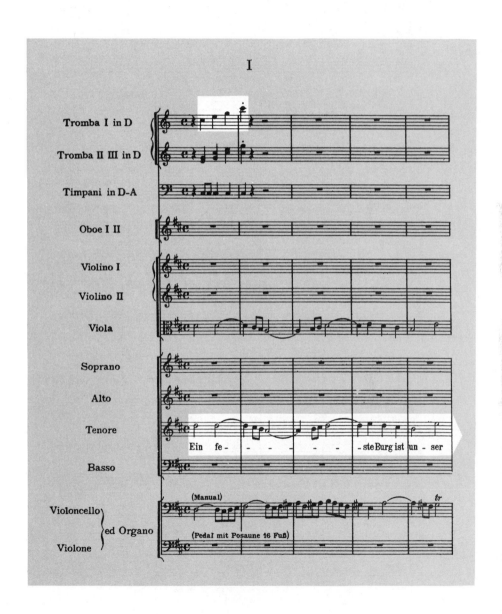

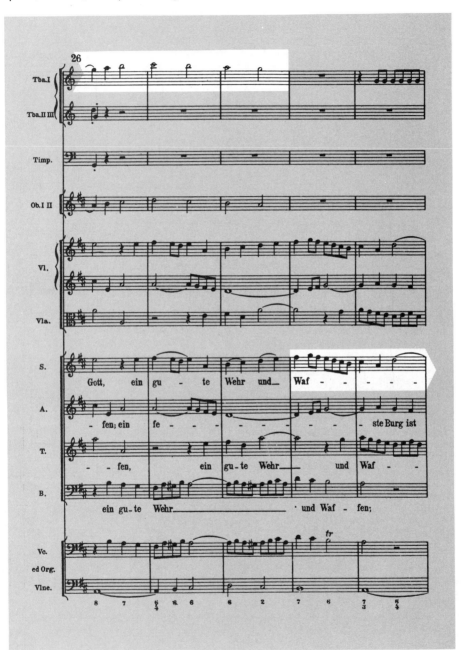

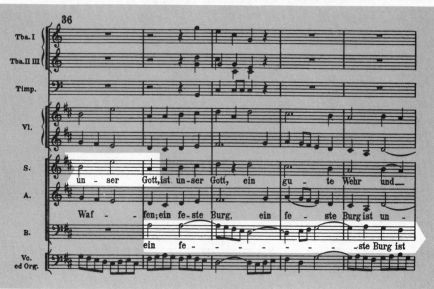

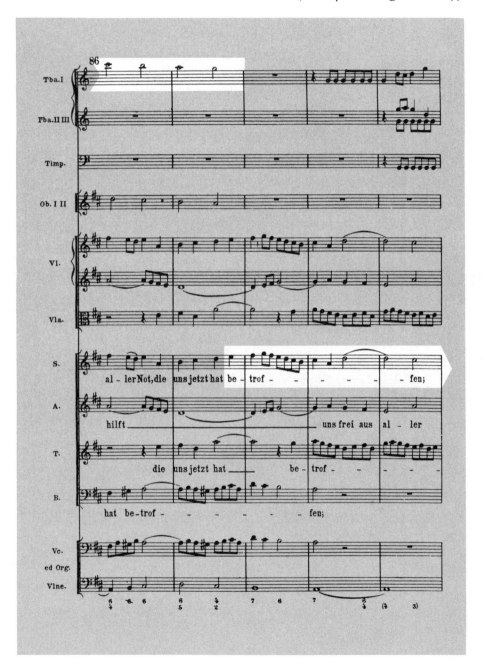

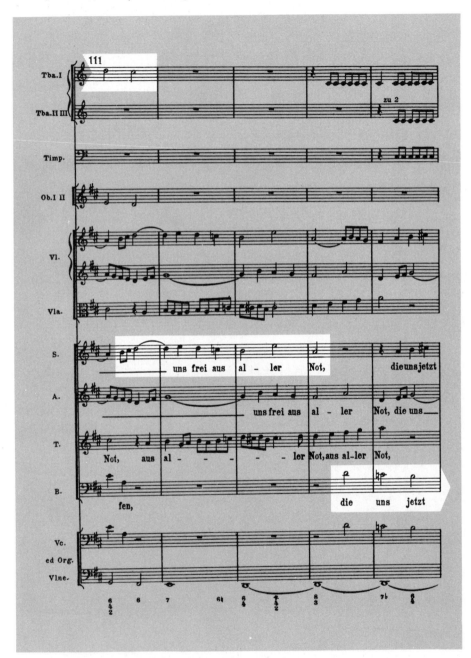

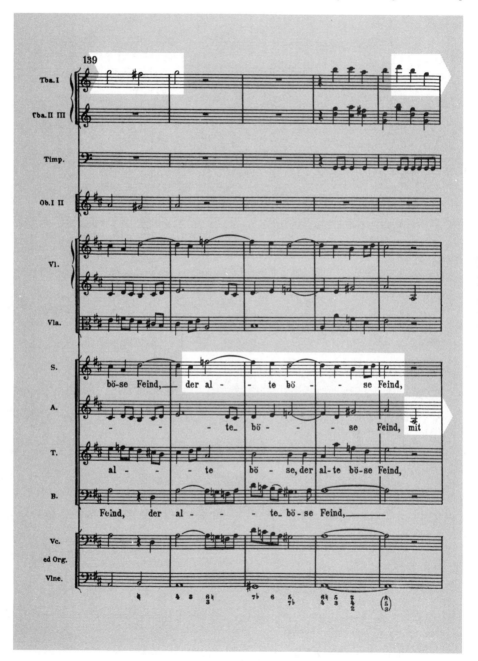

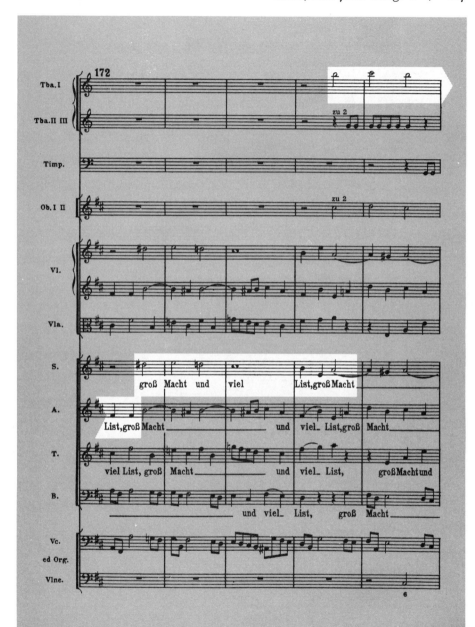

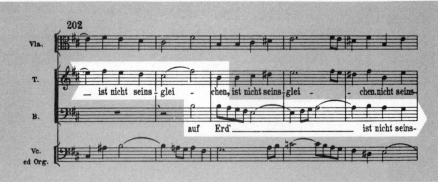

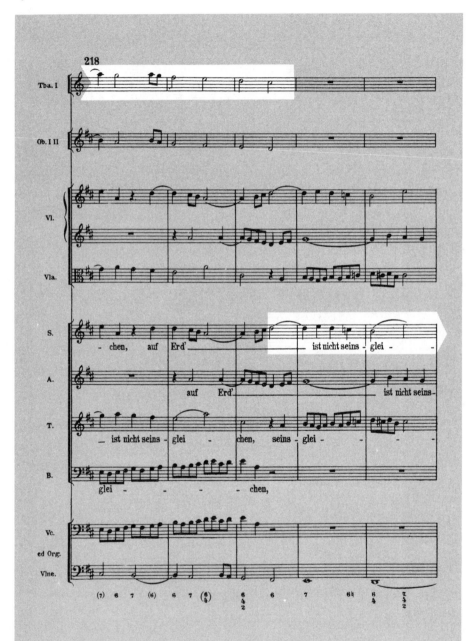

II

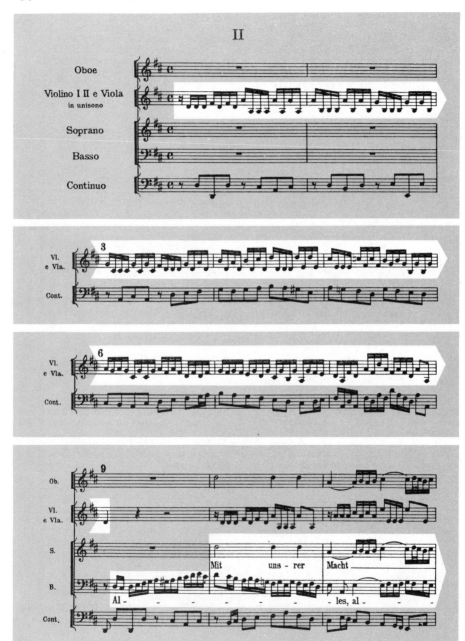

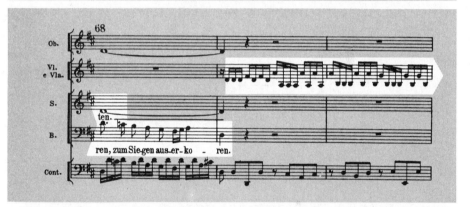

V

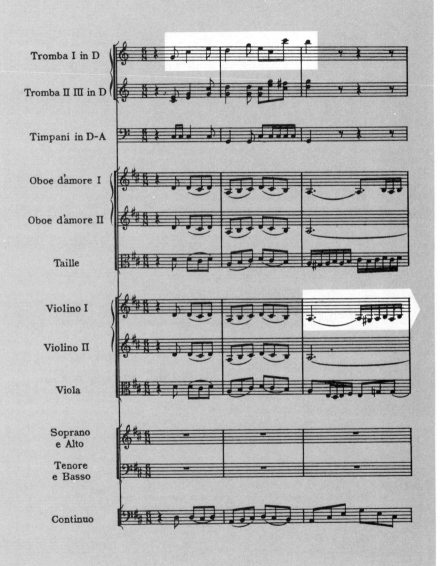

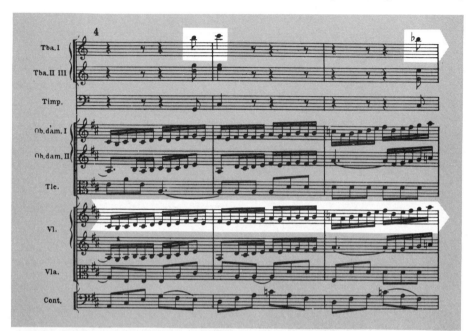

wie saur er sich stellt,

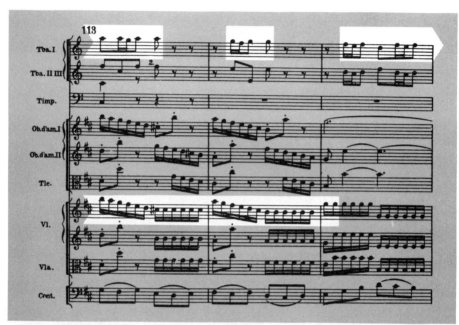

VIII

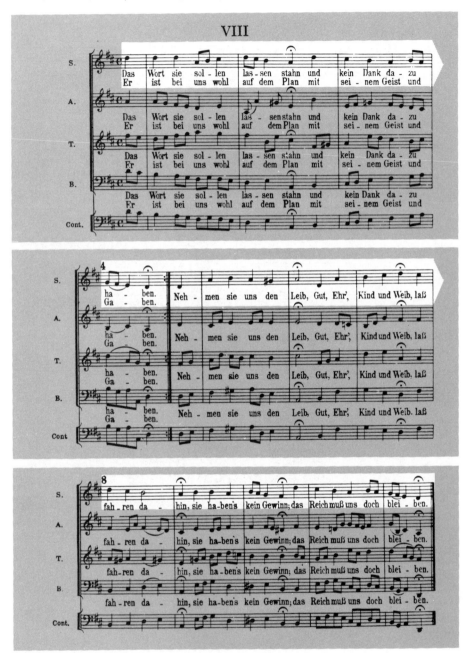

Translation

I

Ein fest Burg ist unser Gott,
  ein' gute Wehr und Waffen;
er hilft uns frei aus aller Not,
  die uns jetzt hat betroffen.

A mighty fortress is our God,
  A good defense and weapon;
He helps free us from all the troubles
  That have now befallen us.

Der alte böse Feind,
mit Ernst er's jetzt meint,
  gross Macht und viel List
  sein grausam Rüstung ist,
auf Erd' ist nicht seinsgleichen.

Our ever evil foe;
In earnest plots against us,
  With great strength and cunning
  He prepares his dreadful plans.
Earth holds none like him.

II

Mit unsrer Macht ist nichts getan,
  wir sind gar bald verloren.
Es streit't für uns der rechte Mann,
  den Gott selbst hat erkoren.

With our own strength nothing is achieved,
  We would soon be lost.
But in our behalf strives the Mighty One,
  whom God himself has chosen.

Fragst du, wer er ist?
Er heisst Jesus Christ,
  der Herre Zebaoth,
  und ist kein andrer Gott,
das Feld muss er behalten.

Ask you, who is he?
He is called Jesus Christ,
  Lord of Hosts,
And there is no other God,
  He must remain master of the field.

Alles was von Gott geboren,
ist zum Siegen auserkoren,
  Wer bei Christi Blutpanier
in der Taufe Treu' geschworen,
  siegt im Geiste für und für.

Everything born of God
  has been chosen for victory.
  He who holds to Christ's banner,
Truly sworn in baptism,
  His spirit will conquer for ever and ever.

V

Und wenn die Welt voll Teufel wär
  und wollten uns verschlingen,
so fürchten wir uns nicht so sehr,
  es soll uns doch gelingen.

Though the world were full of devils
  eager to devour us,
We need have no fear,
  as we will still prevail.

Der Fürst dieser Welt
wie saur er sich stellt,
  tut er uns doch nichts,
  das macht, er ist gericht't,
ein Wörtlein kann ihm fällen.

The Arch-fiend of this world,
No matter how bitter his stand,
  cannot harm us,
  Indeed he faces judgment,
One Word from God will bring him low.

VIII

CHORUS

Das Wort, sie sollen lassen stahn
  und kein Dank dazu haben.
Er ist bei uns wohl auf dem Plan
  mit seinem Geist und Gaben.

Nehmen sie uns den Leib,
Gut, Ehr, Kind und Weib,
  lass fahren dahin,
  sie habens kein Gewinn;
das Reich muss uns doch bleiben.

Now let the Word of God abide
  without further thought.
He is firmly on our side
  with His spirit and strength.

Though they deprive us of life,
Wealth, honor, child and wife,
  we will not complain,
  It will avail them nothing;
For God's kingdom must prevail.

MOVEMENTS I, II, V, AND VIII BY MARTIN LUTHER
MOVEMENTS III, IV, VI, AND VII BY SALOMO FRANCK

17. JOSEPH HAYDN (1732-1809), *Symphony No. 104 in D major (London)* (1795)

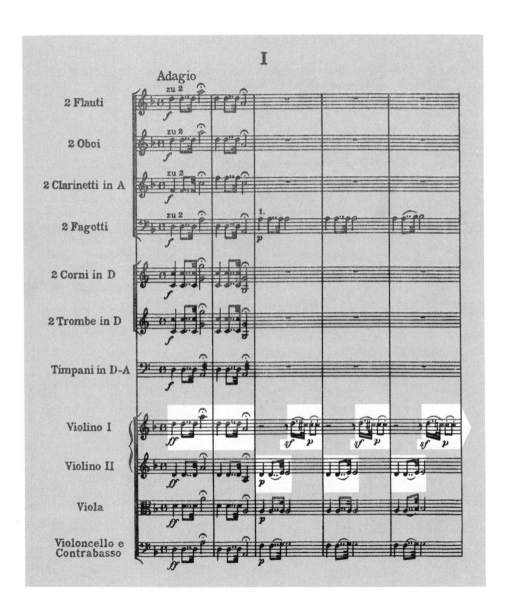

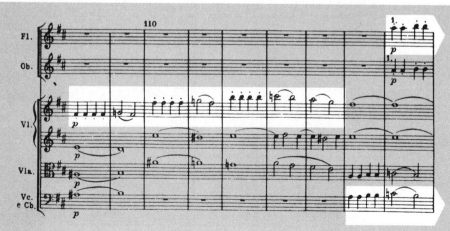

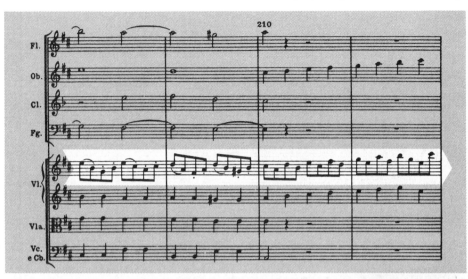

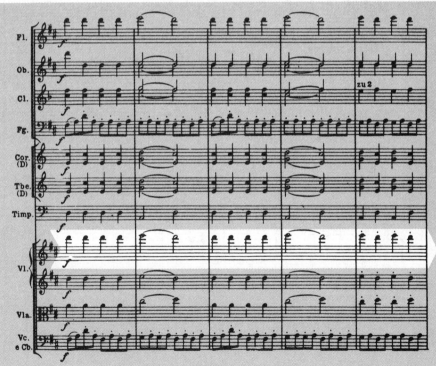

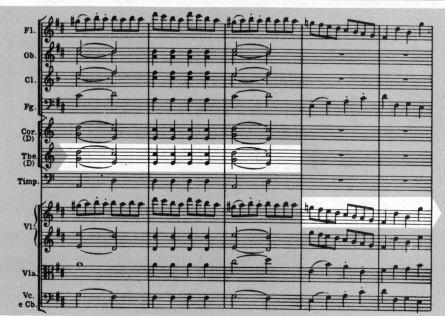

II

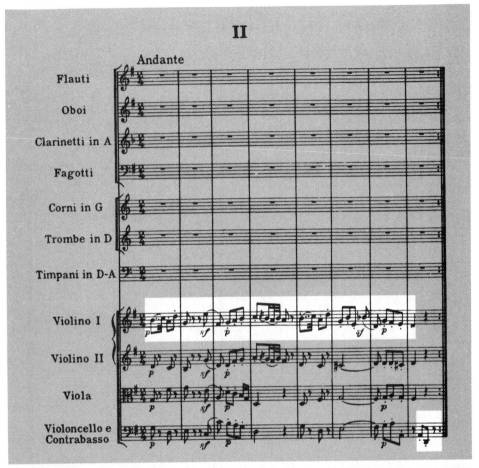

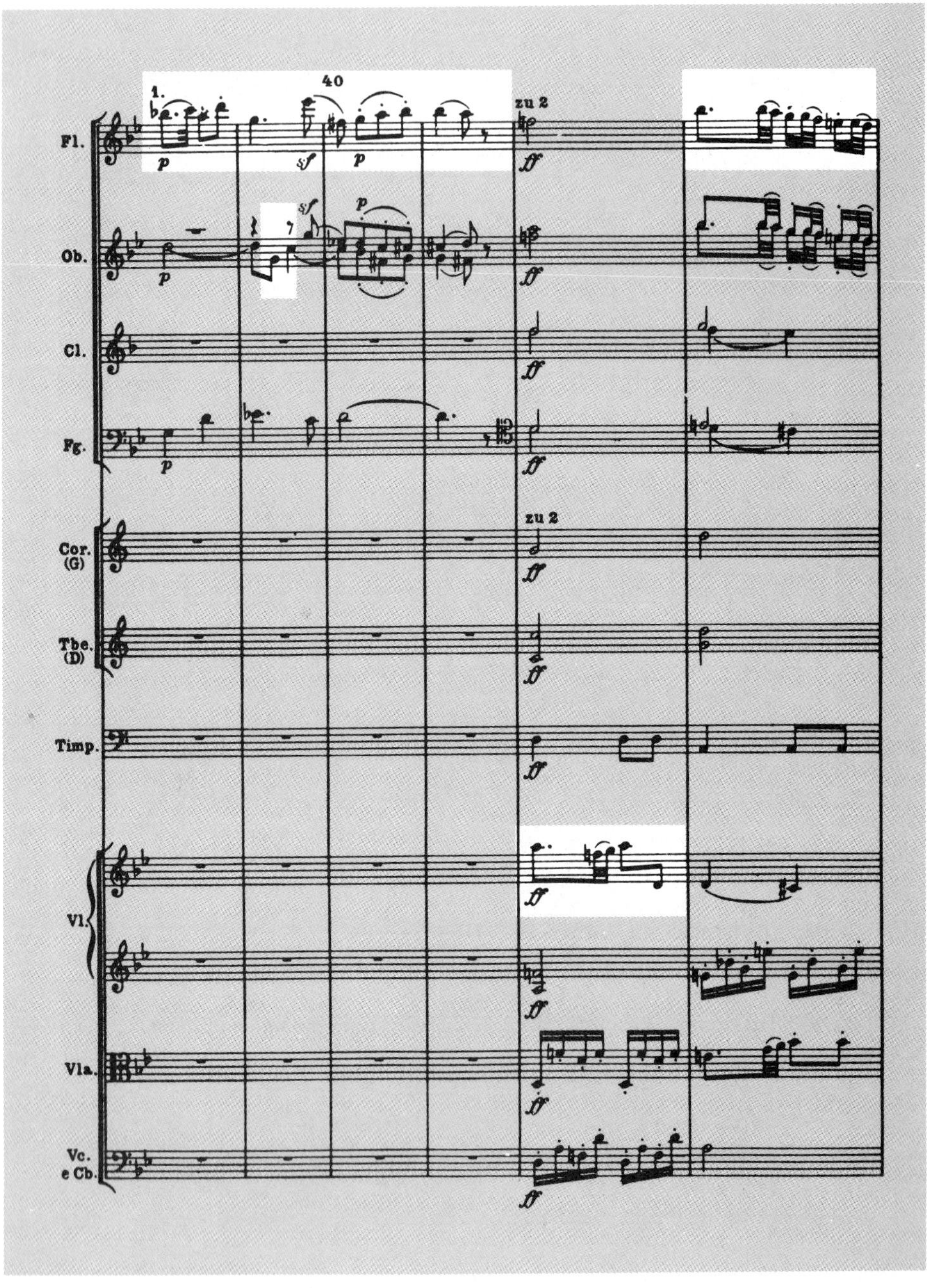

1.
40
zu 2
Fl.
Ob.
Cl.
Fg.
Cor. (G)
Tbe. (D)
Timp.
Vl.
Vla.
Vc. e Cb.
p
sf
ff

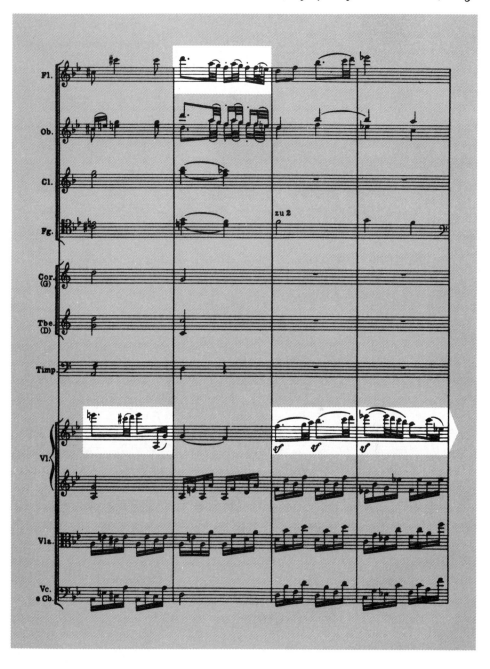

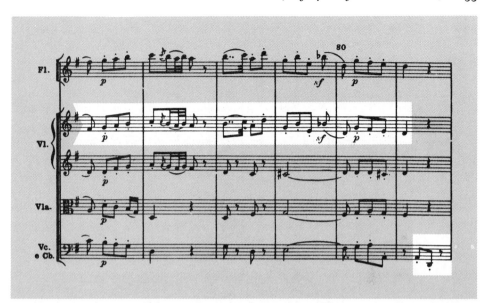

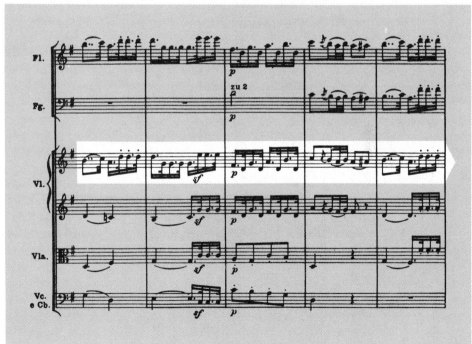

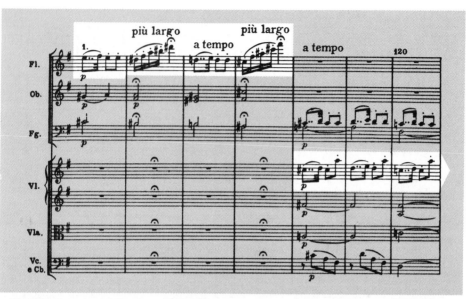

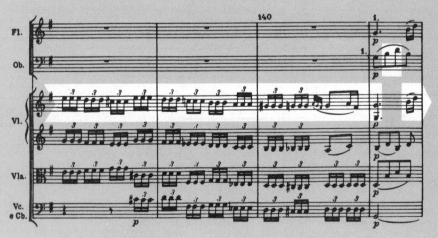

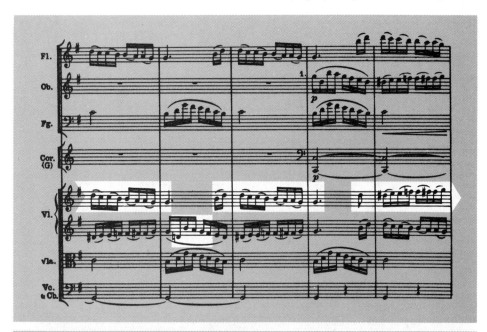

III

Men. D.C.

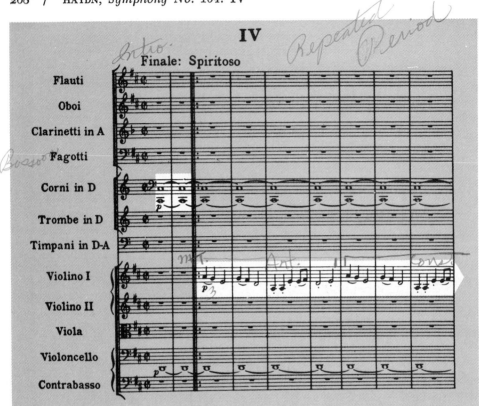

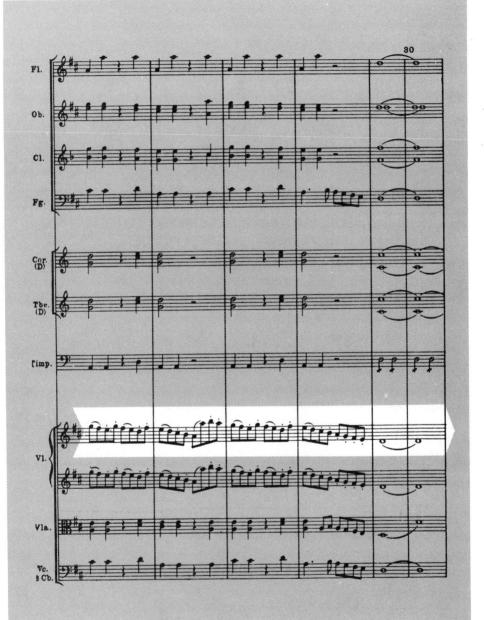

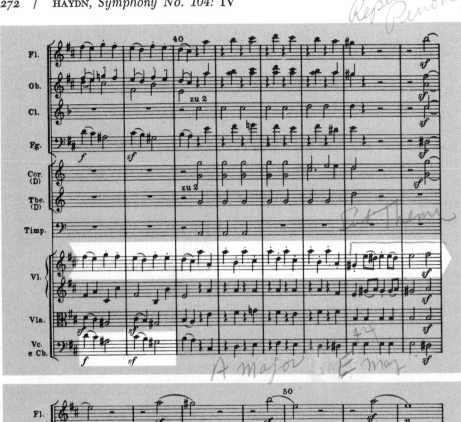

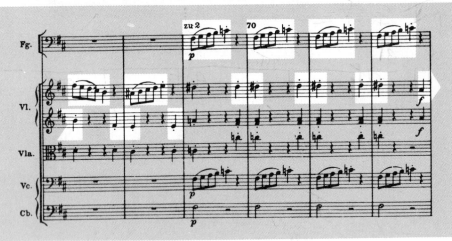

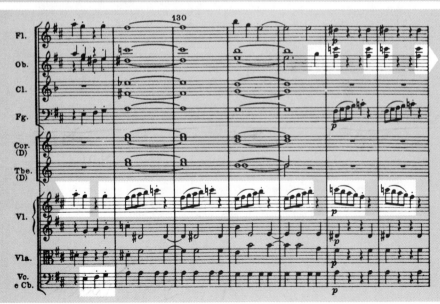

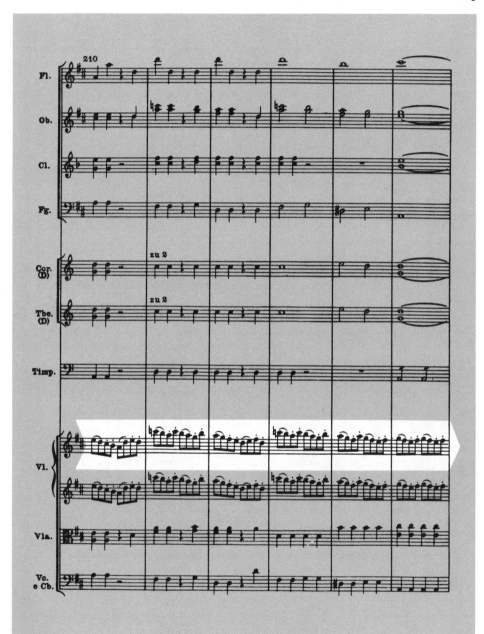

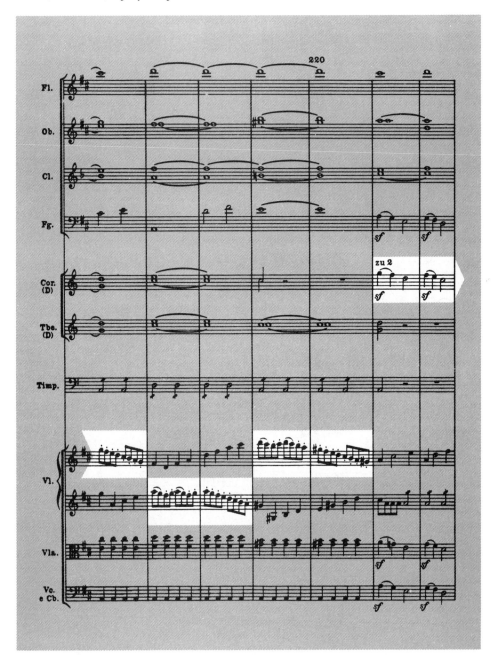

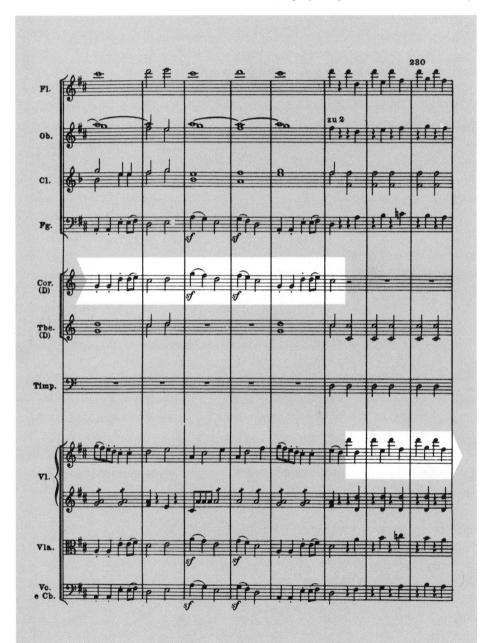

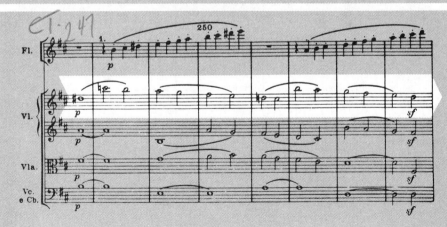

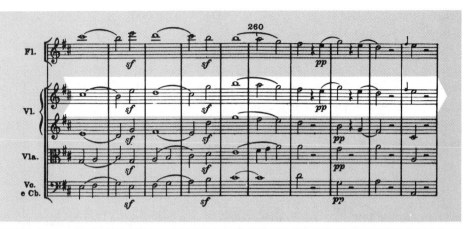

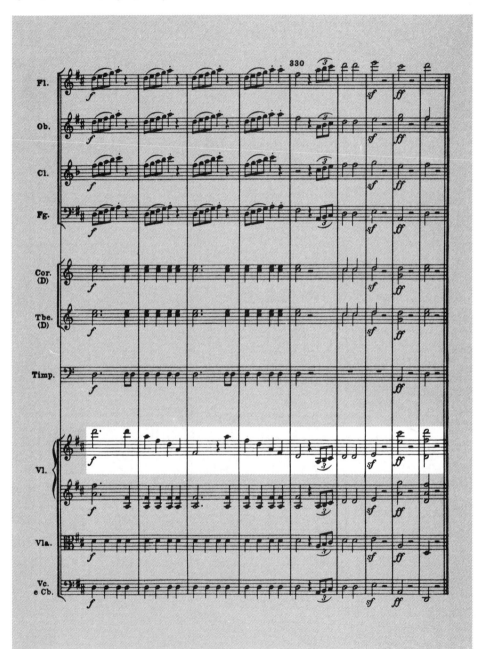

18. WOLFGANG AMADEUS MOZART (1756-1791),
Piano Concerto in C major, K. 467 (1785)

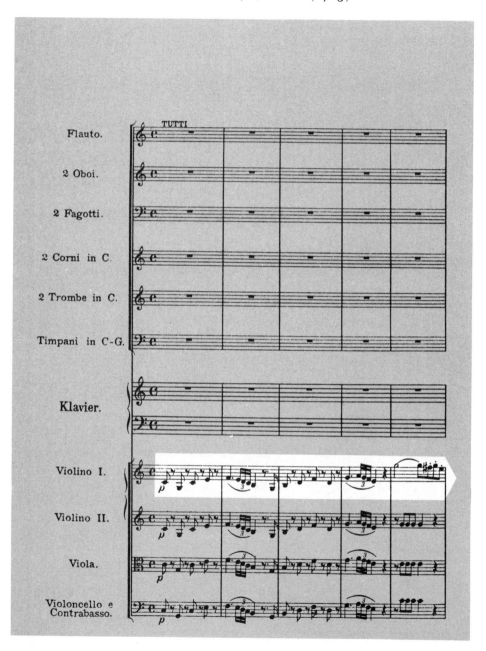

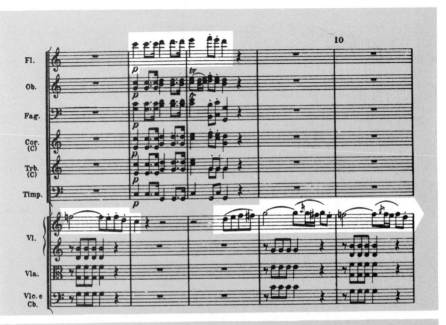

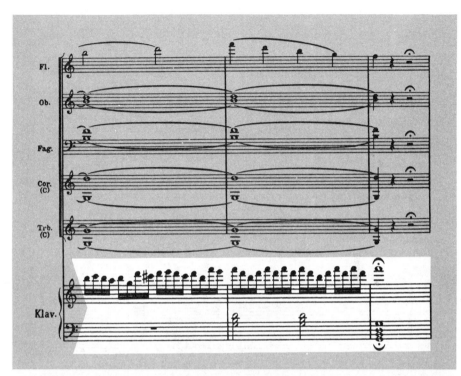

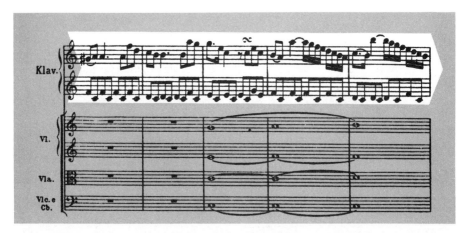

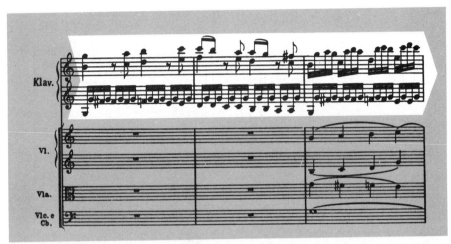

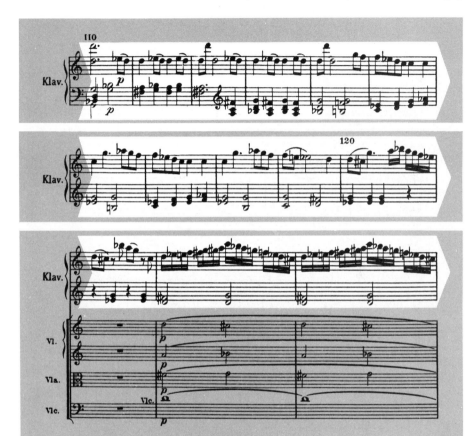

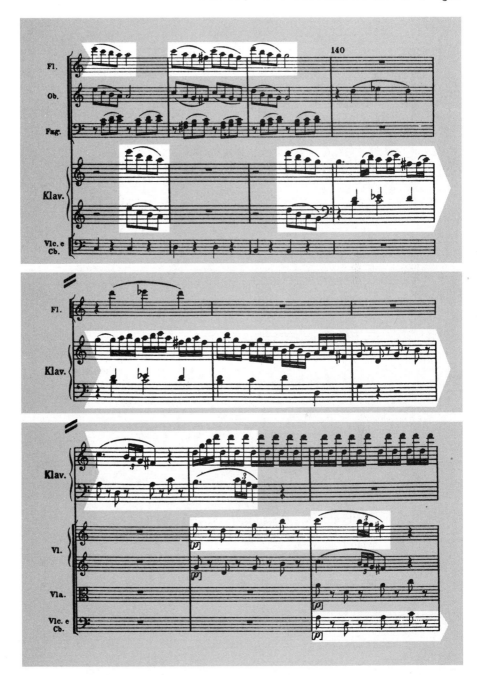

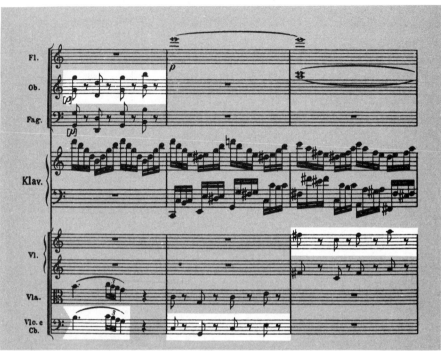

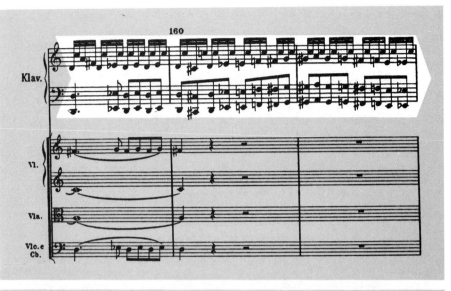

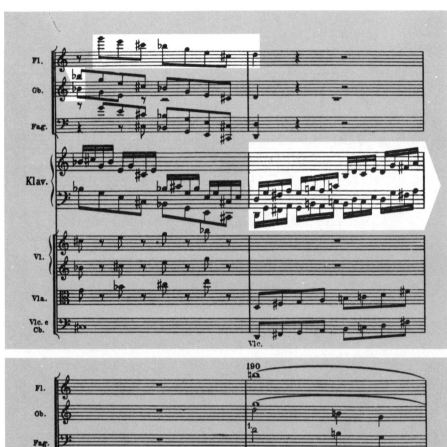

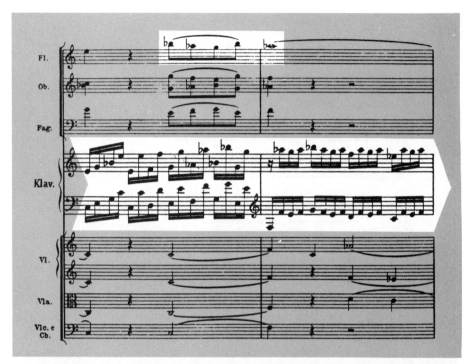

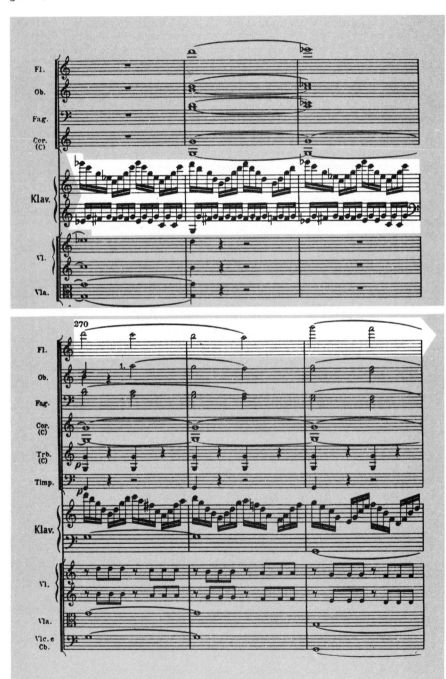

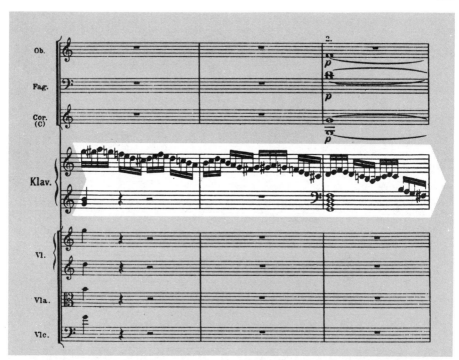

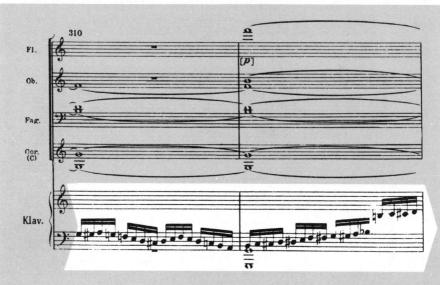

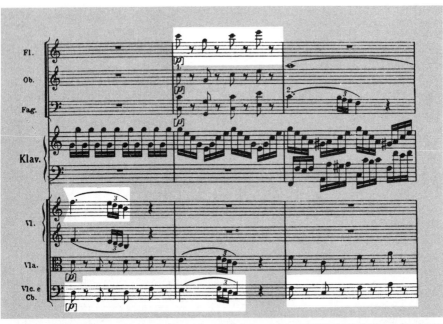

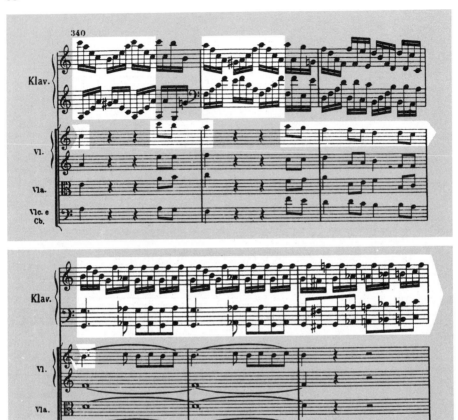

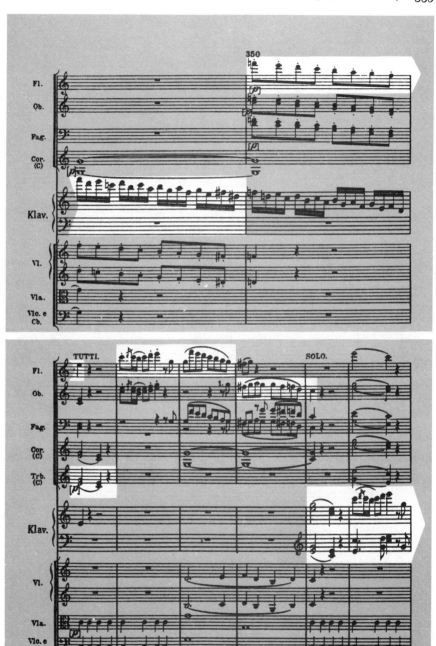

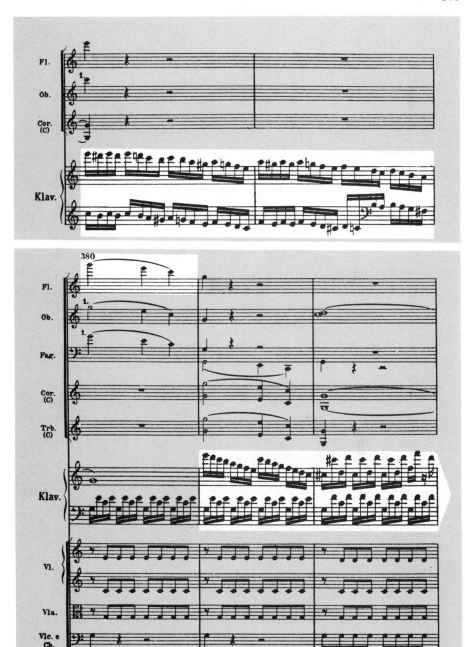

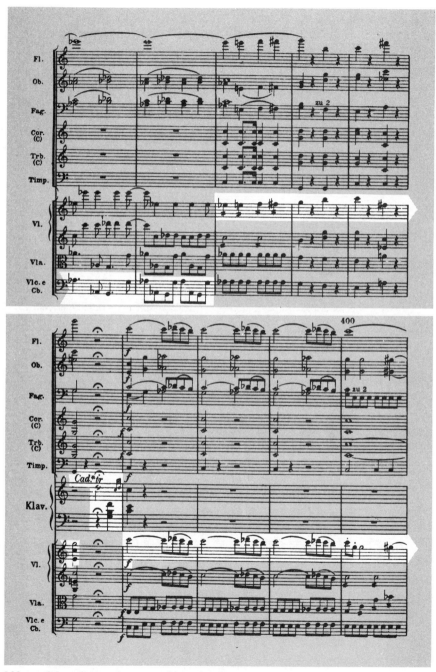

° Mozart did not leave written-out cadenzas for this concerto. Modern pianists supply their own or choose from among various published cadenzas.

II.

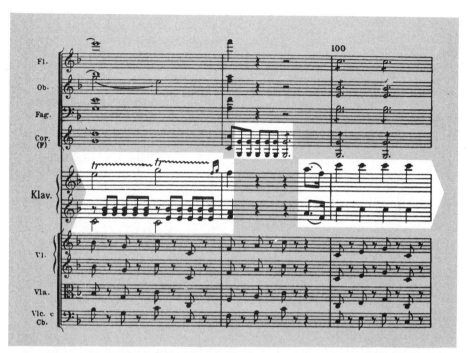

III.

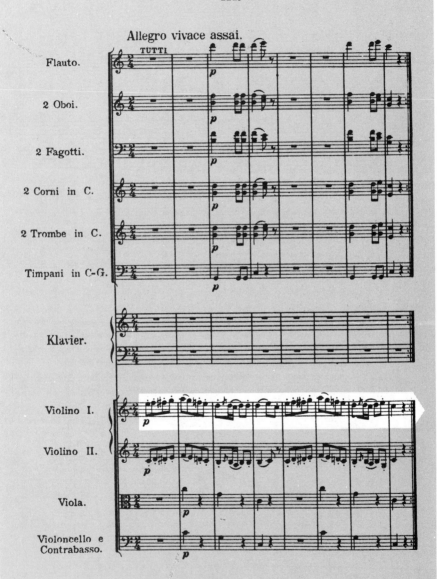

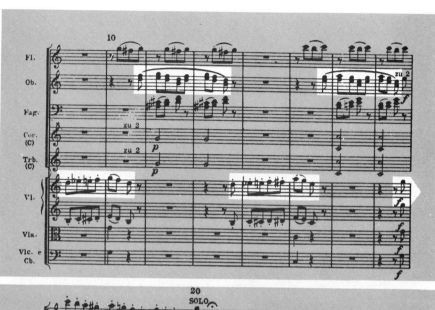

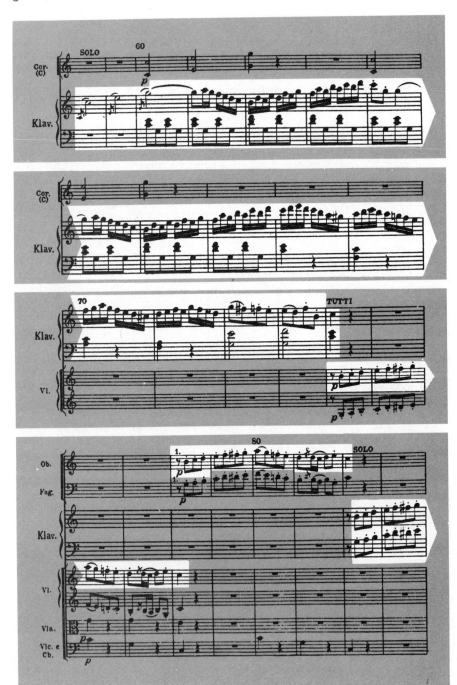

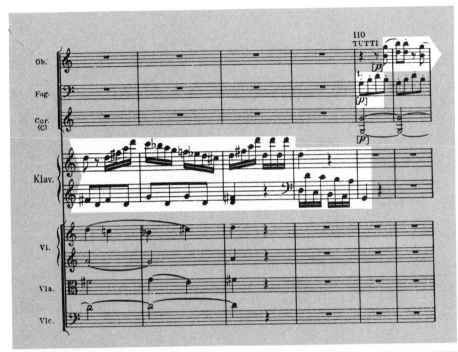

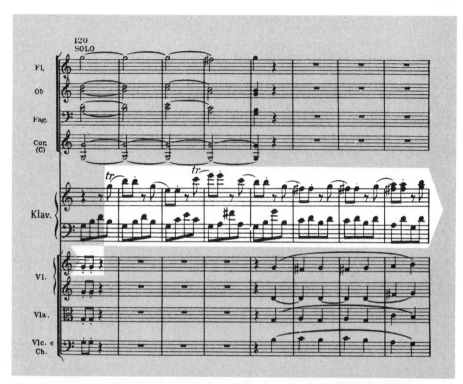

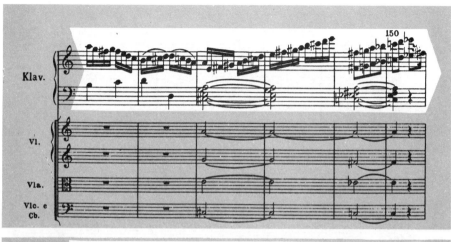

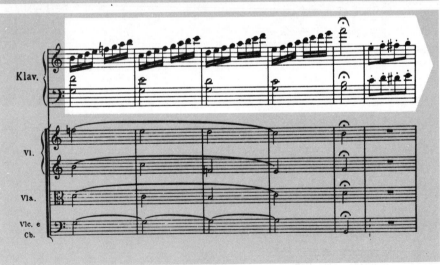

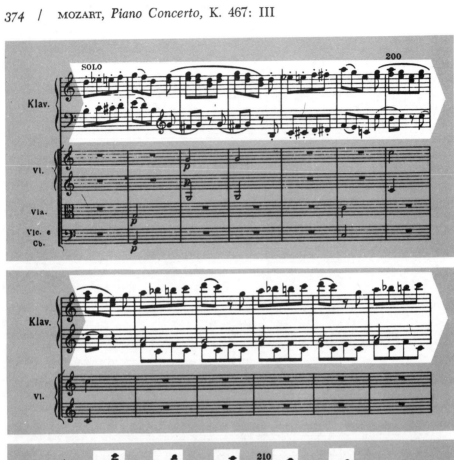

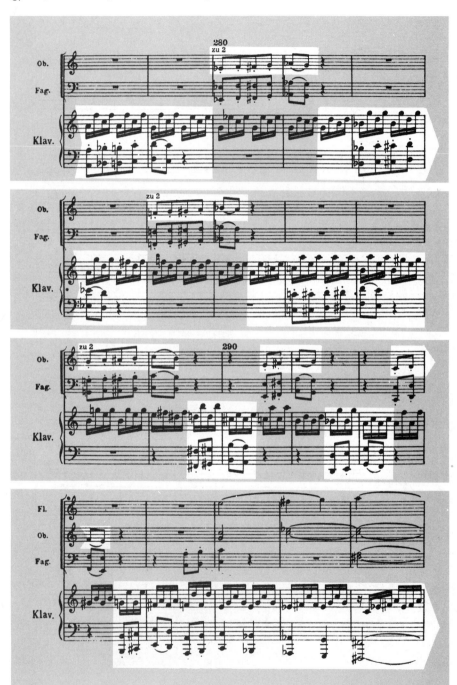

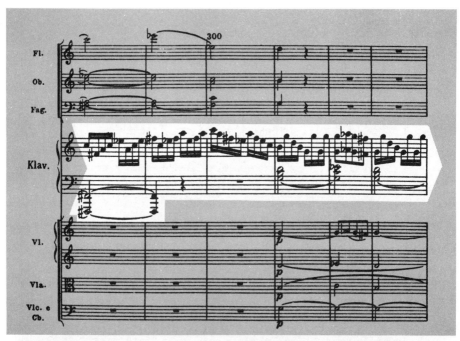

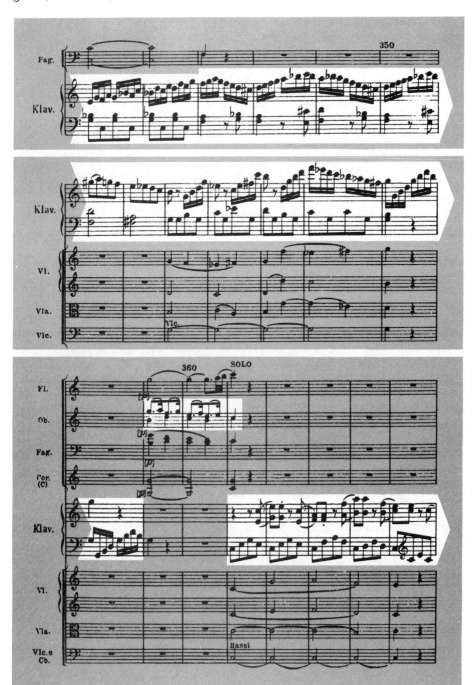

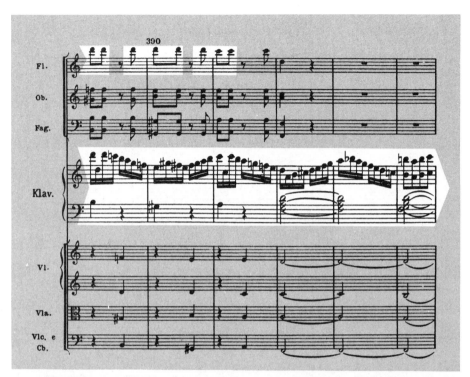

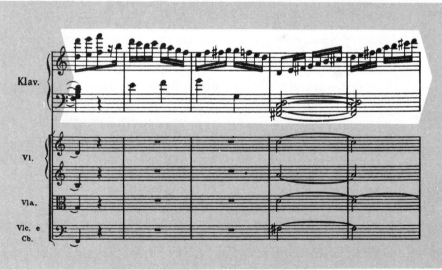

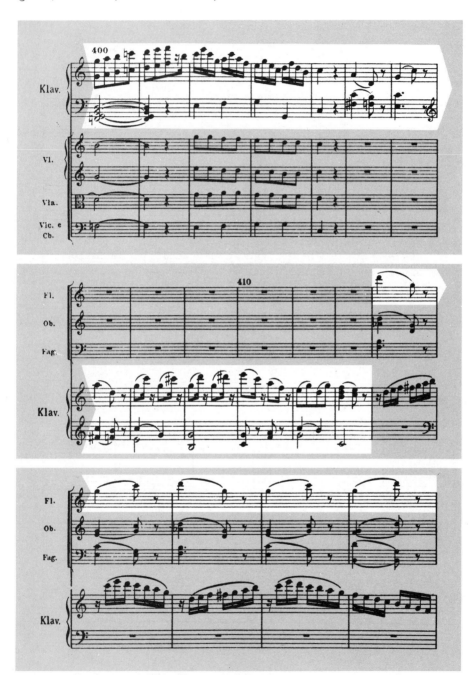

* See note on p. 405.

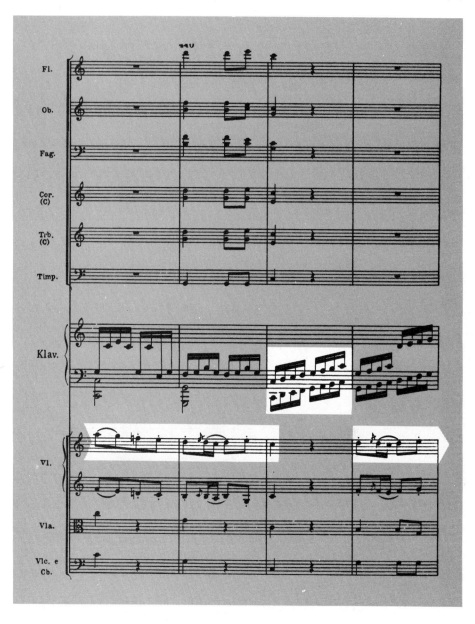

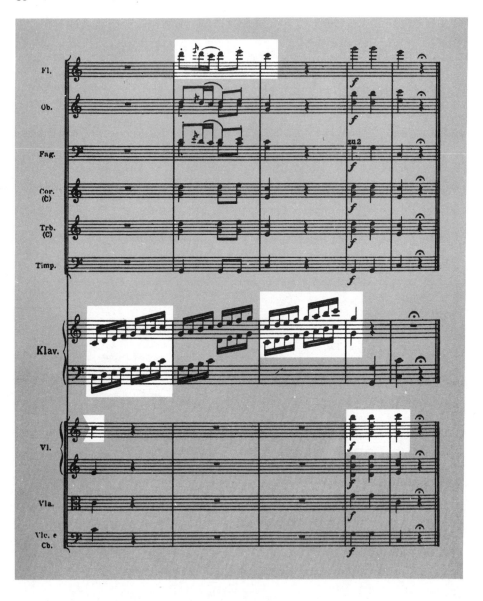

19. WOLFGANG AMADEUS MOZART (1756-1791),
Eine kleine Nachtmusik (1787)

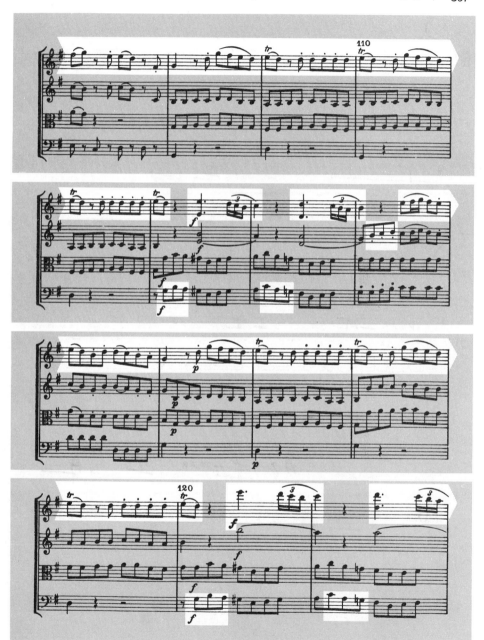

III

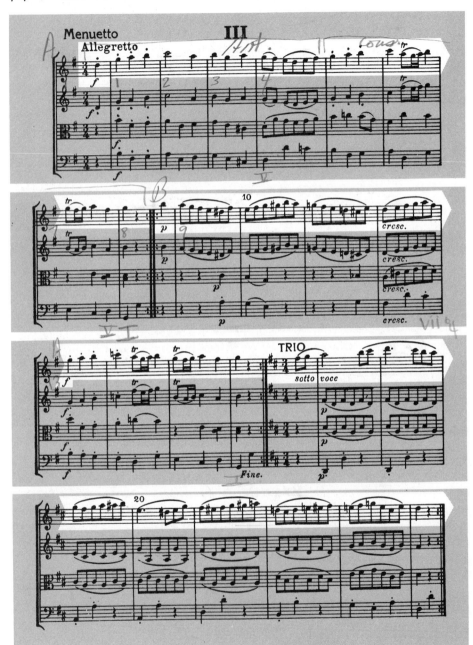

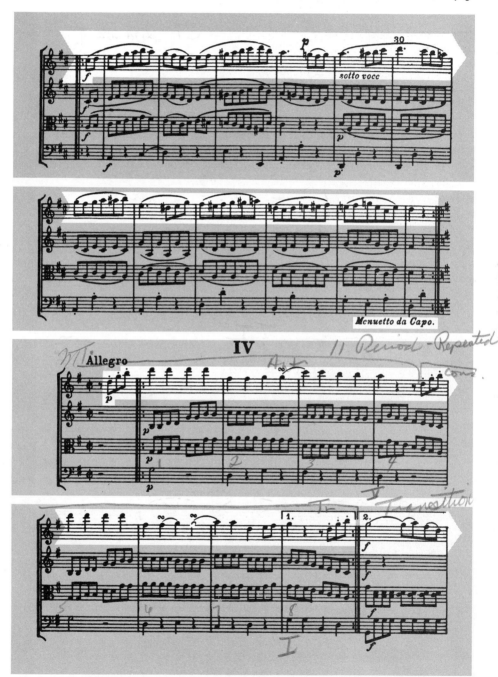

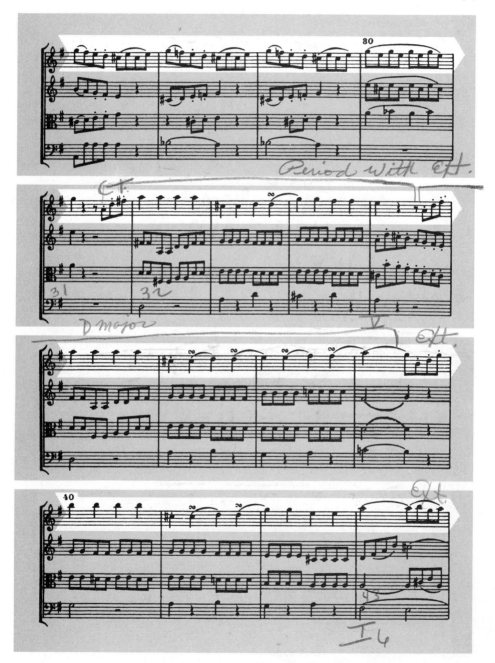

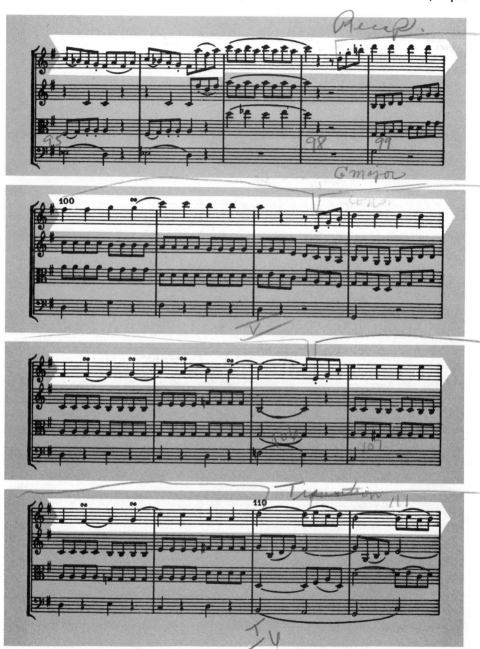

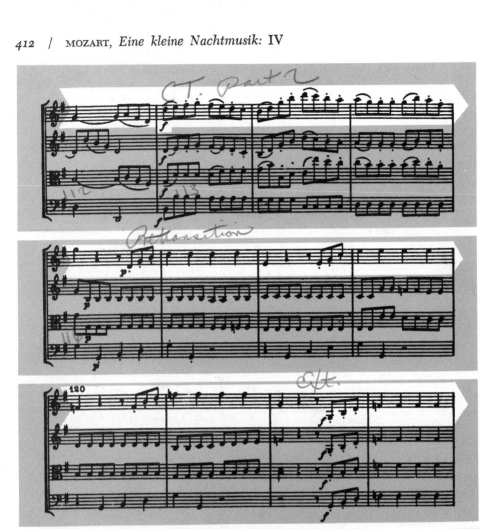

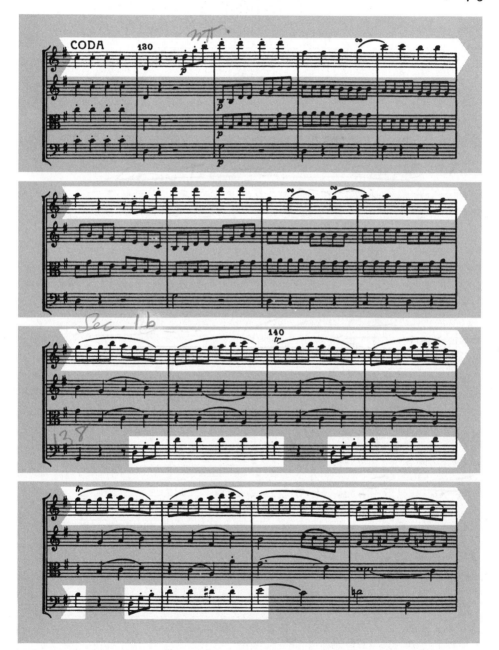

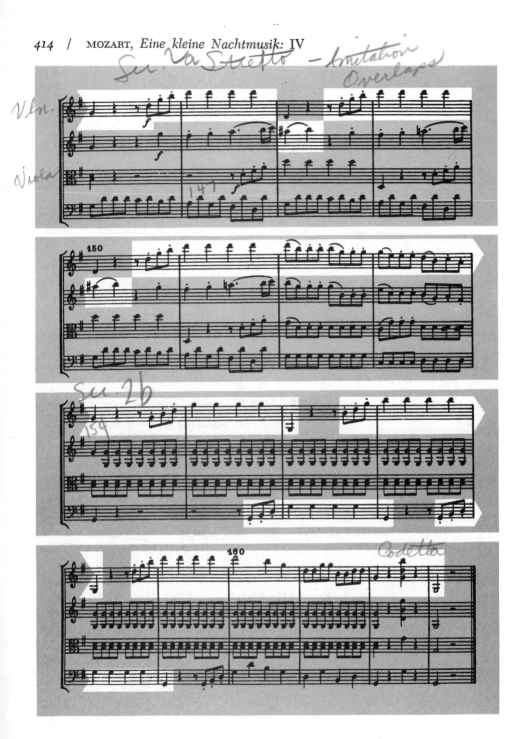

20. MOZART, Excerpts from *Don Giovanni* (1787)

No. 4: *Catalogue Aria*

in Al - ma-gna due cen-to e trent' u - na,
Down for Eng-land, a hun - dred-e - lev - en;

cen - to in Francia, in Turchia no-vant' u - na; ma, in I -
For San Ma - ri - no a mere nine-ty - sev-en; But prim and

spa-gna, ma in I - spa-gna son già mille e tre! mil-le e tre!
prop-er Spain con - tri-butes a thou-sand-and-three! Can that be?

mil - le e tre! V'han fra que-ste con-ta - di - ne,
Yes, it's three. There are bar-maids, bas-ket-weav-ers,

ca - me-rie - re, cit-ta-di - ne, V'han contesse, ba - ro - nes-se,
There are dair-y-maids and di-vas, Count-less count-ess-es, prin-cess-es,

marchesa-ne, prin-ci-pesse, e v'han don-ne d'o-gni gra-do, d'o-gni for-ma, d'ogni e-
In the ranks of his suc-cess-es, Ev-'ry pos-si-ble con-di-tion, Oc-cu-pa-tion, form and

tà, d'o-gni for-ma, d'o-gni e-tà,   In I-ta-li-a
age All a-rouse his gal-lant rage!   In A-ra-bia,

sei cen-to e qua-ran-ta,   in Al-ma-gna
ten doz-en were fool-ish;   In Dal-ma-tia,

due cen-to e trent' u-na,   cen - to in Fran - cia, in Tur-
a hun-dred were wan-ton;   Here's   Hel - ve - tia— a

chia   no   vant' u-na, ma, ma,— ma   in I-spa-gna! ma in I-
gross   in   each Can-ton; But, but,— but over-prud-ish Spain con-

No. 7: Duet: *Là ci darem la mano*

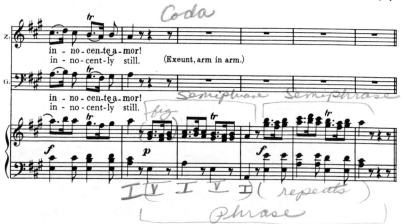

21. LUDWIG VAN BEETHOVEN (1770-1827),
Piano Sonata in C minor, Opus 13 (*Pathétique*) (1799)

attacca subito il Allegro.

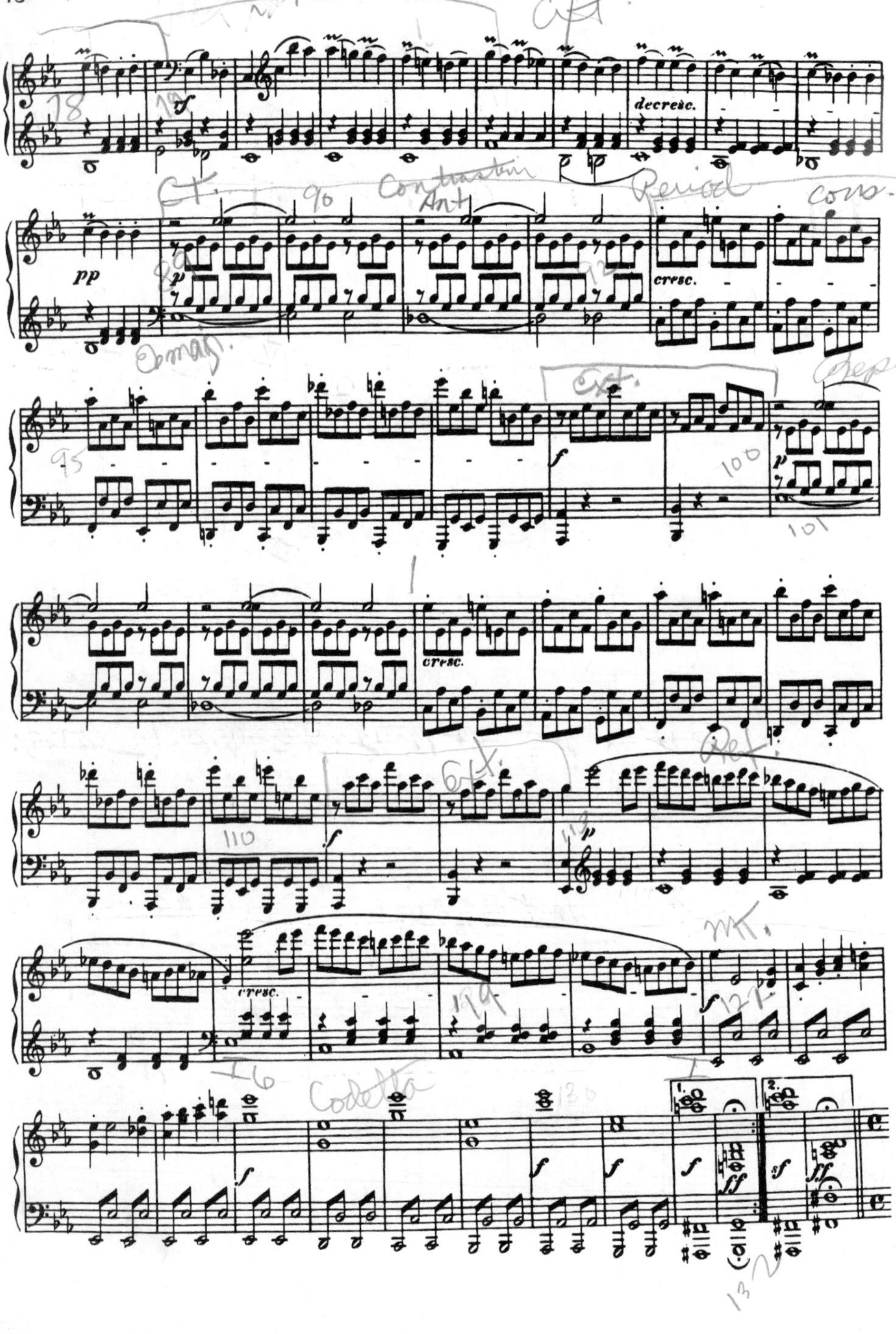
decresc.
pp
p
cresc.
f
p
cresc.
f
p
cresc.
f
ff

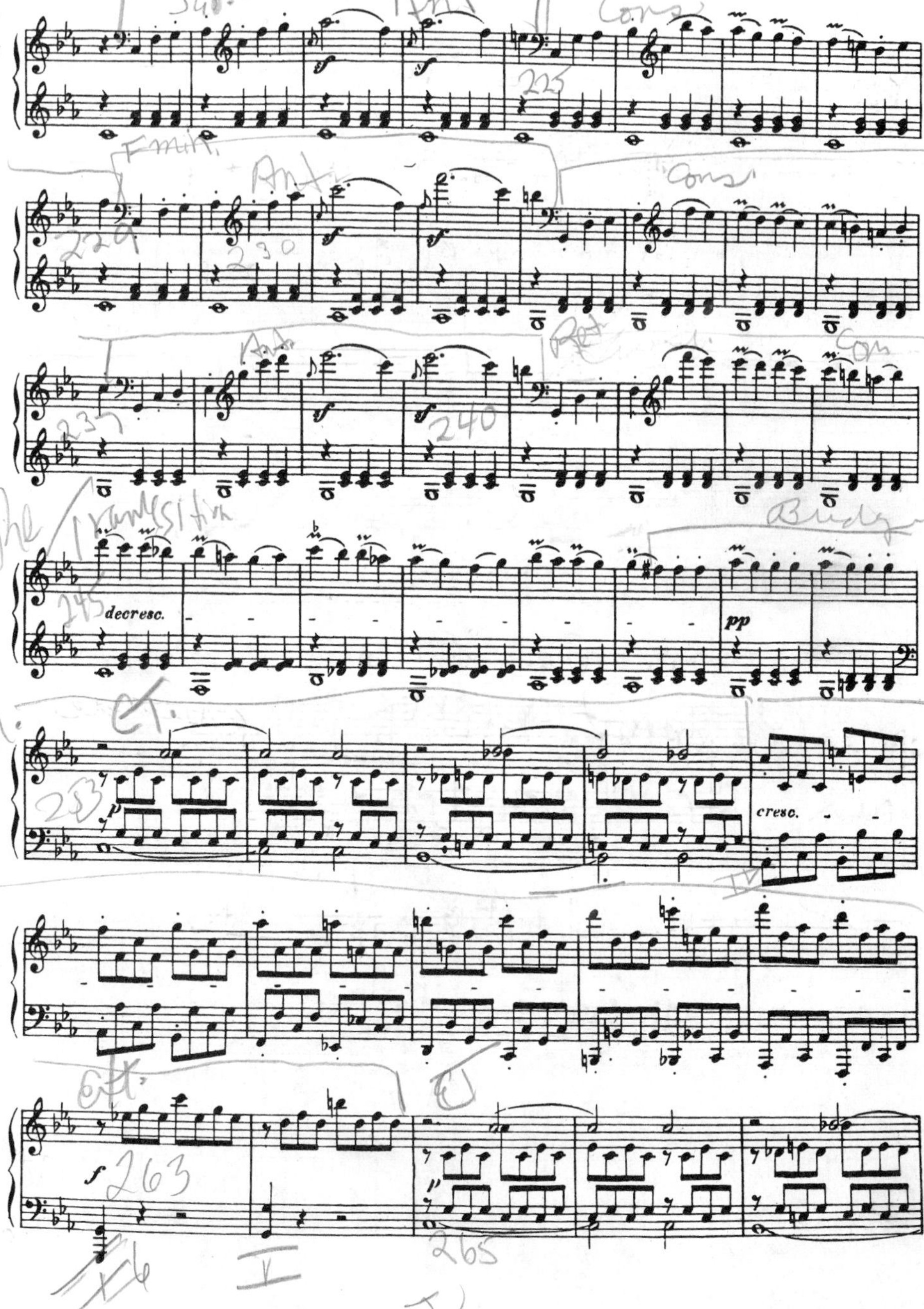
sf
sf
sf
sf
sf
sf
decresc.
pp
p
cresc.
f
p

22. BEETHOVEN, *Symphony No. 5 in C minor* (1807)

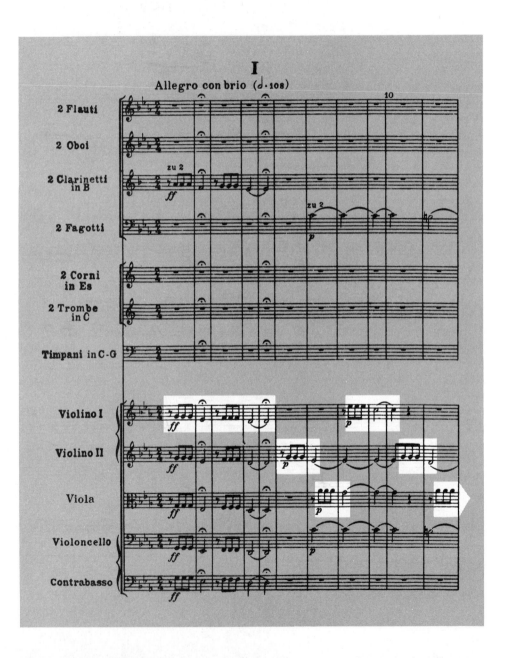

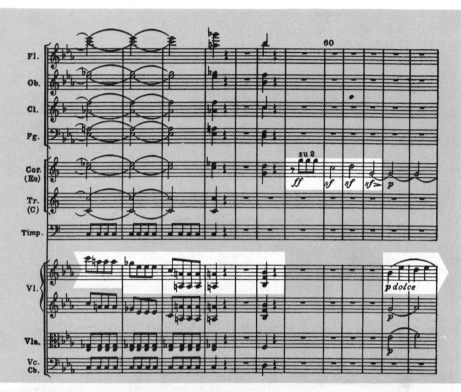

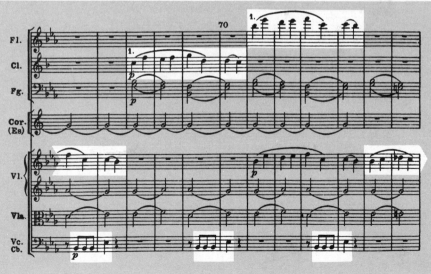

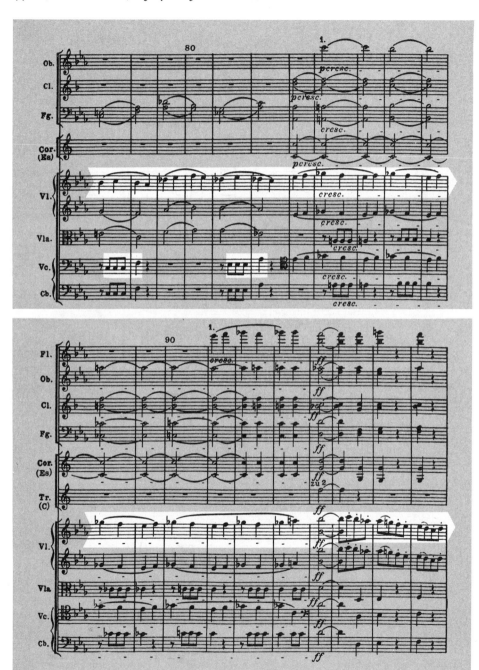

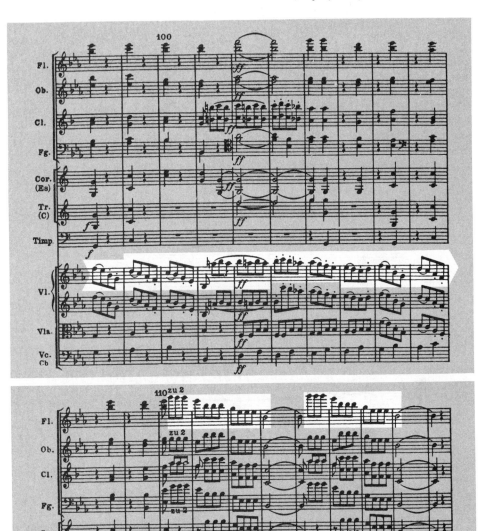

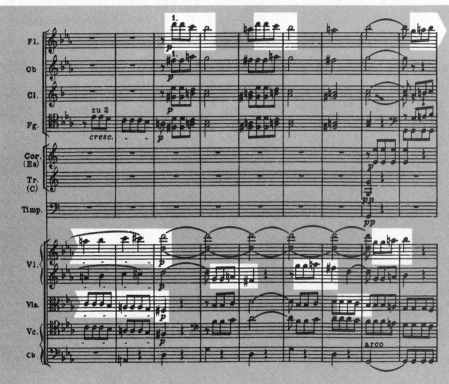

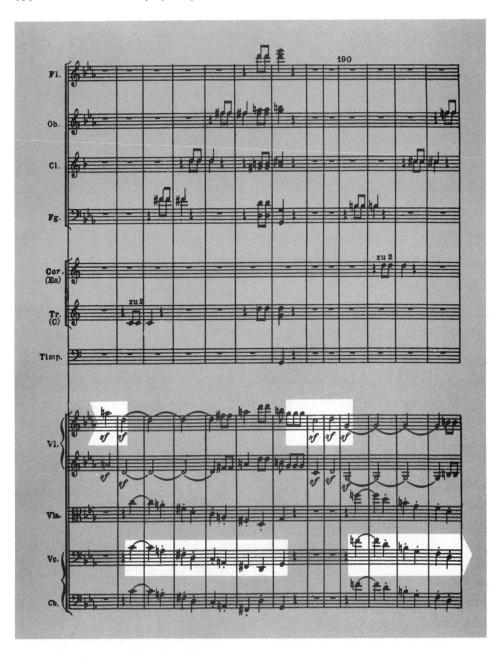

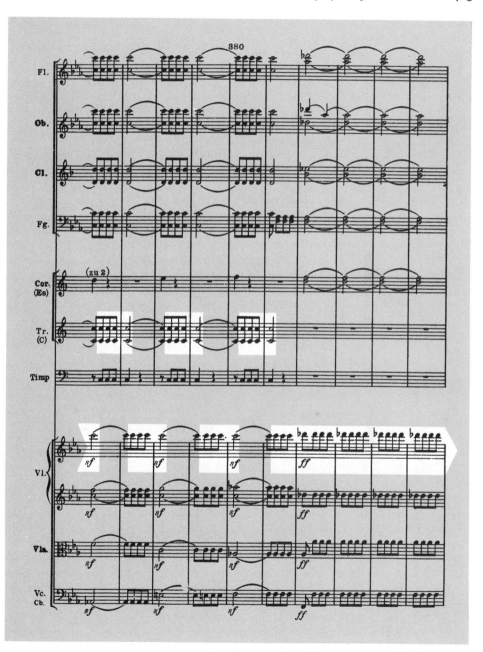

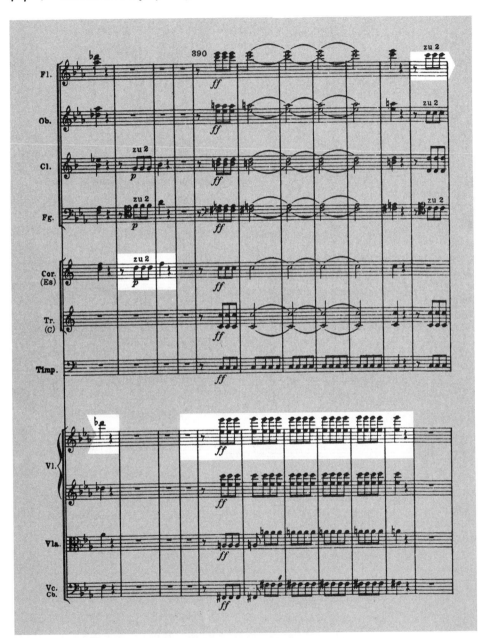

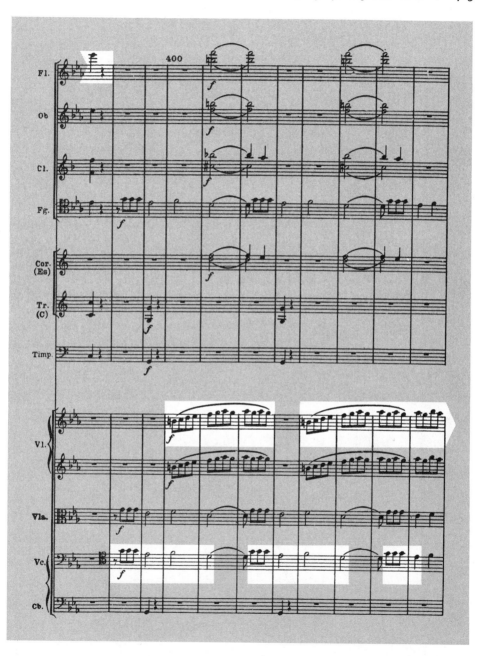

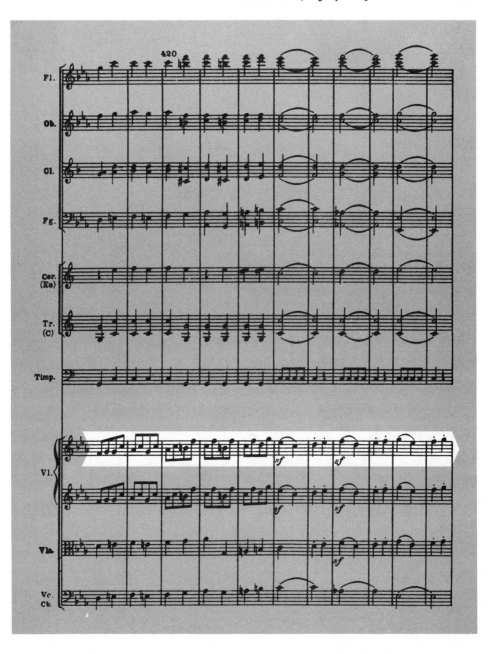

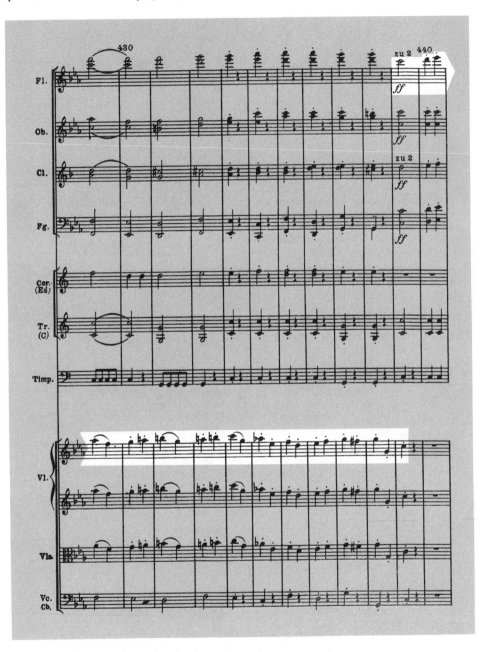

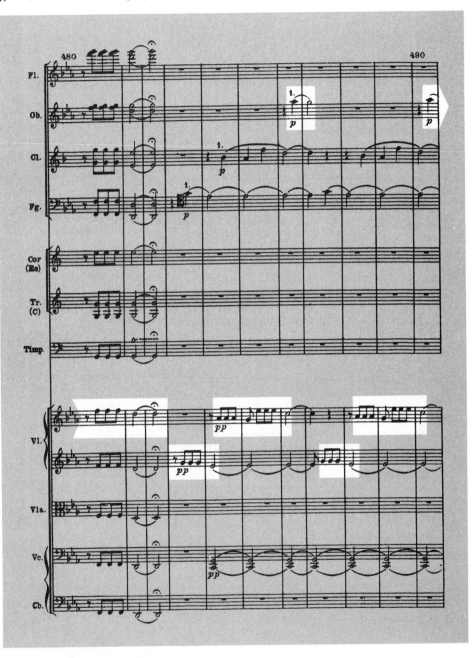

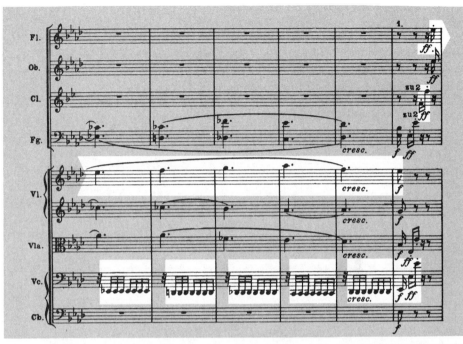

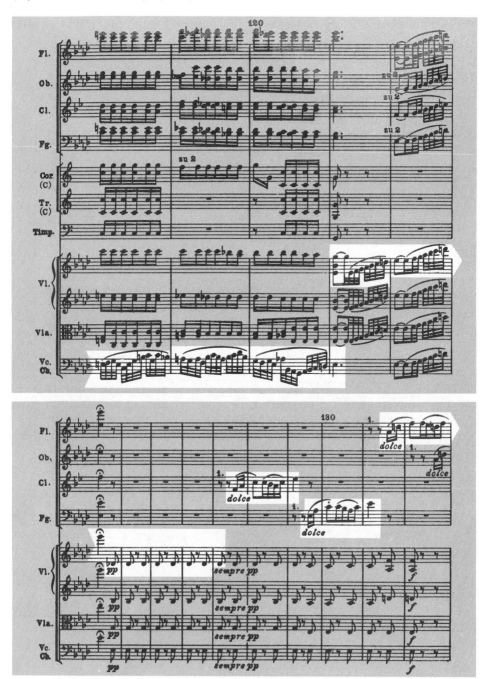

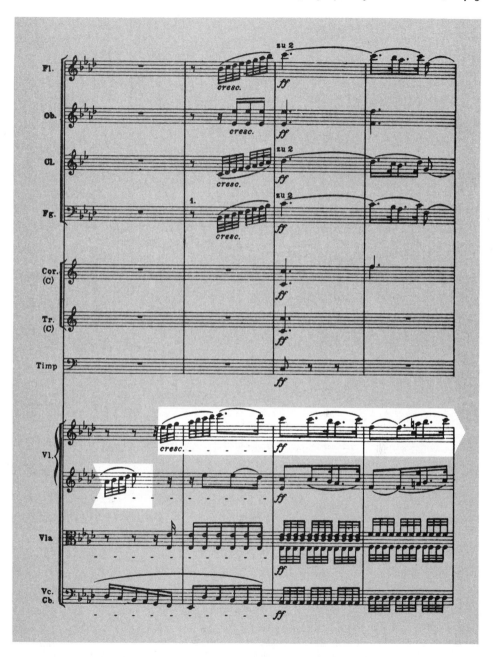

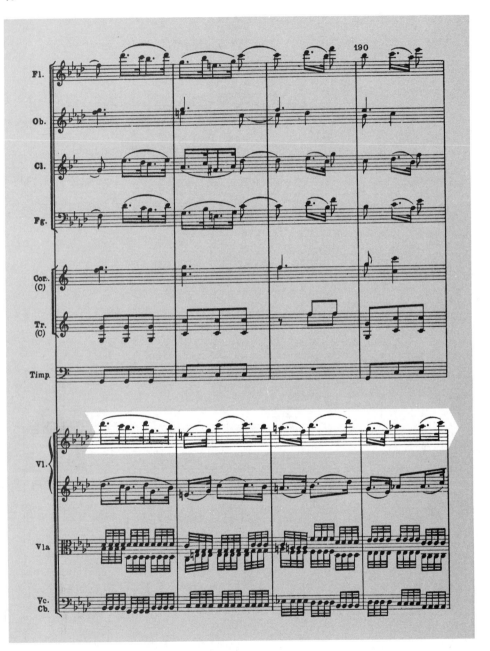

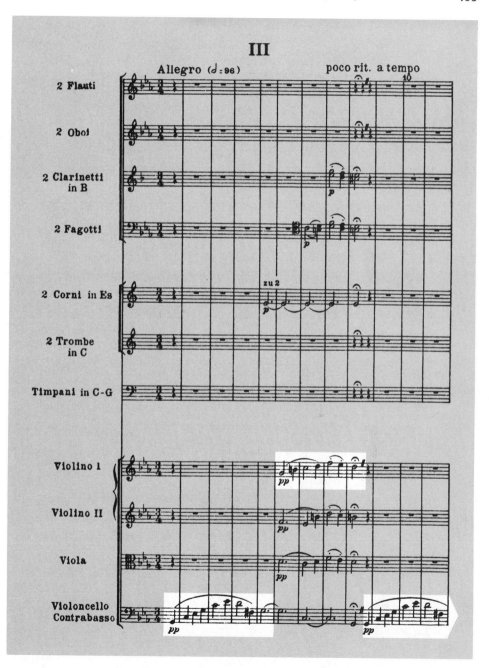

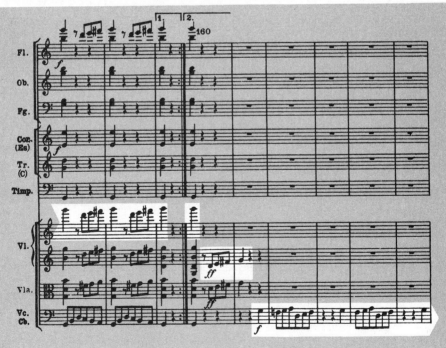

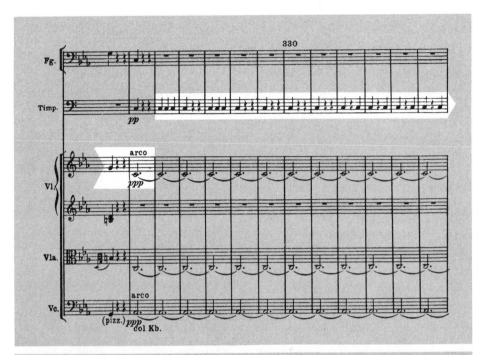

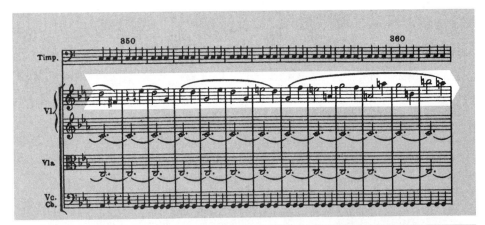

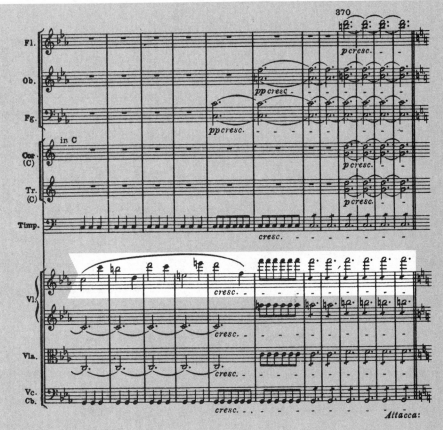

IV

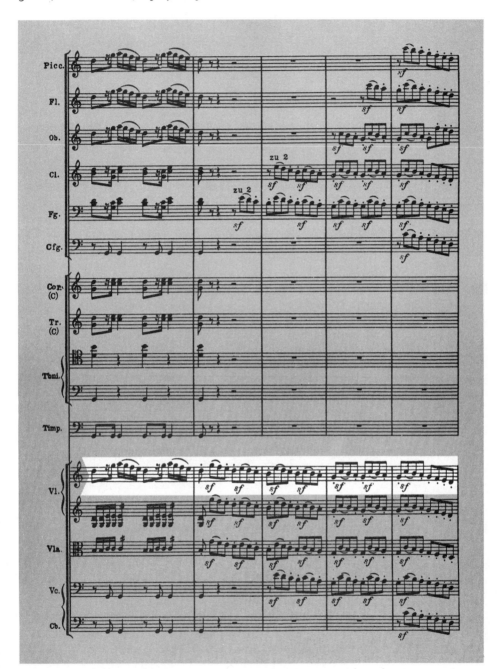

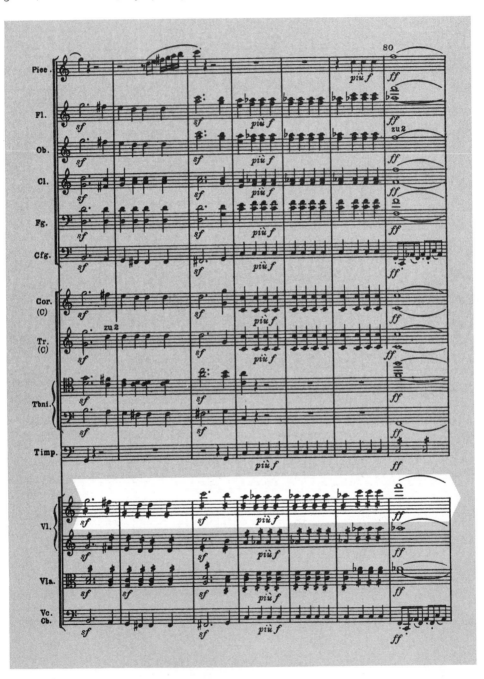

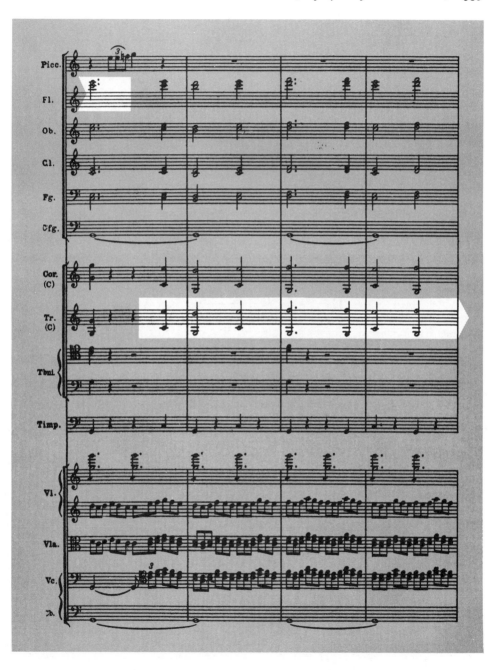

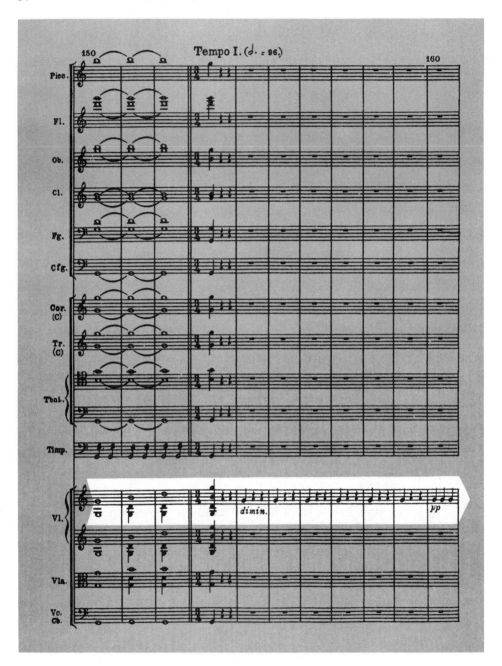

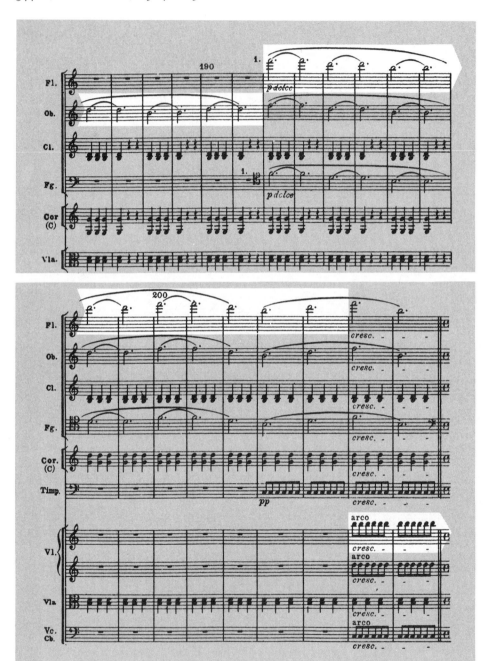

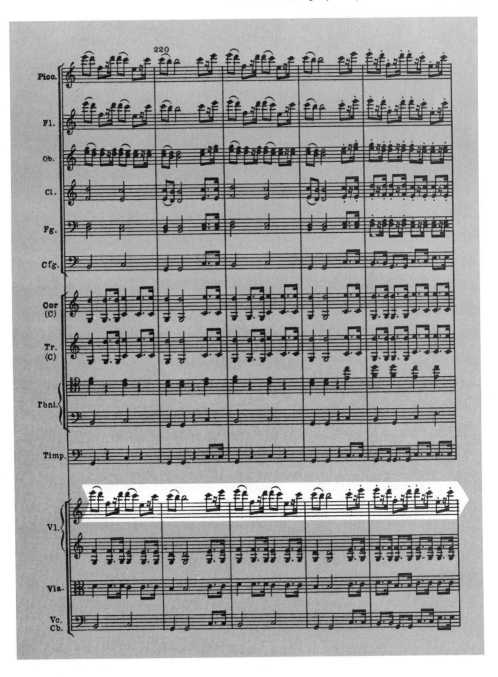

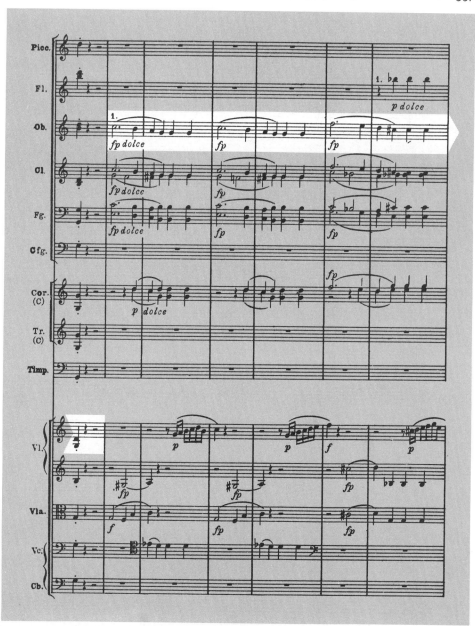

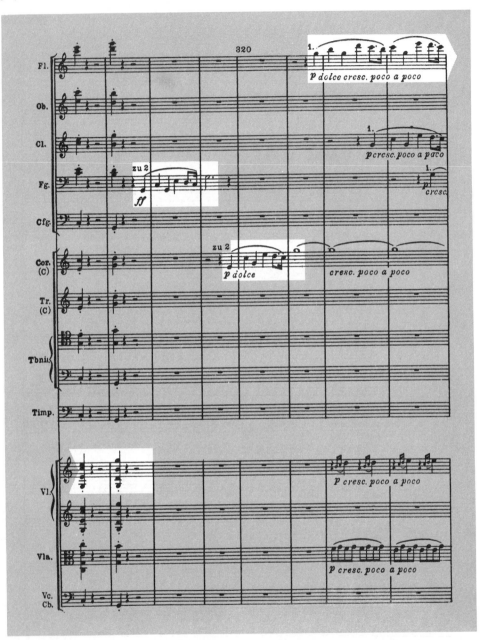

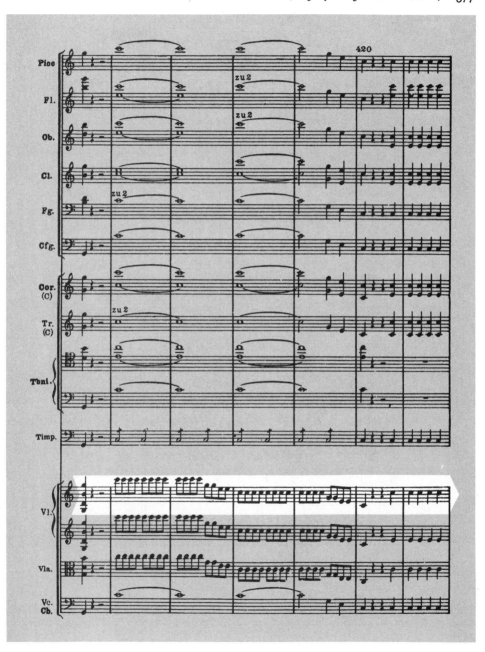

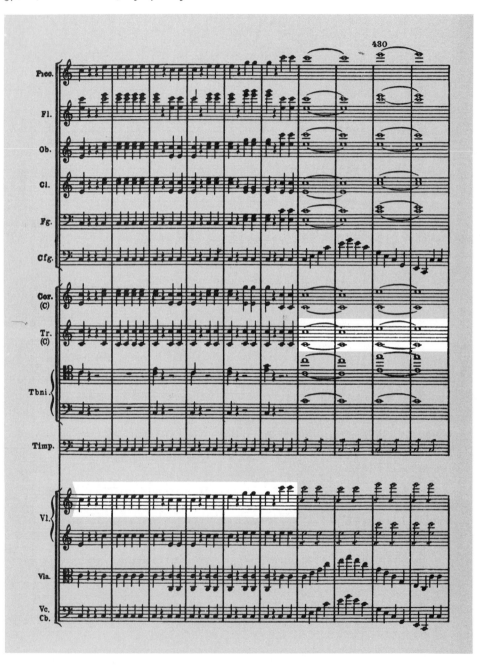

23. FRANZ SCHUBERT (1797-1828), *Erlkönig* (1815)

Translation

Wer reitet so spät durch Nacht
  und Wind?
Es ist der Vater mit seinem Kind;
er hat den Knaben wohl in dem Arm,
er fasst ihn sicher, er hält ihn warm.

"Mein Sohn, was birgst du so bang dein
  Gesicht?"
"Siehst, Vater, du den Erlkönig nicht?
den Erlenkönig mit Kron' und Schweif?"
"Mein Sohn, es ist ein Nebelstreif."

"Du liebes Kind, komm, geh' mit mir!
gar schöne Spiele spiel' ich mit dir;
manch' bunte Blumen sind an dem Strand;
meine Mutter hat manch' gülden Gewand."

"Mein Vater, mein Vater, und hörest du
  nicht,
was Erlenkönig mir leise verspricht?"
"Sei ruhig, bleibe ruhig, mein Kind;
in dürren Blättern säuselt der Wind."

"Willst, feiner Knage, du mit mir geh'n?
meine Töchter sollen dich warten schön;
meine Töchter führen den nächtlichen
  Reih'n
und wiegen und tanzen und singen dich ein."

"Mein Vater, mein Vater, und siehst du nicht
  dort
Erlkönigs Töchter am düstern Ort?"
"Mein Sohn, mein Sohn, ich seh' es genau,
es scheinen die alten Weiden so grau."

"Ich liebe dich, mich reizt deine schöne
  Gestalt,
und bist du nicht willig, so brauch' ich
  Gewalt."
"Mein Vater, mein Vater, jetzt fasst er
  mich an!
Erlkönig hat mir ein Leid's gethan!"

Dem Vater grauset's, er reitet geschwind,
er hält in Armen das ächzende Kind,
erreicht den Hof mit Müh' und Noth:
in seinem Armen das Kind war todt!

      JOHANN WOLFGANG VON GOETHE

Who rides so late through the night
  and the wind?
It is the father with his child;
he folds the boy close in his arms,
he clasps him securely, he holds him warmly.

'My son, who do you hide your face so
  anxiously?"
"Father, don't you see the Erlking?
The Erlking with his crown and his train?"
"My son, it is a streak of mist."

"Dear child, come, go with me!
I'll play the prettiest games with you.
Many colored flowers grow along the shore;
my mother has many golden garments."

"My father, my father, and don't you
  hear
the Erlking whispering promises to me?"
"Be quiet, stay quiet, my child;
the wind is rustling in the dead leaves."

"My handsome boy, will you come with me?
My daughters shall wait upon you;
my daughters lead off in the dance every
  night,
and cradle and dance and sing you to sleep."

"My father, my father, and don't you
  see there
the Erlking's daughters in the shadows?"
"My son, my son, I see it clearly;
the old willows look so gray."

"I love you, your beautiful figure
  delights me!
And if you are not willing, then I
  shall use force!"
"My father, my father, now he is taking
  hold of me!
The Erlking has hurt me!"

The father shudders, he rides swiftly on;
he holds in his arms the groaning child,
he reaches the courtyard weary and anxious:
in his arms the child was dead.

      PHILIP L. MILLER

24. SCHUBERT, Fourth movement (Theme and Variations) from
Quintet in A major (Trout) for Violin, Viola, Cello, Double
Bass, and Piano (1819?)

Tema. Andantino

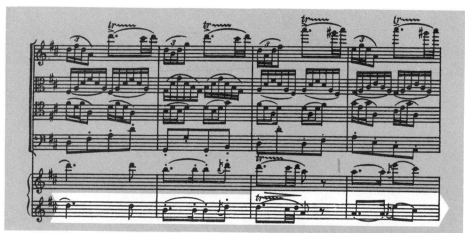

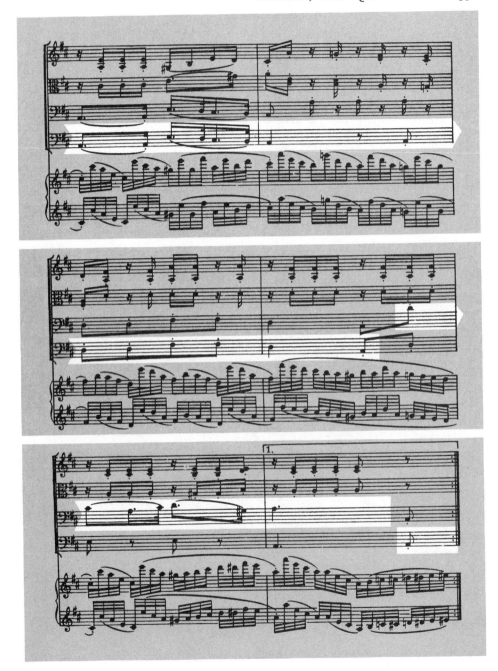

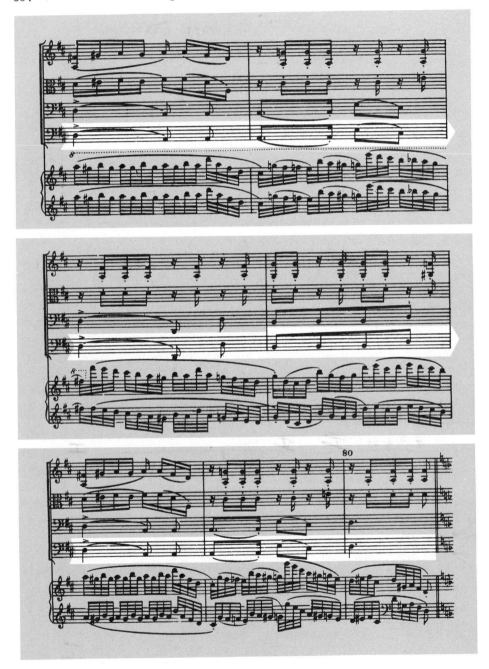

Dmin ff - pp.

Var. IV

F Major

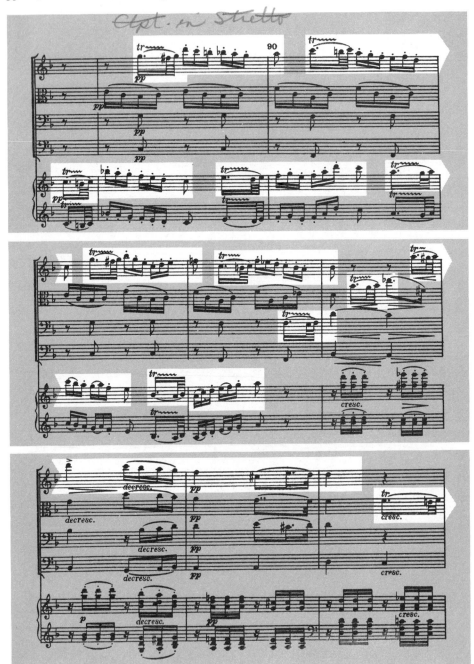

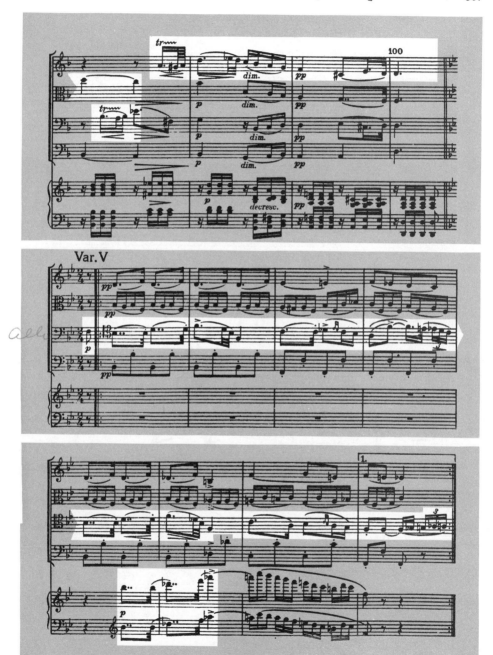

25. HECTOR BERLIOZ (1803-1869),
Fifth movement from *Symphonie fantastique* (1830)

Dream of a Witches' Sabbath

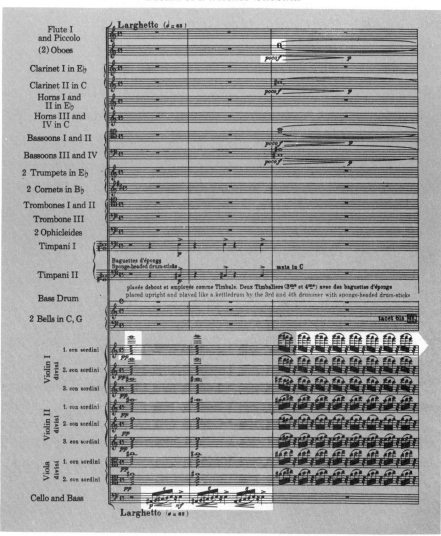

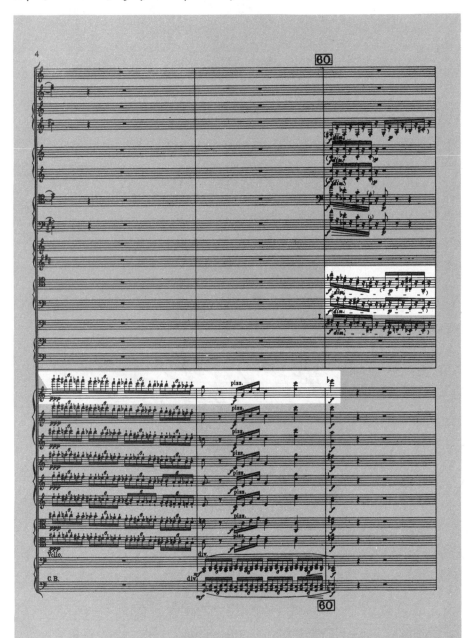

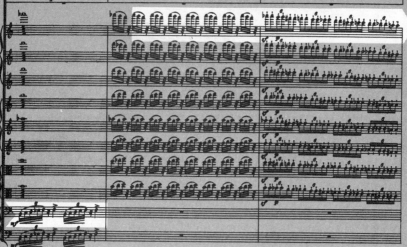

21
Allegro (♩. = 112)
Allegro assai (o = 76)
Solo
lointain
distant
ppp
cresc.
ouvert avec les cylindres
open, with valves
a 2.
I.
p cresc. poco a poco
Sur les deux timbales
p
cresc. poco a poco
sans sourdine
sans sourdine
Allegro (♩. = 112)
Allegro assai (o = 76)

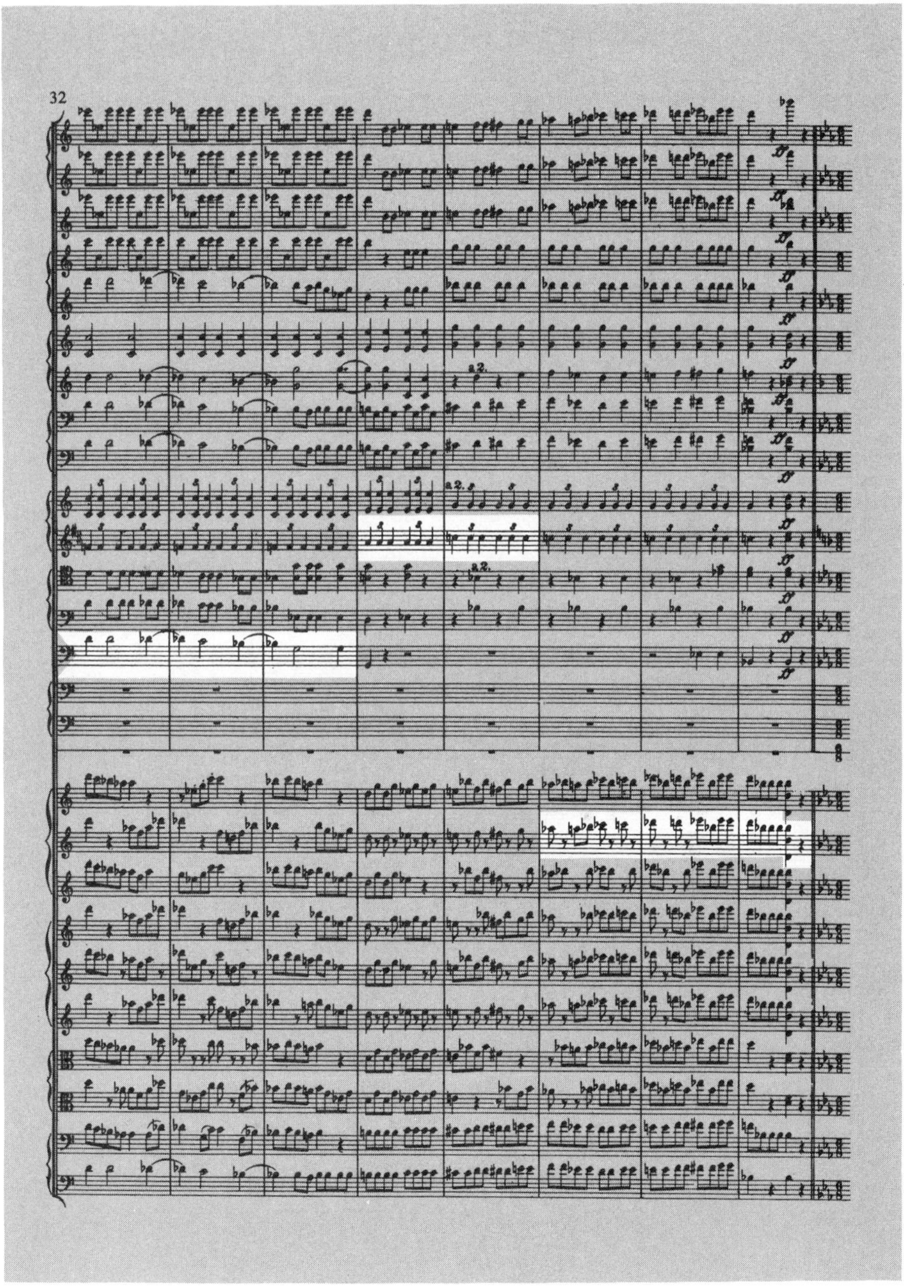
32
a2.
a2.
a2.
ff

67
Fl.
Fl. picc.
Ob.
Clar.
a 2.
Cor.
a 2.
unis.
Fag.
Tr.
Cttі
Tromb.
Oph.
Timp.
Viol.

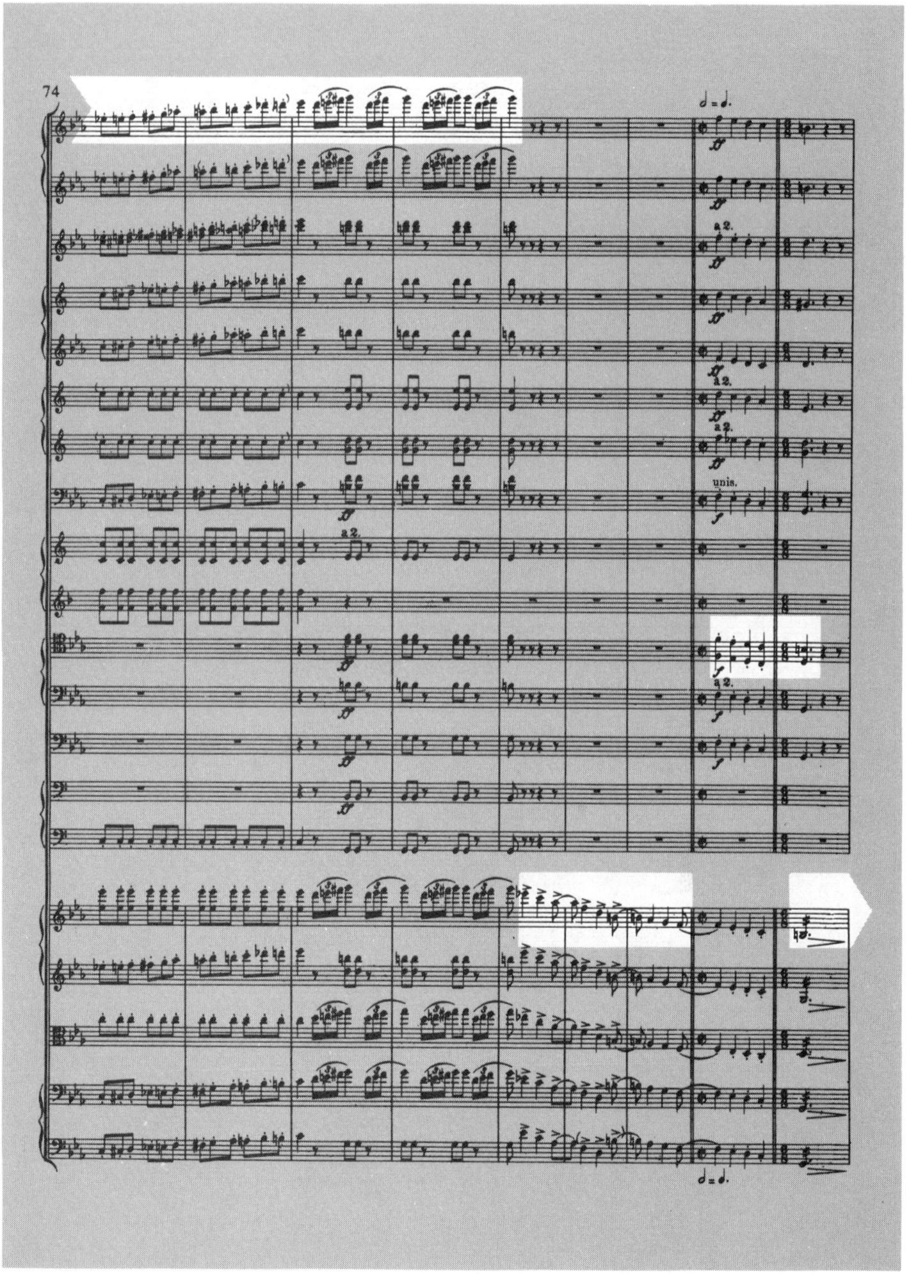
74
a 2.
unis.

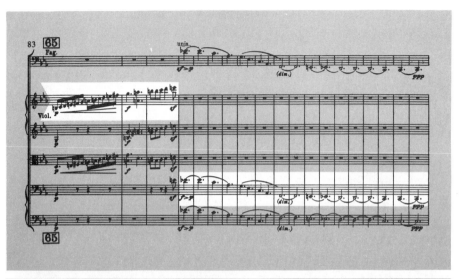

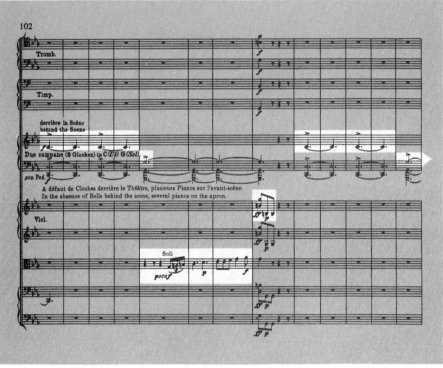

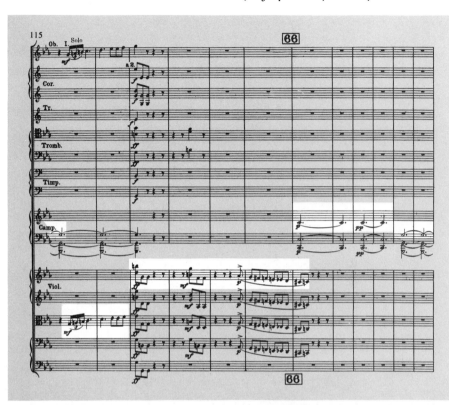

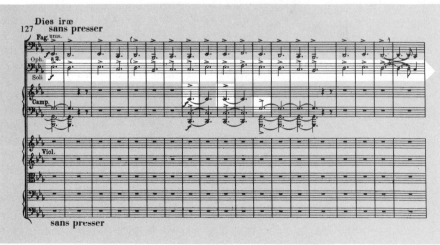

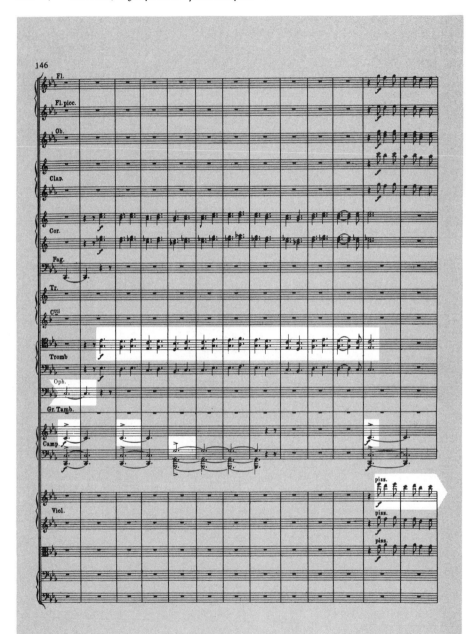

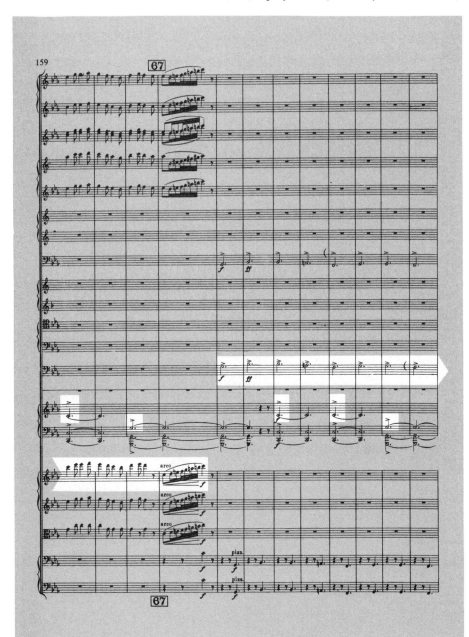

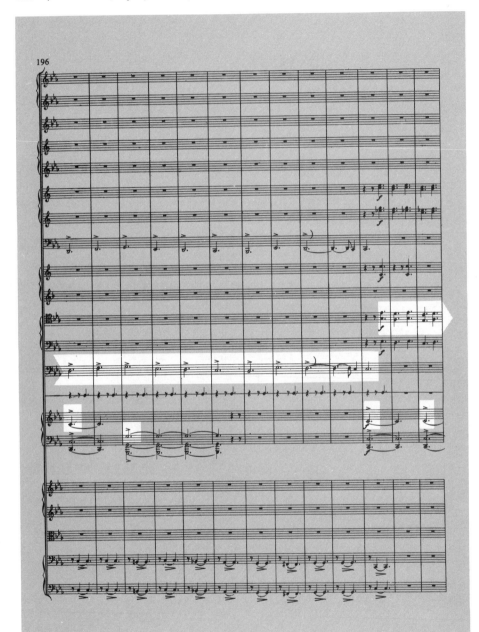

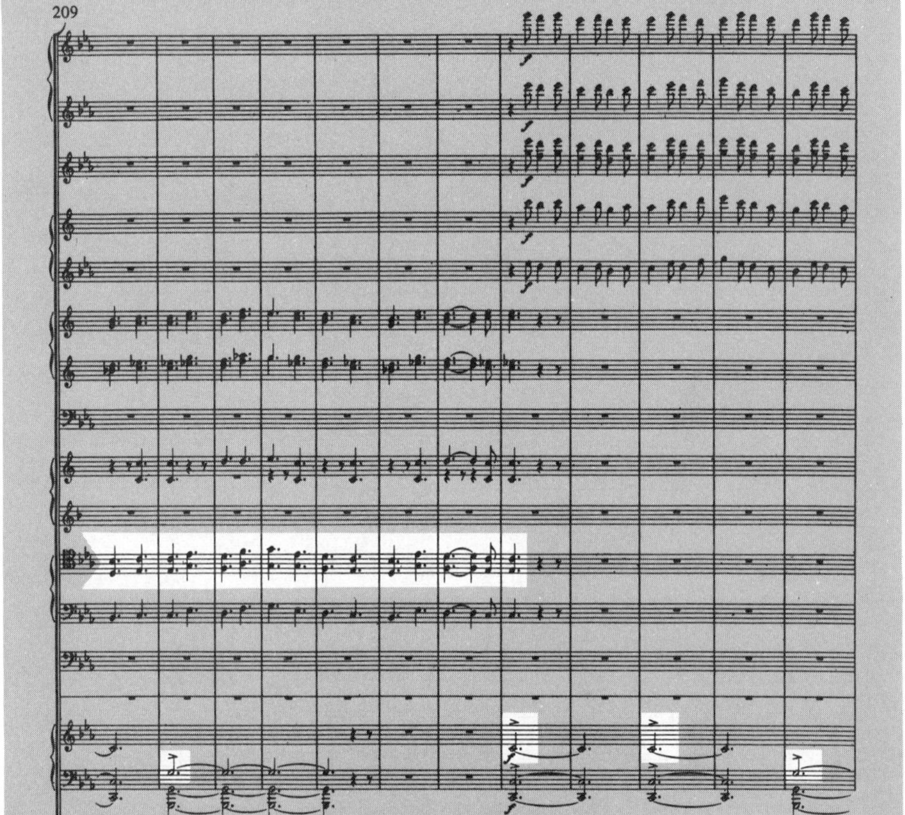
209
pizz.
pizz.
pizz.

Ronde du Sabbat
Witches' round dance
241 Un peu retenu

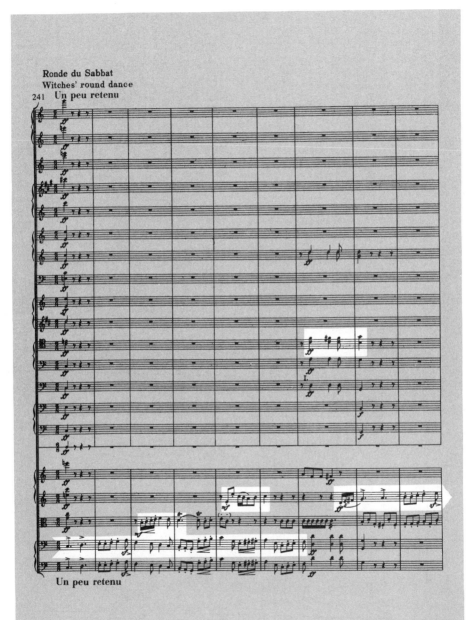

Un peu retenu

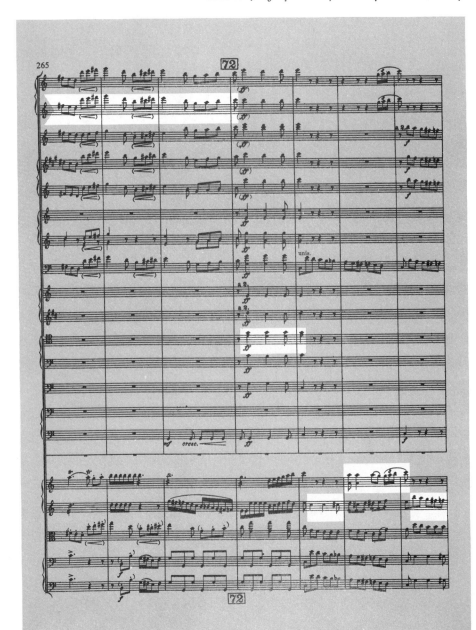

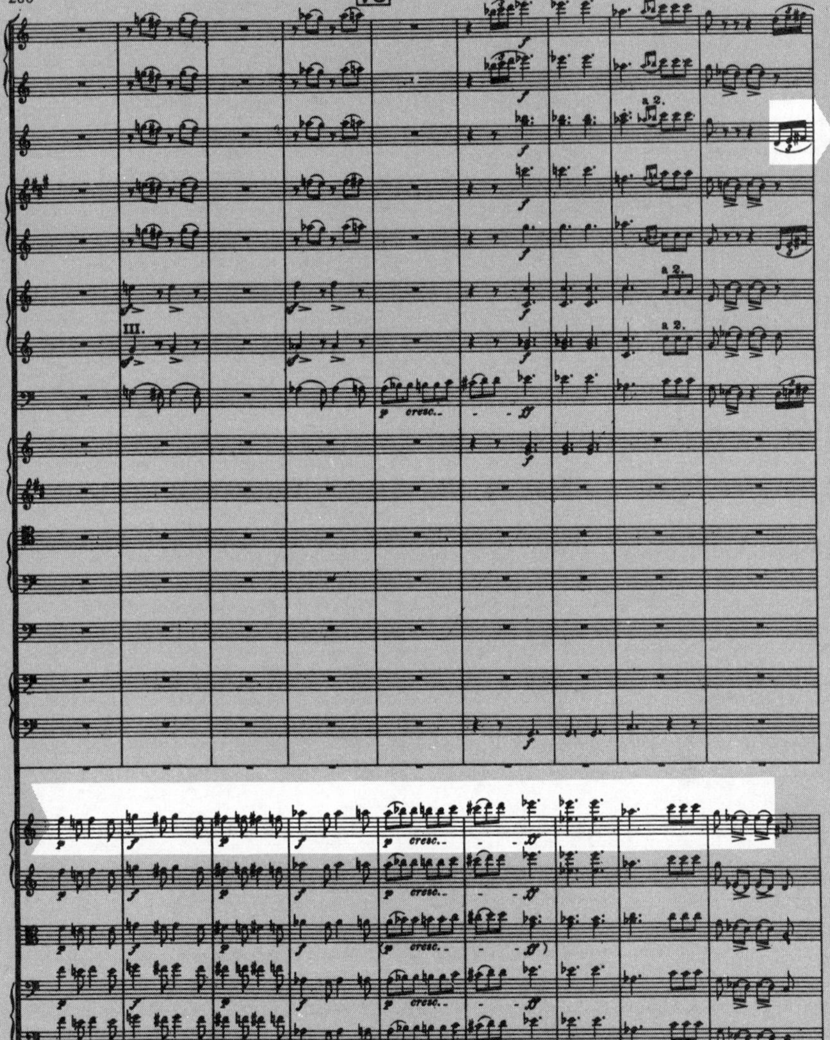
280
73
III.
a 2.
a 2.
a 2.
cresc.
73

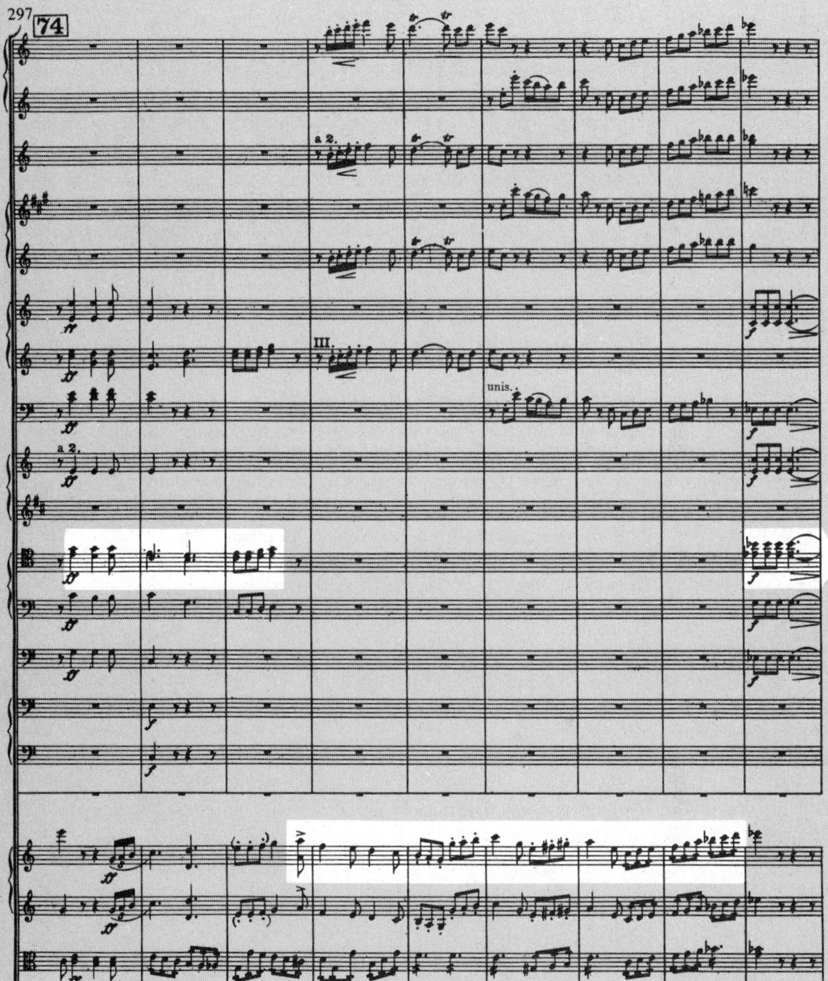
297
74
a 2.
III.
unis.
a 2.
74

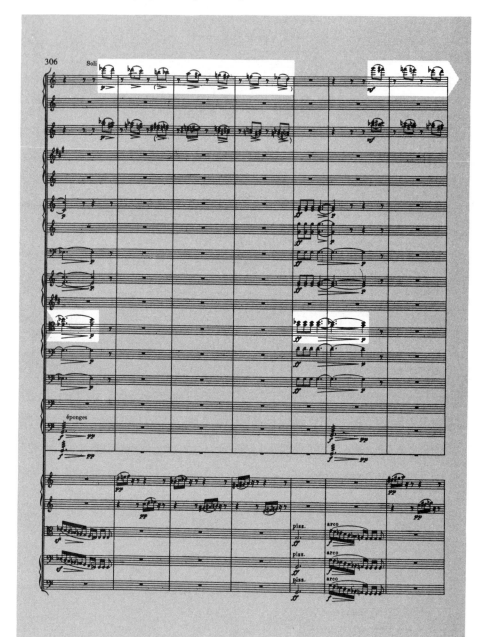

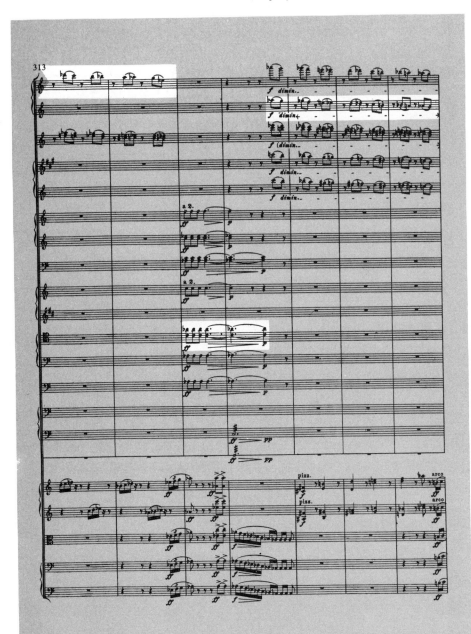

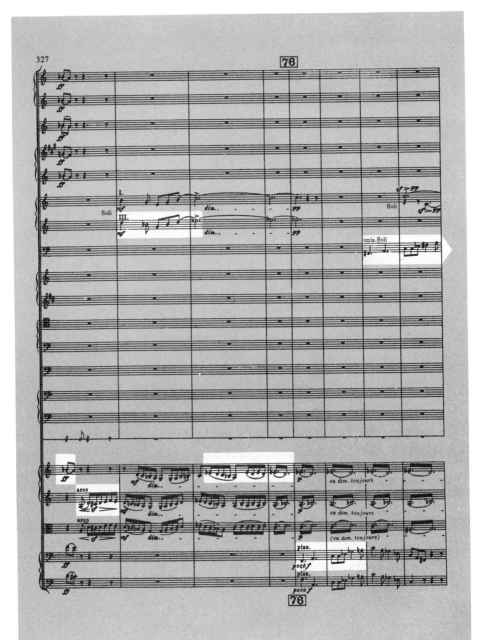

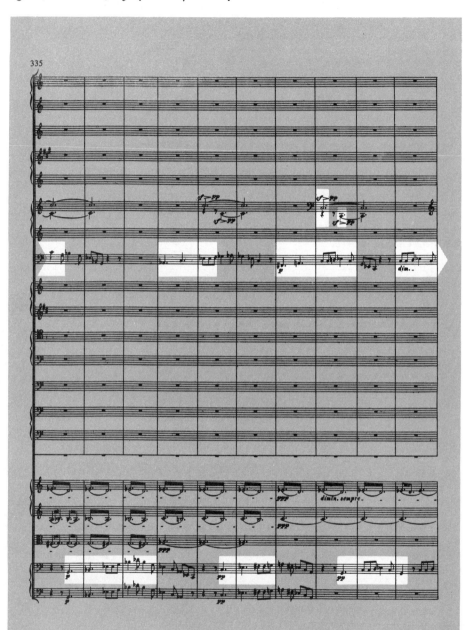

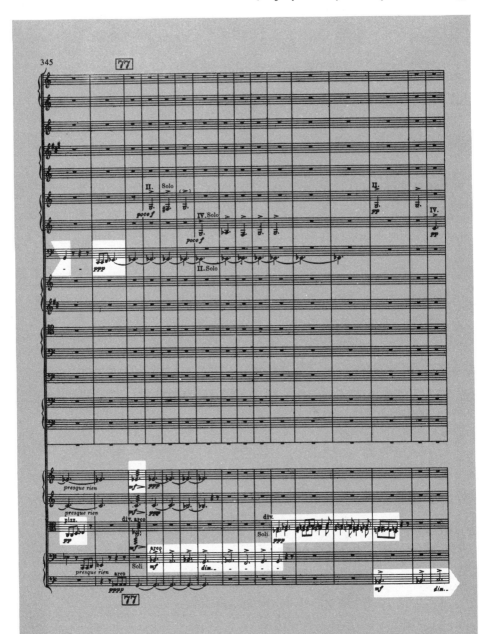

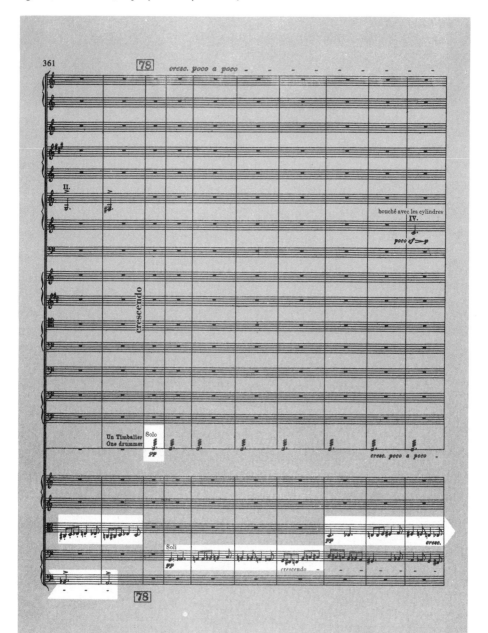

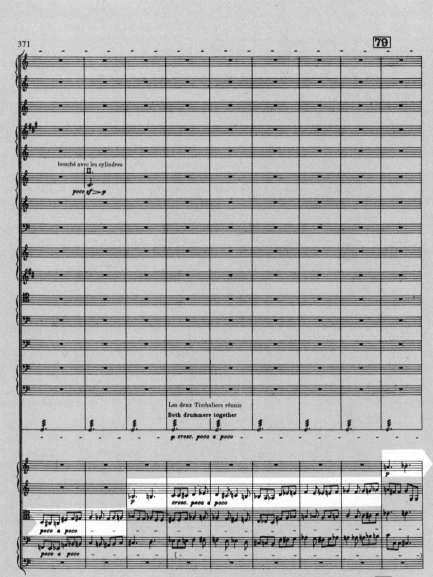

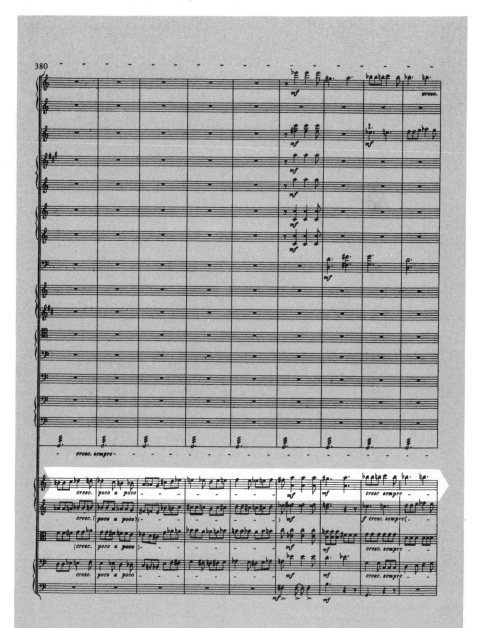

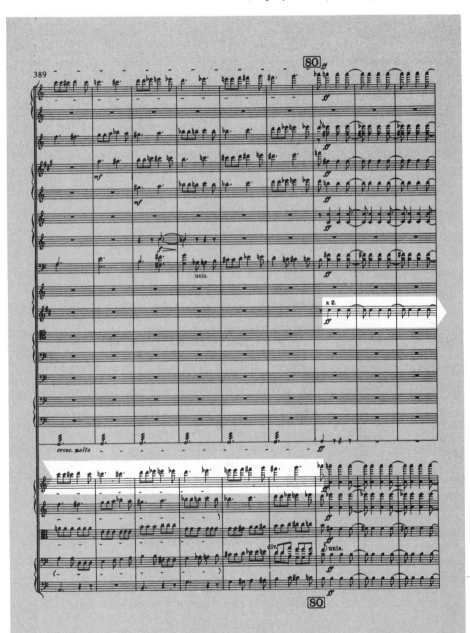

Dies irae et Ronde du Sabbat ensemble
414 Dies irae and witches' round dance together

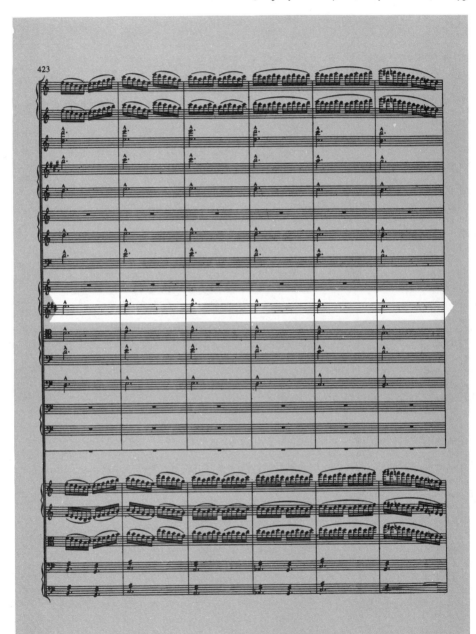

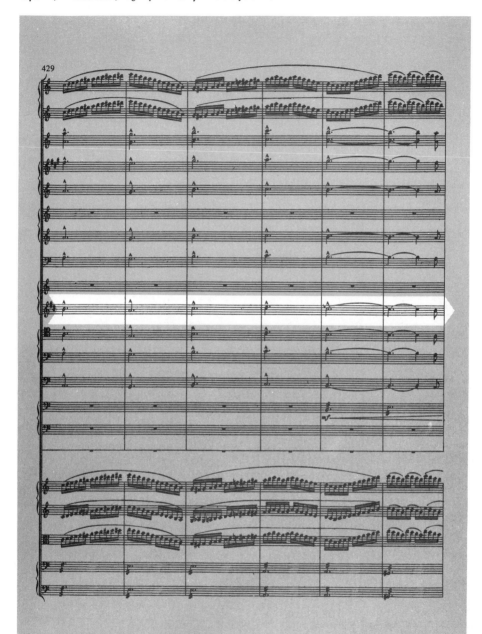

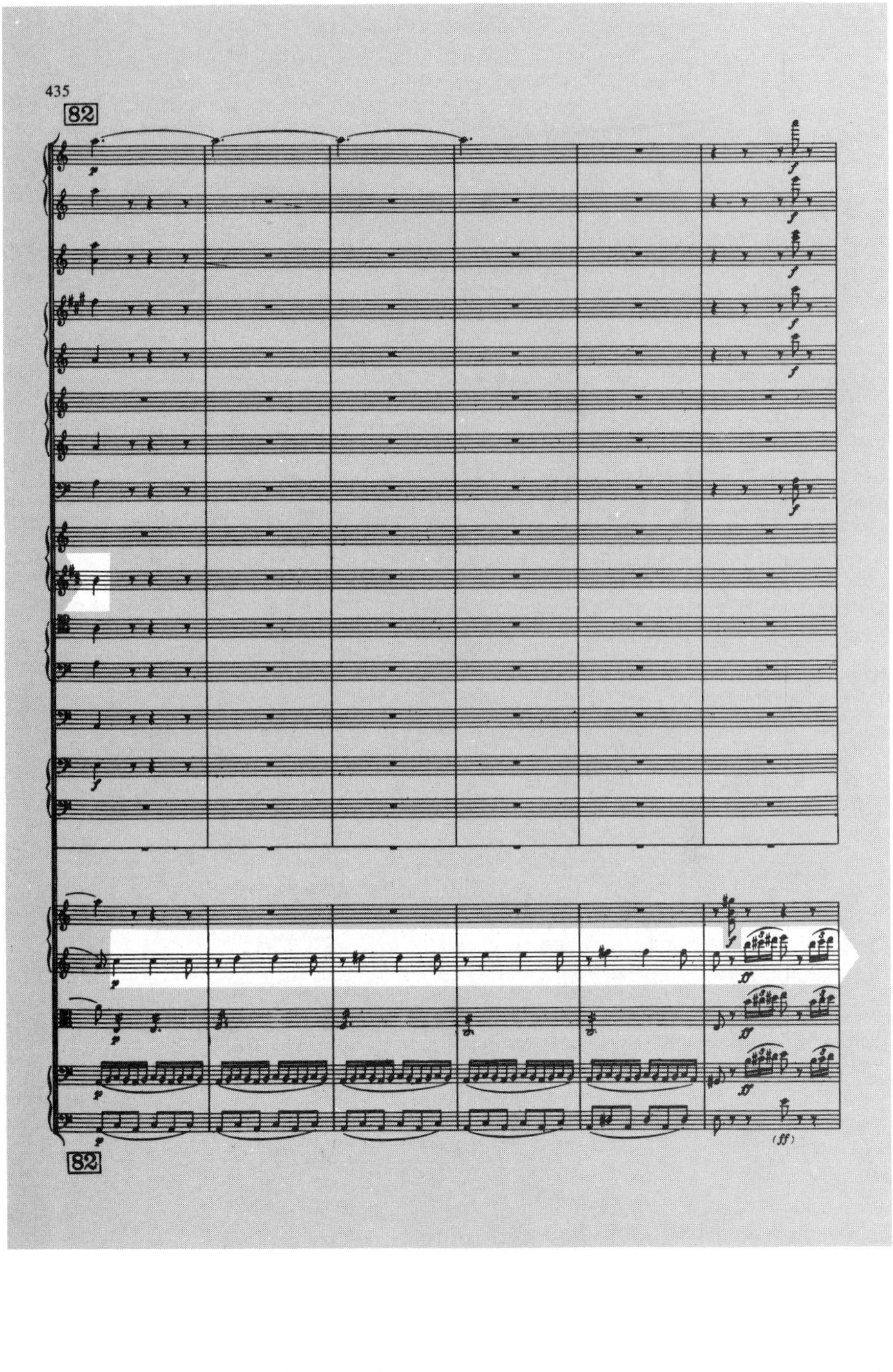
435
82
82

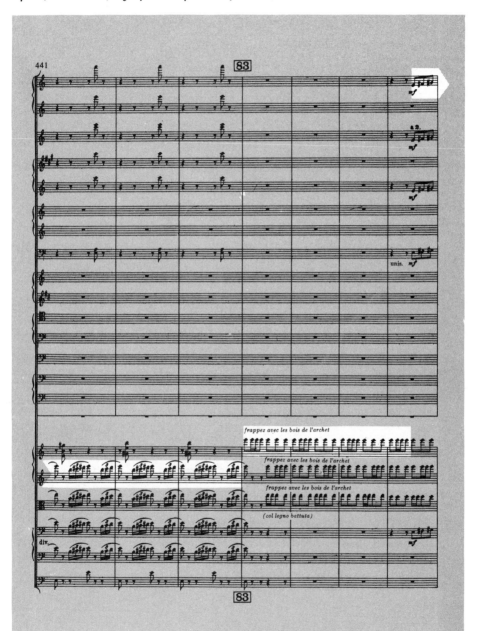

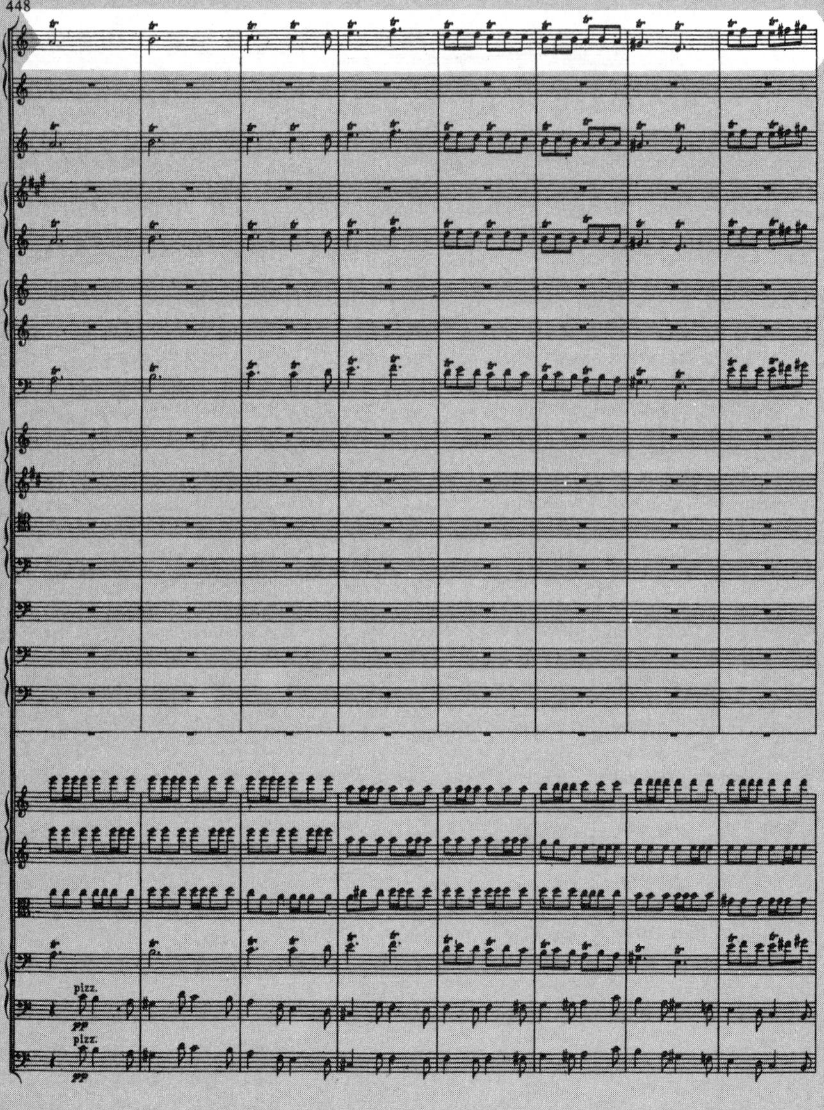
448
tr
pizz.
pp
pizz.
pp

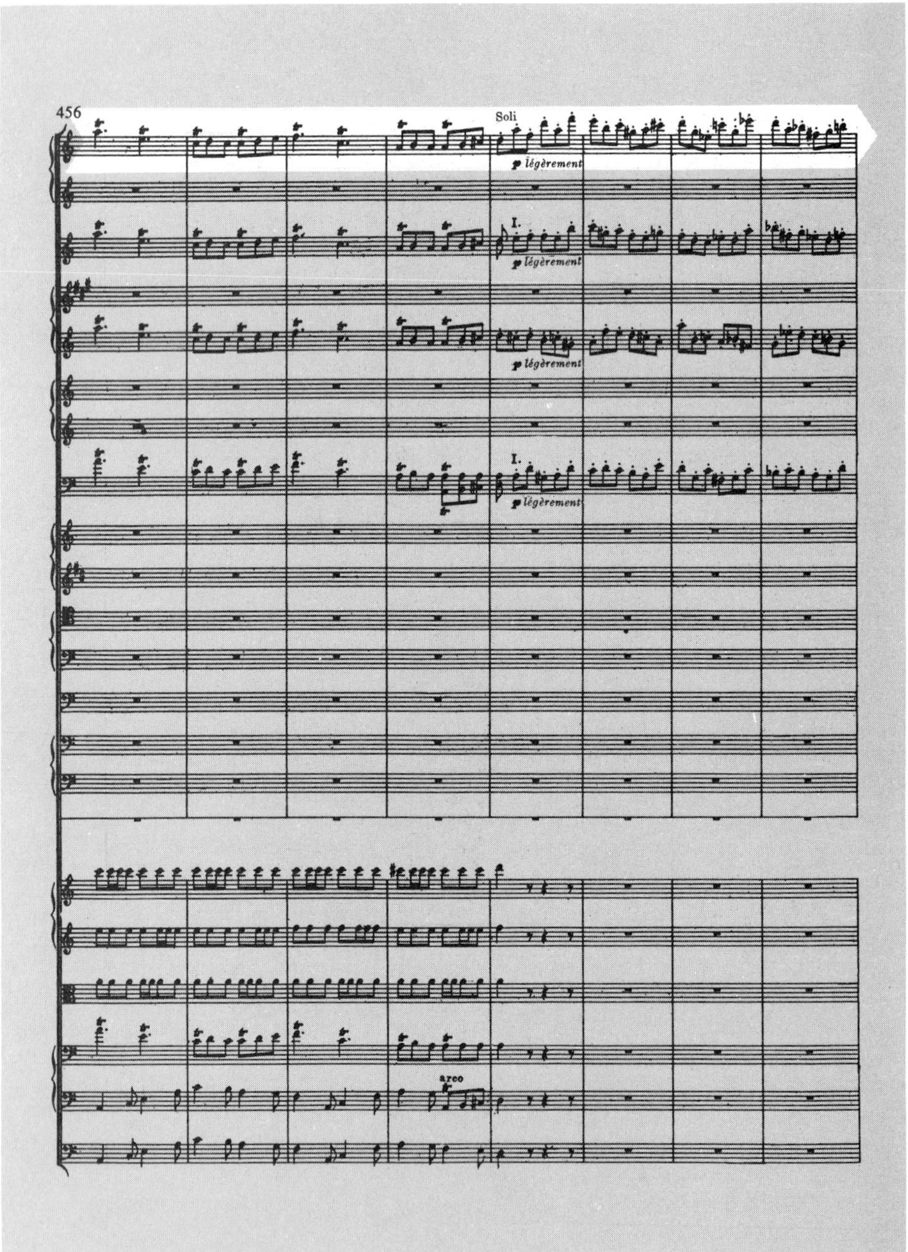
456
Soli
p légèrement
I.
p légèrement
p légèrement
I.
p légèrement
arco

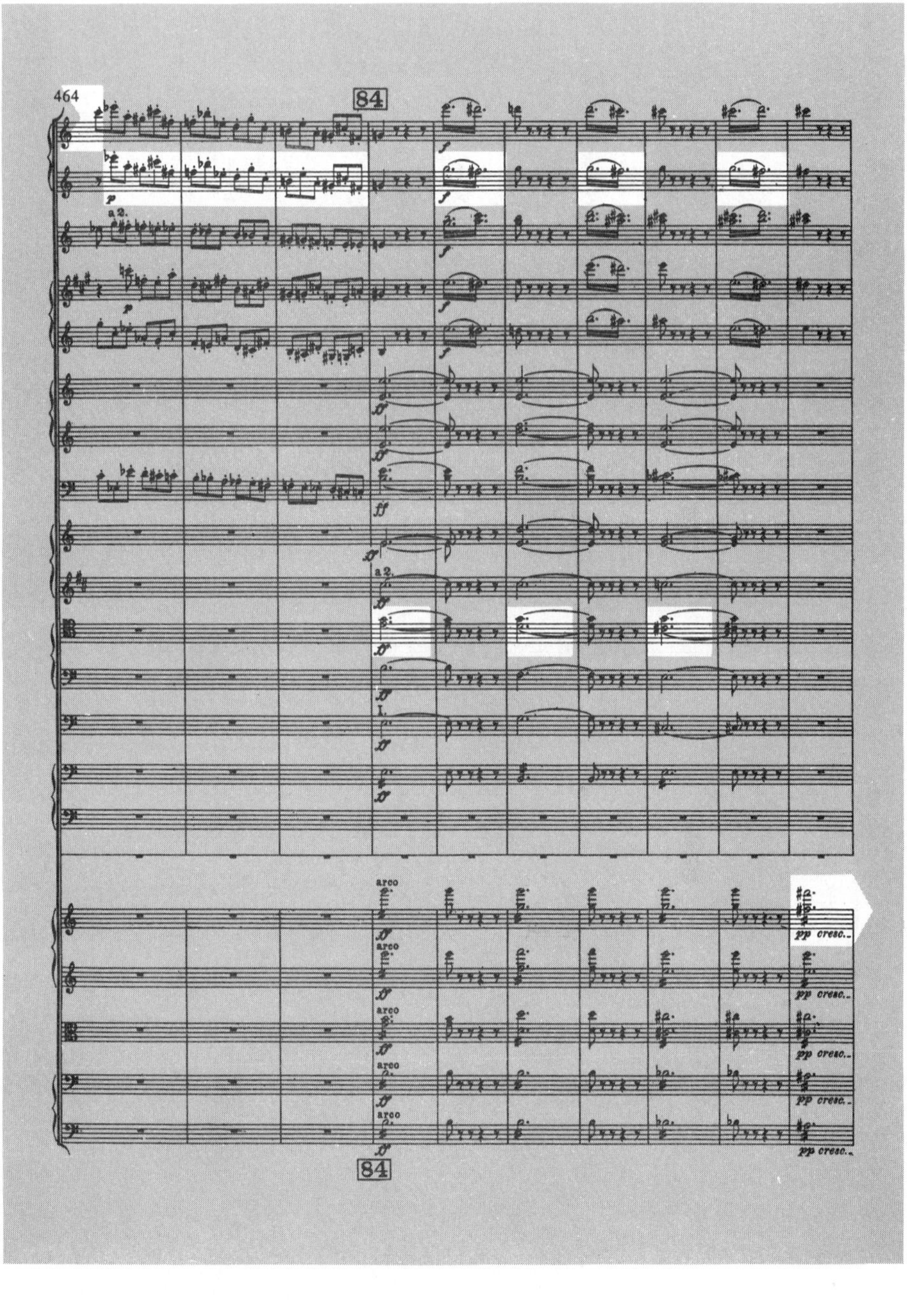
464
84
a 2.
a 2.
I.
arco
pp cresc.
84

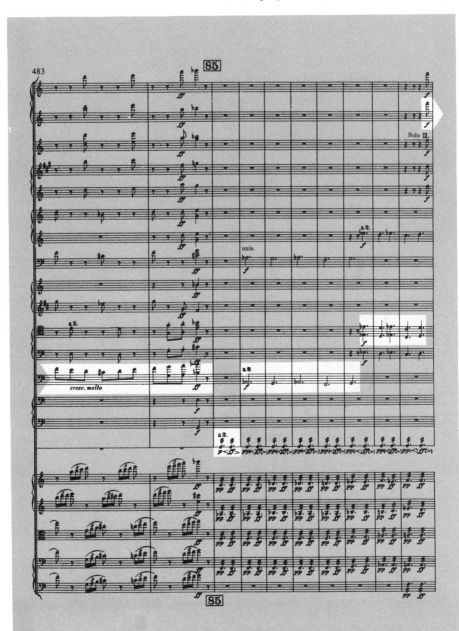

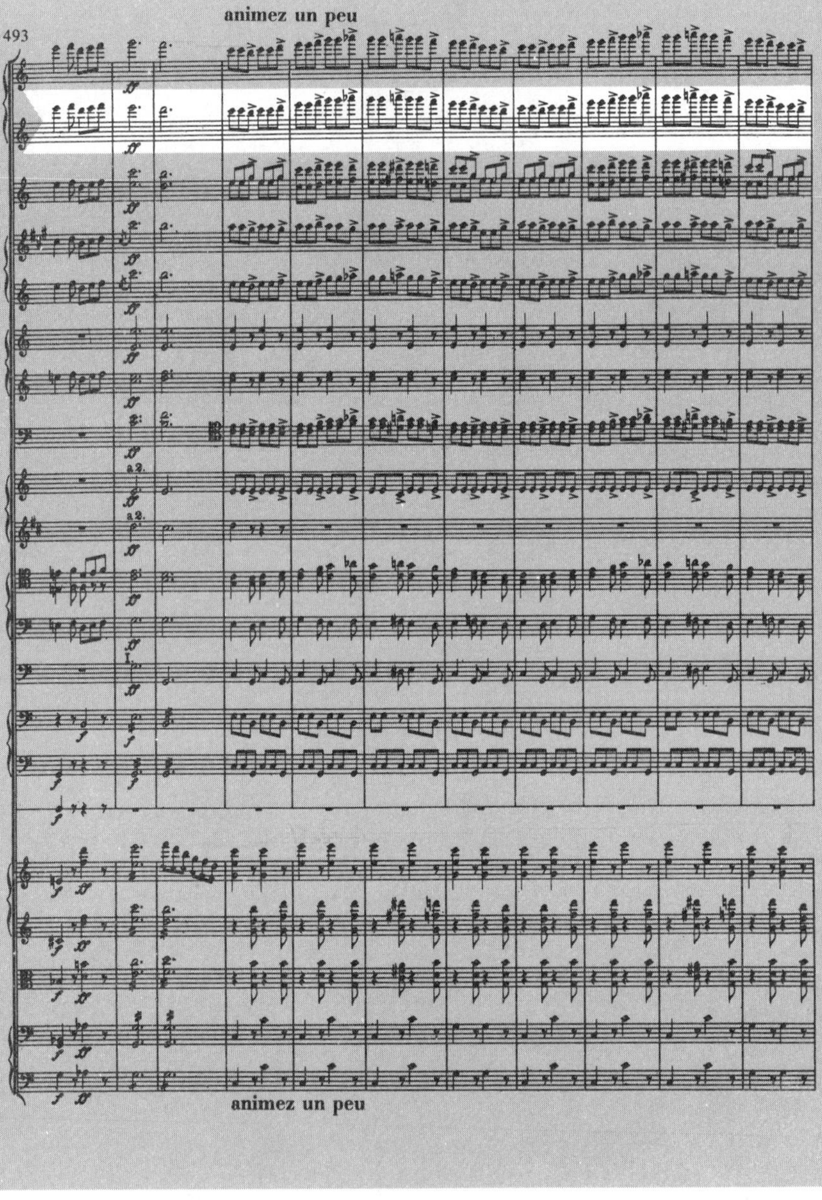
animez un peu
493
a 2.
a 2.
animez un peu

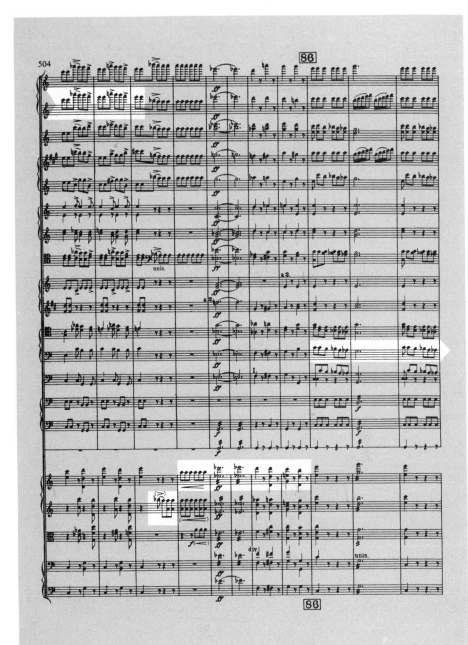

515
tenu
unis.
Cinelli.
Coup frappé sur une Cymbale avec une baguette couverte d'éponge ou un tampon
Struck on a cymbal with a sponge-headed drum-stick or a padded stick

26. FELIX MENDELSSOHN (1809-1847), First movement from *Violin Concerto in E minor* (1844)

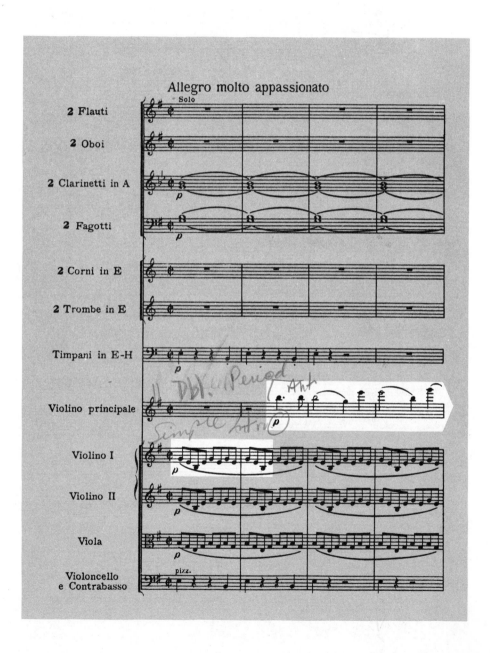

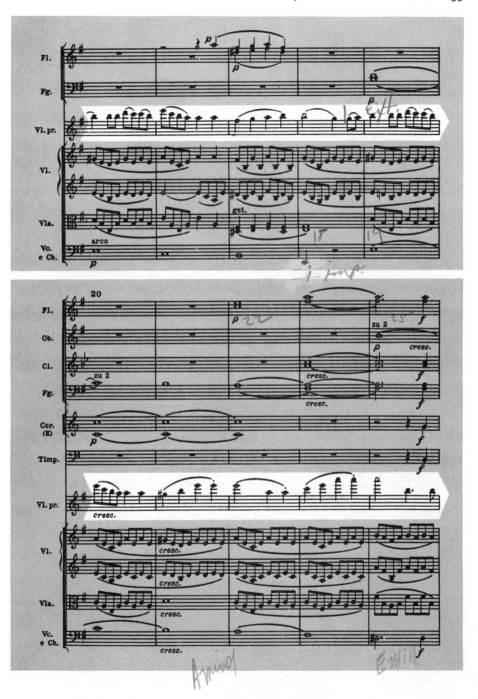

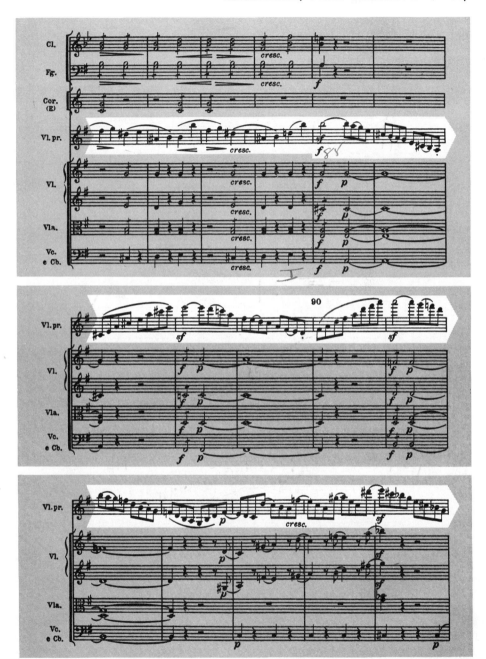

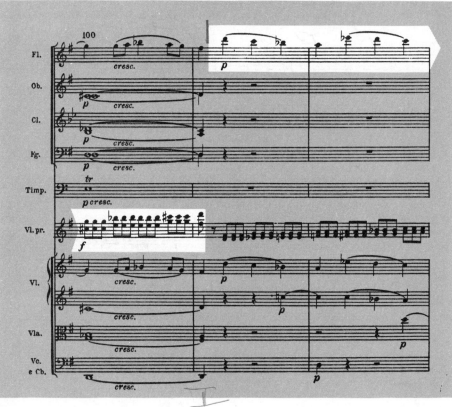

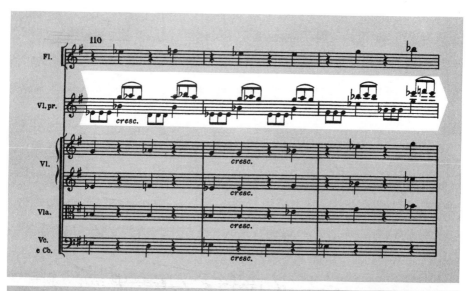

Dev.

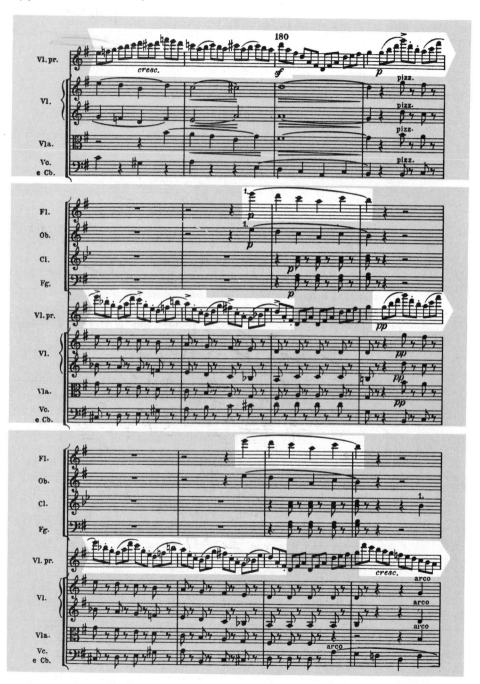

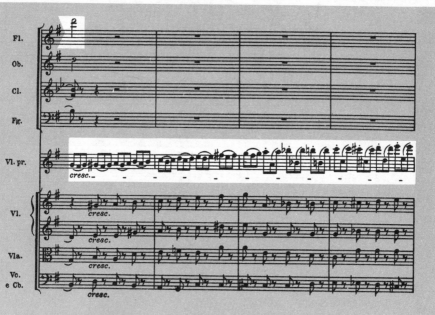

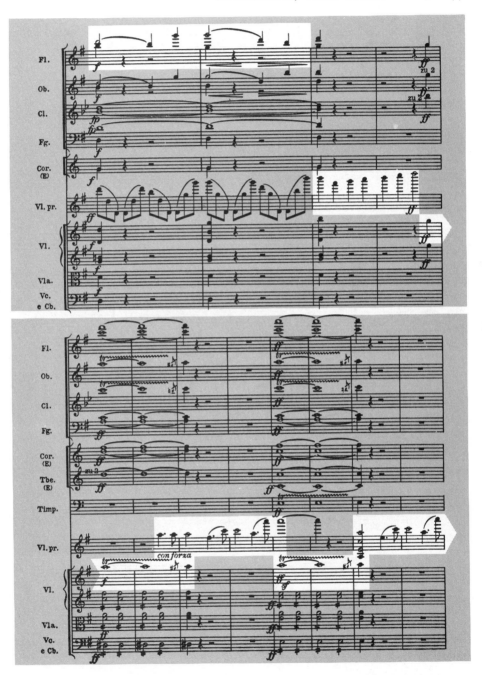

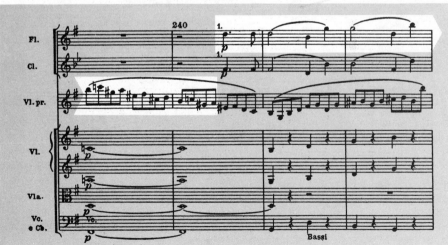

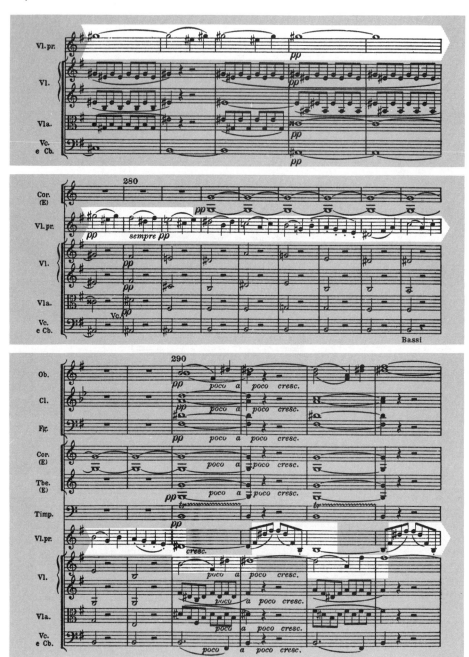

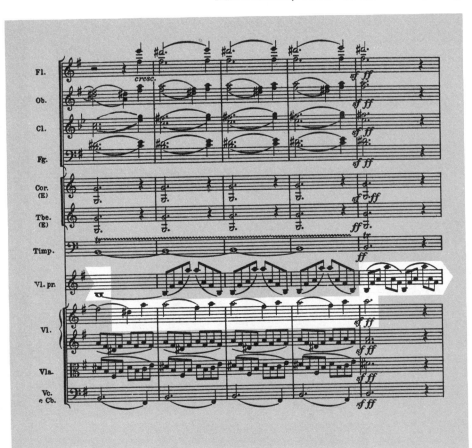

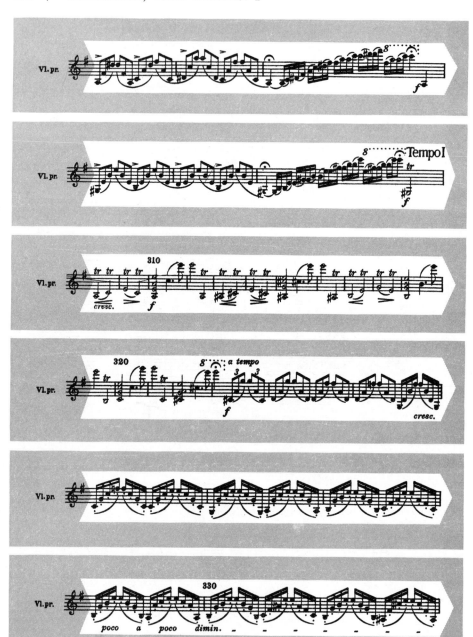

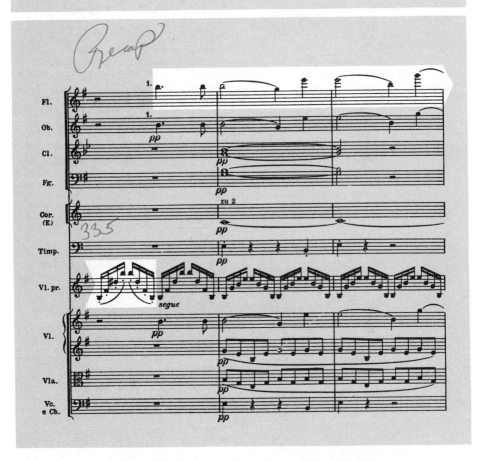

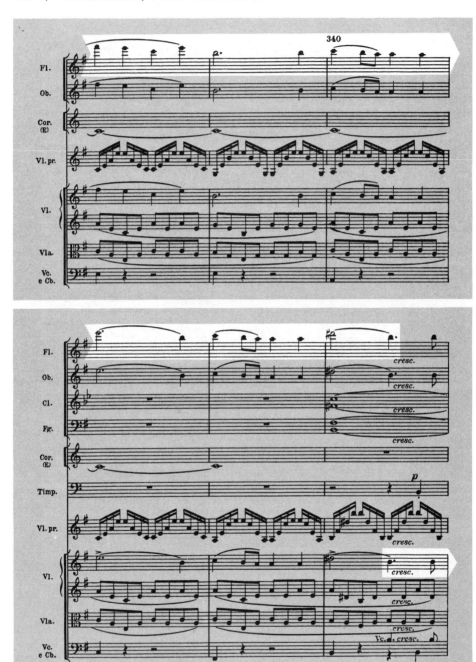

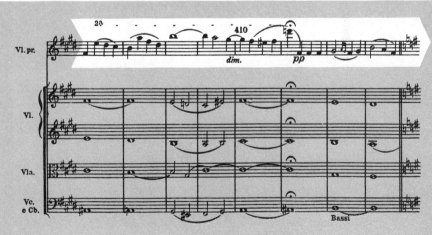

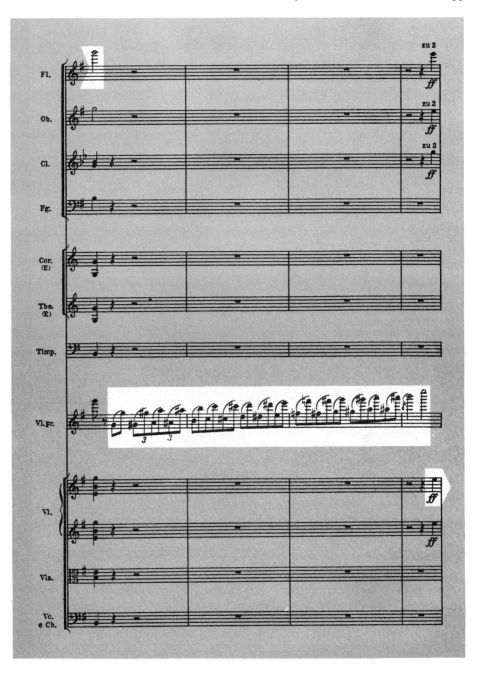

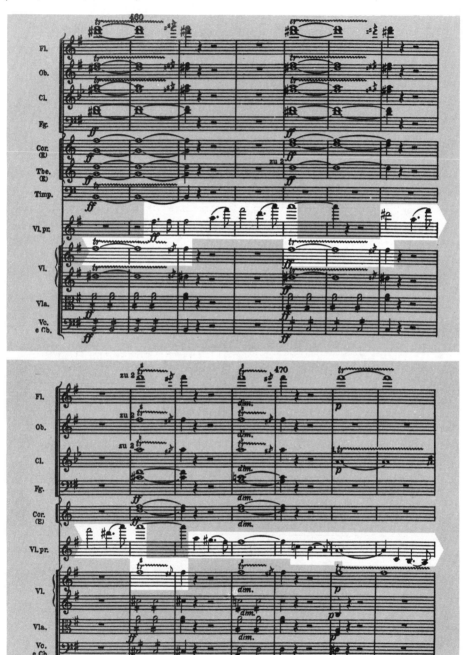

27. FRÉDÉRIC FRANÇOIS CHOPIN (1810-1849),
Polonaise in A-flat major, Op. 53 (1842)

29. CHOPIN, *Prelude in E minor*, Opus 28, No. 4 (PUBL. 1839)

30. ROBERT SCHUMANN (1810–1856), *Ich grolle nicht* from *Dichterliebe* (1840)

Translation

Ich grolle nicht und wenn das Herz
  auch bricht.
Ewig verlor'nes Lieb, ich grolle nicht.
Wie du auch strahlst in
  Diamantenpracht,
Es fällt kein Strahl in deines
  Herzens Nacht.

Das weiss ich längst. Ich sah dich ja im
  Traume,
Und sah die Nacht in deines Herzens
  Raume,
Und sah die Schlang', die dir am
  Herzen frisst,
Ich sah, mein Lieb, wie sehr du elend
  bist.

HEINRICH HEINE

I bear no grudge, even though my
  heart may break,
eternally lost love! I bear no grudge.
However you may shine in the
  splendor of your diamonds,
no ray of light falls in the darkness
  of your heart.

I have long known this. I saw you in
  a dream,
and saw the night within the void of
  your heart,
and saw the serpent that is eating
  your heart—
I saw, my love, how very miserable
  you are.

PHILIP L. MILLER

31. LISZT, *Les Préludes* (1856)

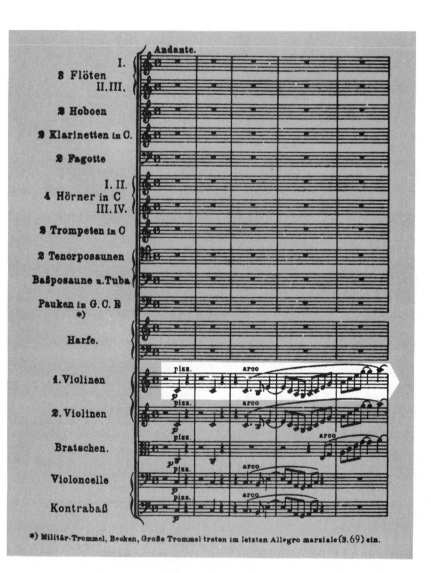

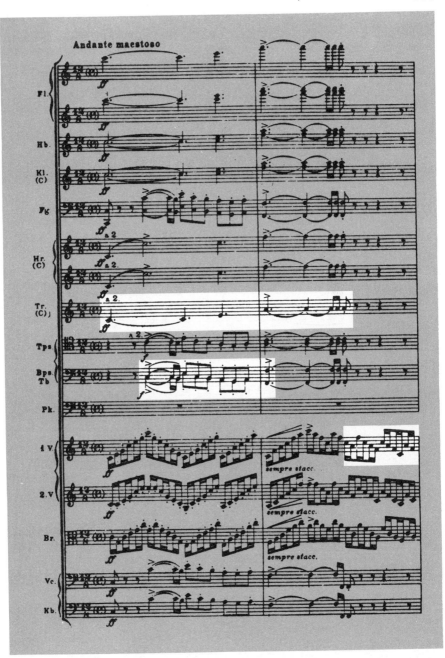

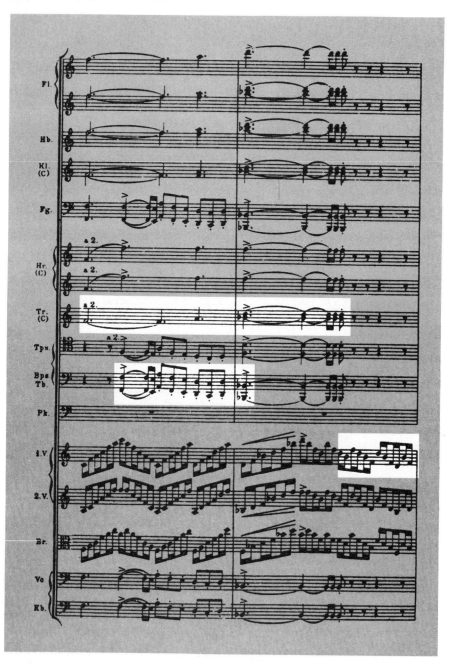

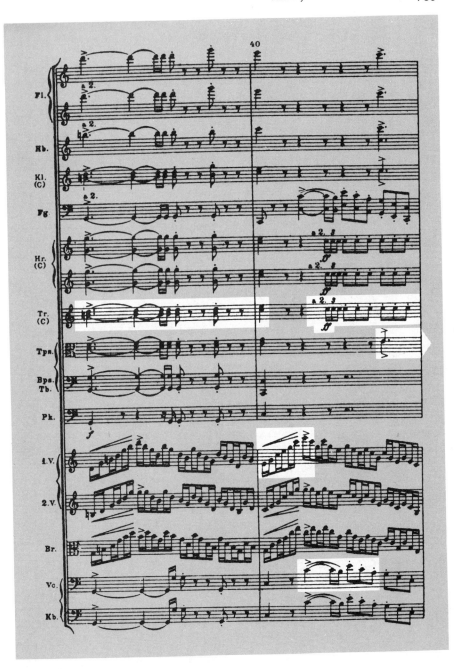

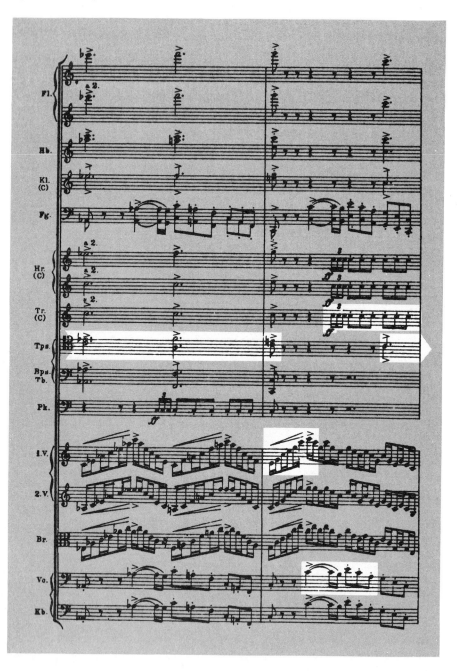

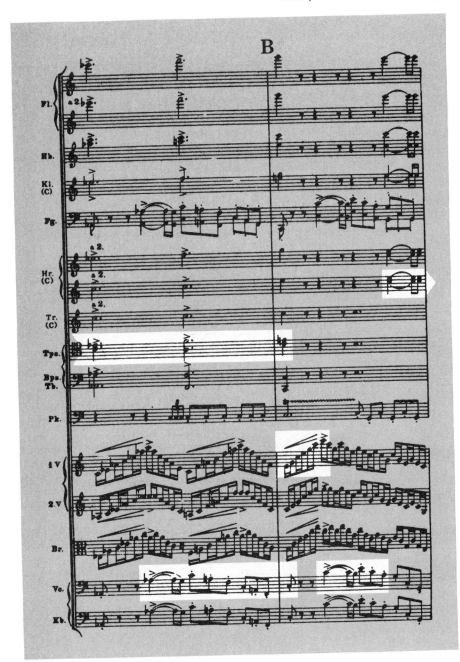

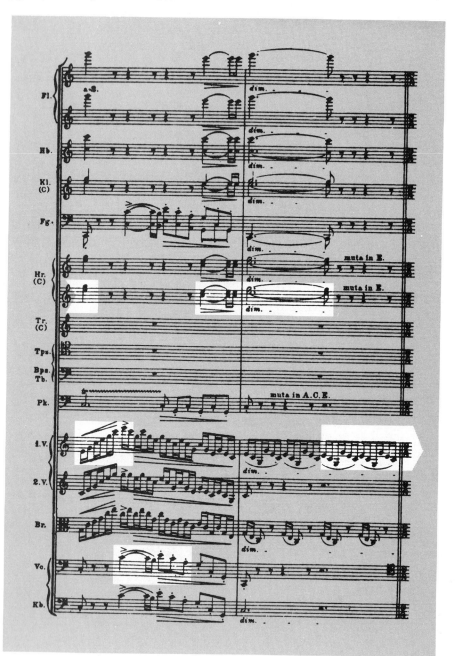

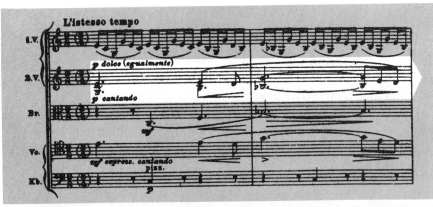

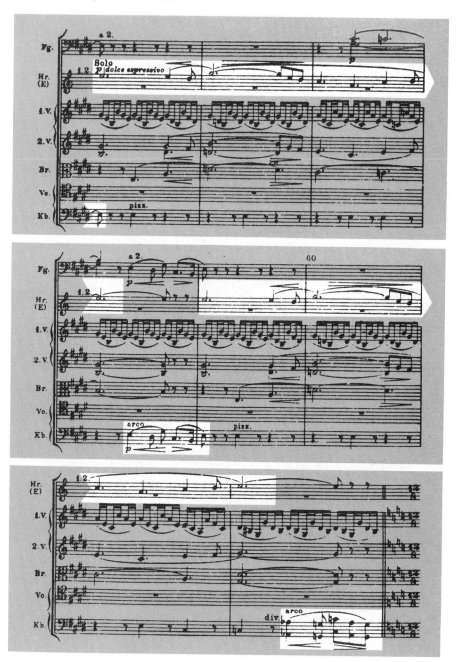

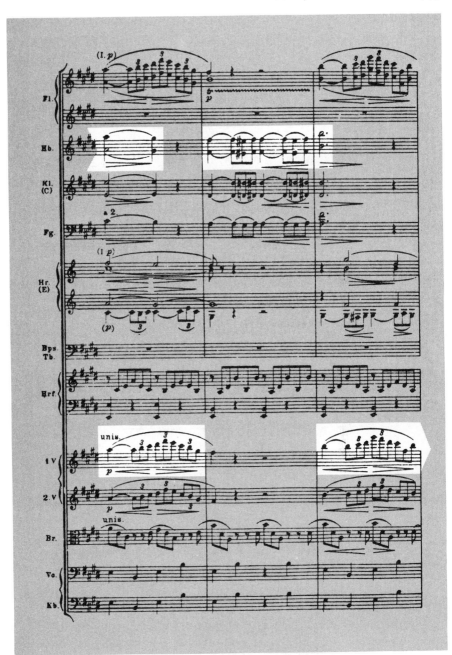

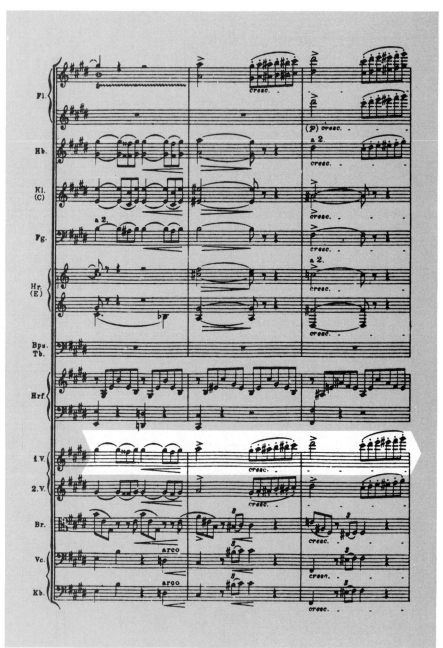

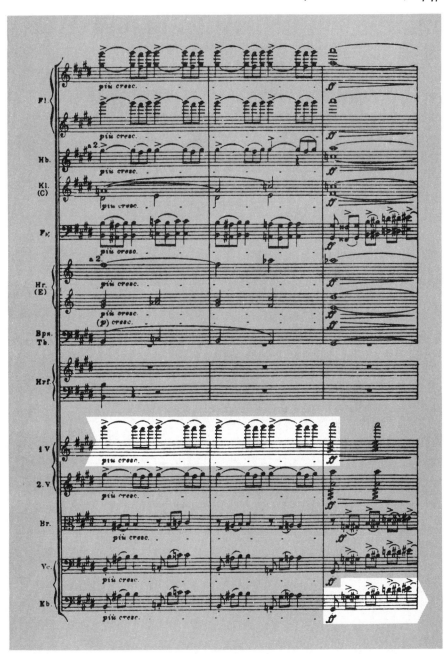

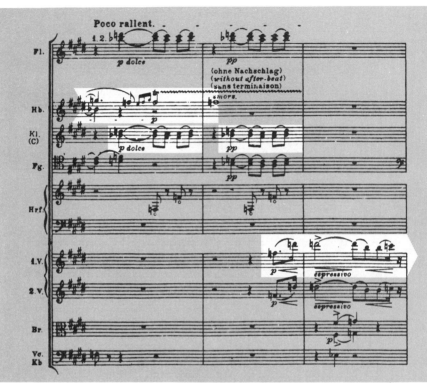

150

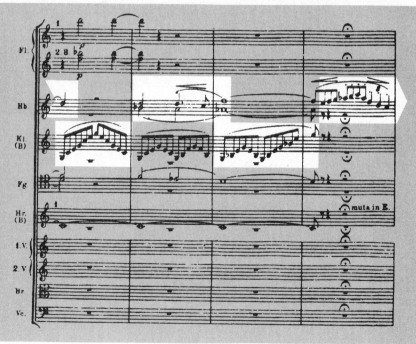

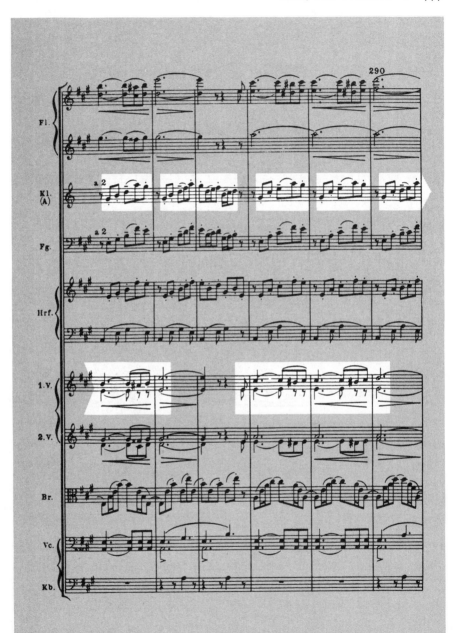

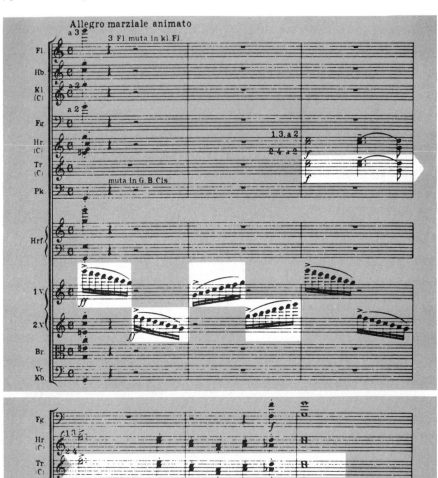

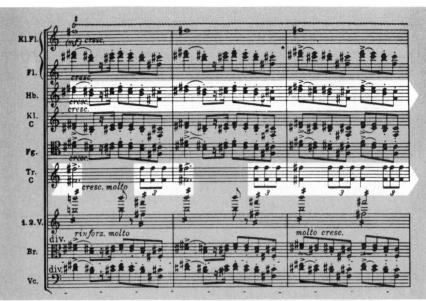

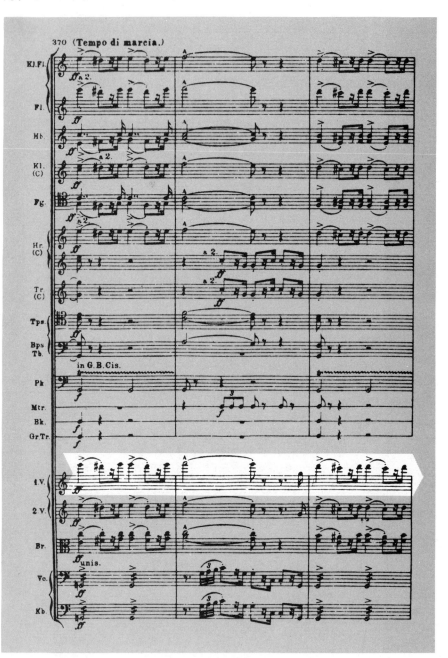

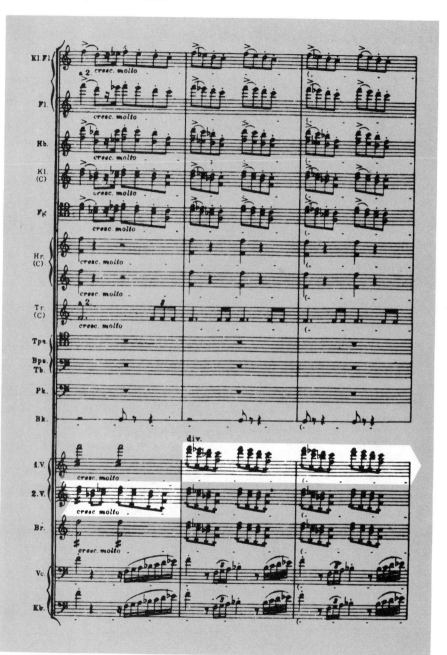

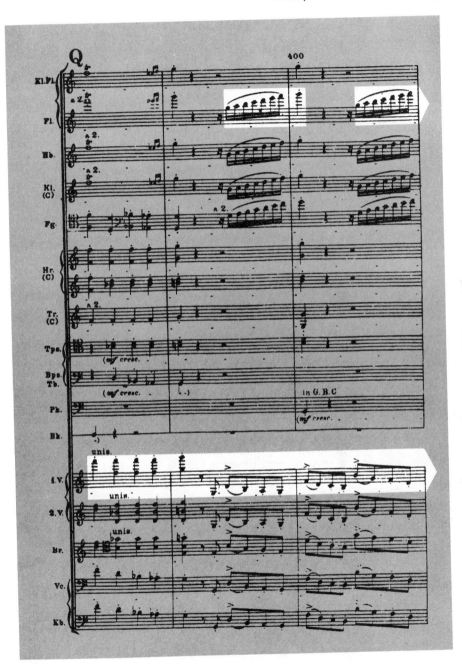

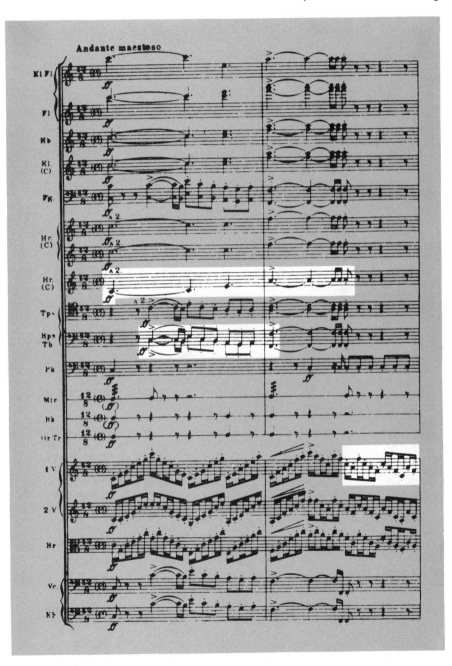

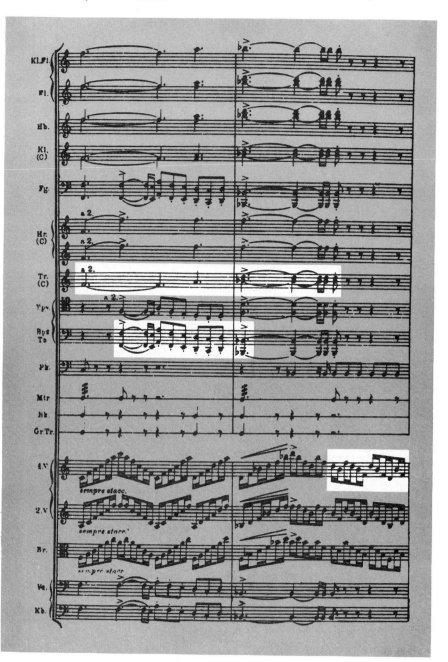

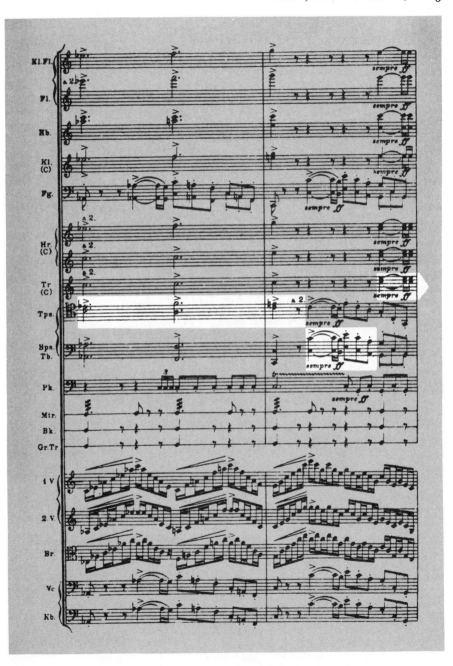

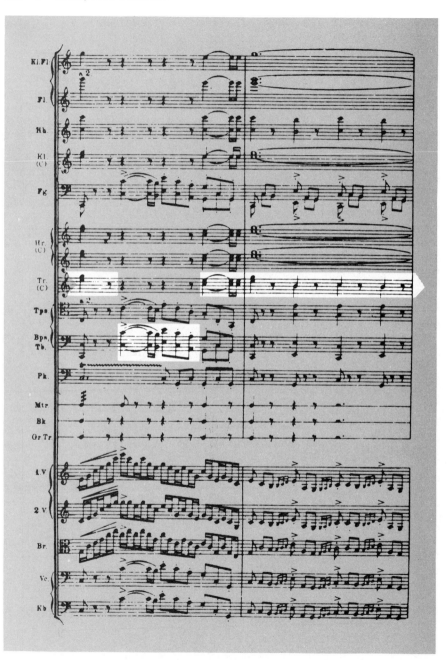

32. RICHARD WAGNER (1813-1883),
Excerpts from *Tristan und Isolde* (1859)

(Completely carried away. Tristan and Isolda sink down and remain lying on the flowery bank, their heads side by side)

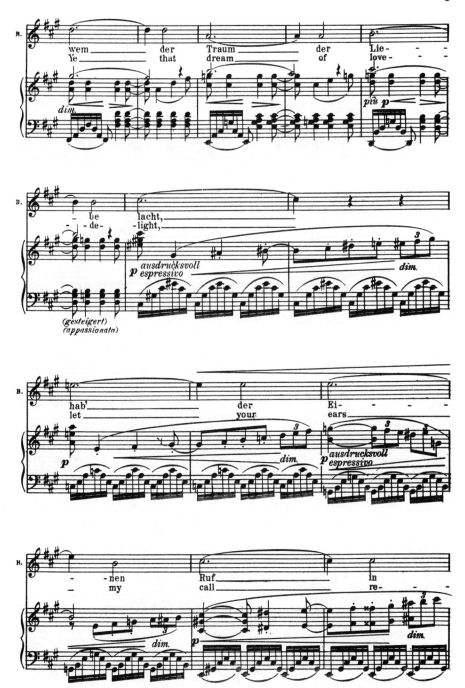

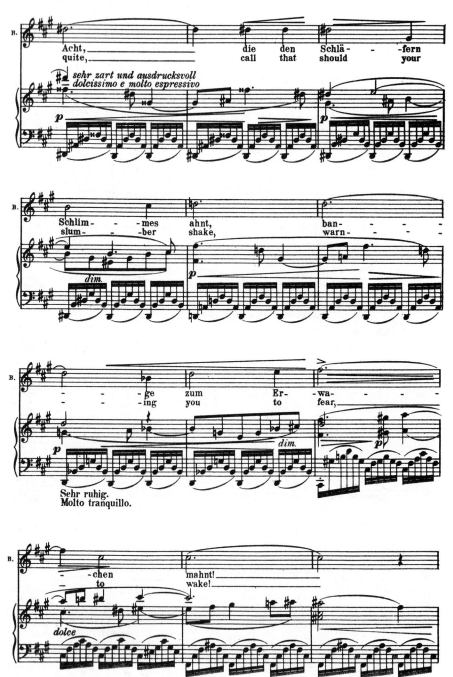

33. GIUSEPPE VERDI (1813-1901),
Opening of Act III from *Aïda* (1871)

Shores of the Nile._ Granite rocks overgrown with palm-trees. On the summit of the rocks, a
temple dedicated to Isis, half hidden in foliage. Night; stars and a bright moon.

(From a boat which approaches the shore descend Amneris and Ramphis, followed by some women closely veiled. Guards.)

vie-ni_a re-car-mi,o cru-del, l'ul-ti-mo_ad-di-o, del
came for a fi-nal fare-well. cruel-ly to leave me... The

Ni - lo i cu-pi vor - ti-ci
Nile soon will be a tomb to me,

mi da-ran tom - ba
end my de-spair for-ev - er.

e pa-ce for-se e pa-ce for-se_e o-bli - o.
Si-lent and som-ber, calm of the deep, re-ceive me!

morendo

Andante mosso. (♩ = 92.)

p legato

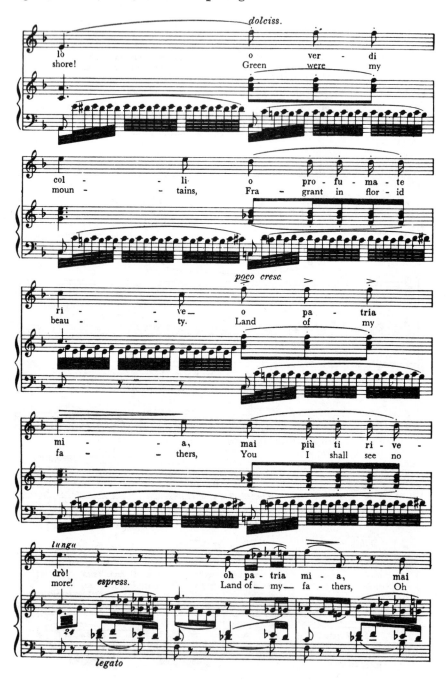

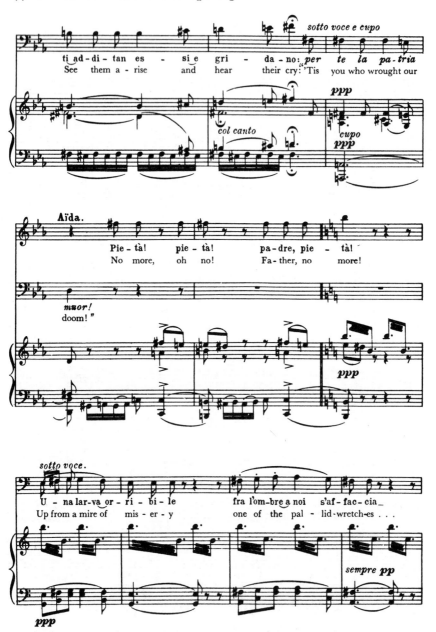

sotto voce e cupo

ti ad-di-tan es - si e gri - da - no: *per te la pa-tria*
See them a-rise and hear their cry: "'Tis you who wrought our

col canto

ppp

cupo
ppp

Aïda.

Pie - tà! pie - tà! pa-dre, pie - tà!
No more, oh no! Fa-ther, no more!

muor!
doom! "

ppp

sotto voce.

U - na lar-va or - ri - bi - le fra l'om-bre a noi s'af-fac-cia_
Up from a mire of mis-er-y one of the pal - lid-wretch-es . . .

sempre pp

ppp

34. VERDI, Opening of the Dies irae from *Messa da Requiem* (1874)

35. BEDŘICH SMETANA (1824-1884),
The Moldau from *Má Vlast* (1874-1879)

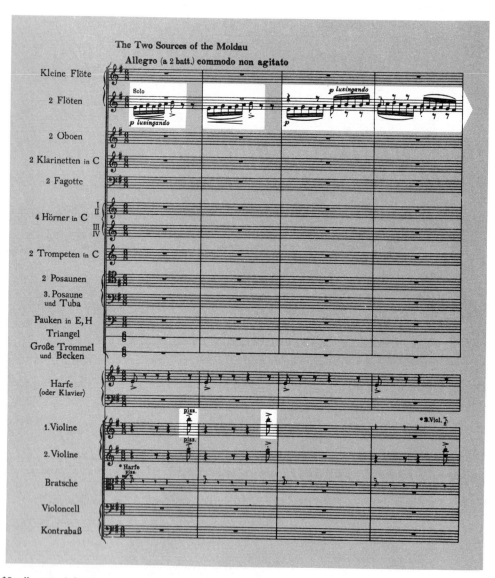

*Smaller notes indicate an alternate version for reduced orchestra.

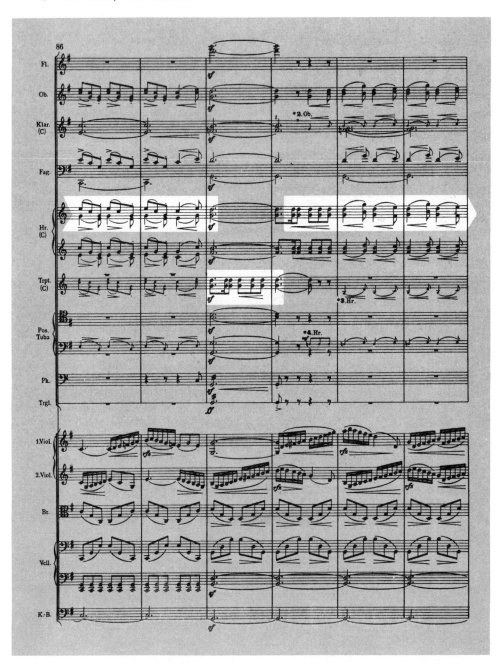

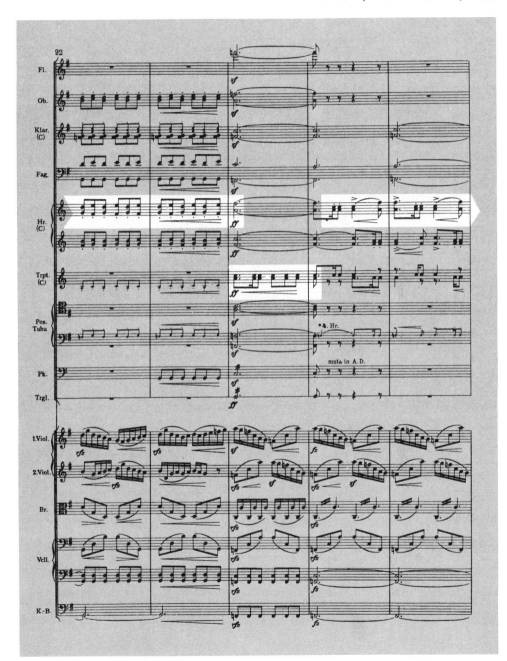

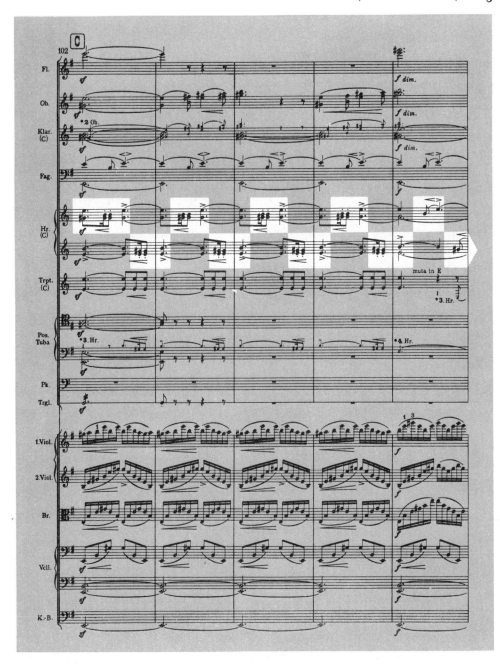

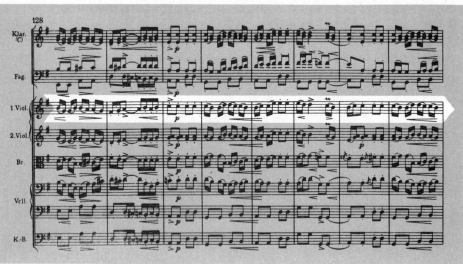

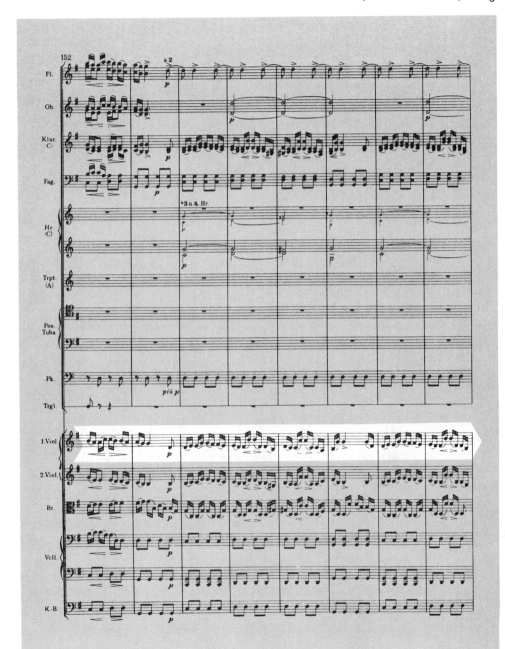

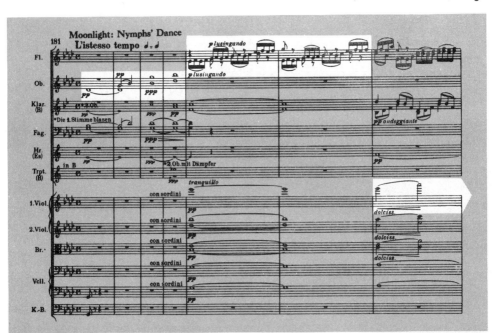

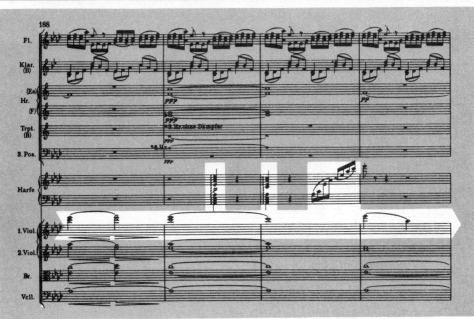

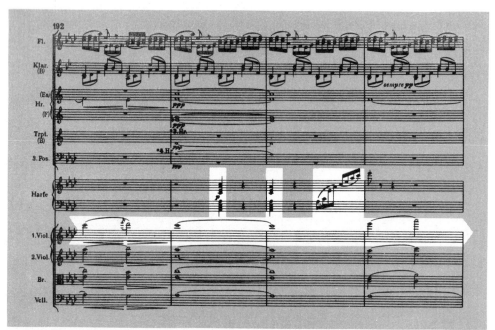

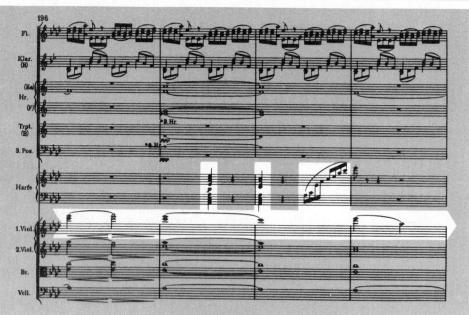

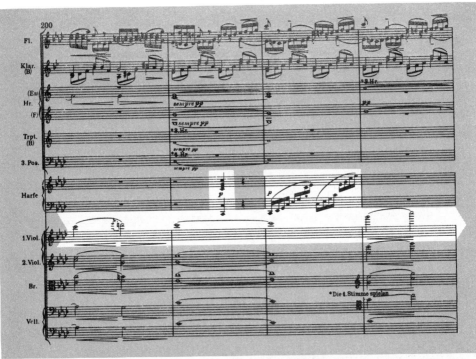

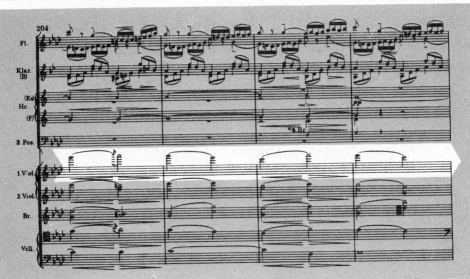

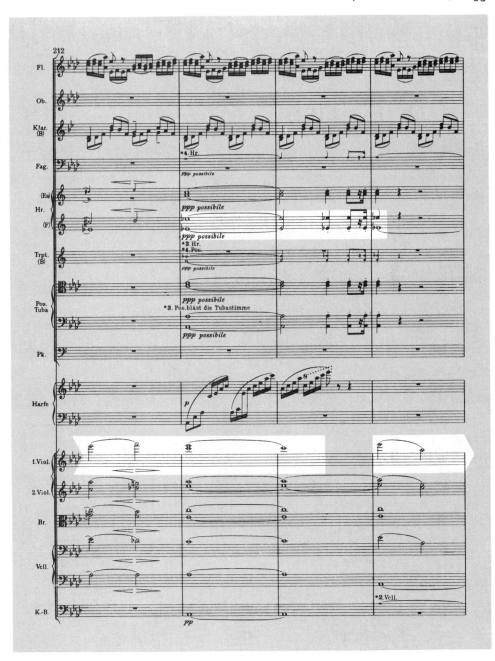

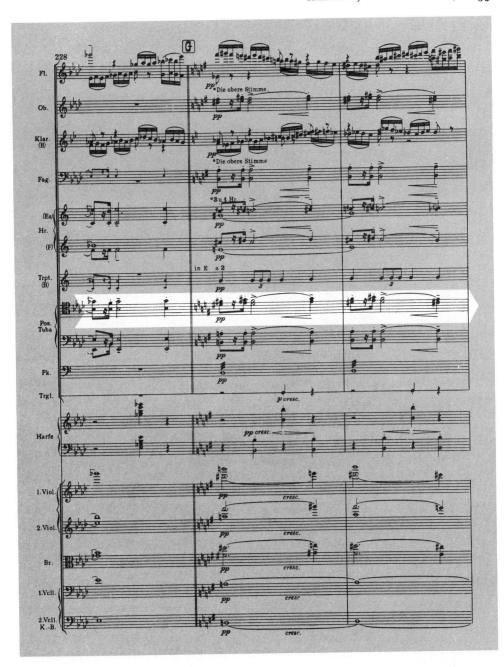

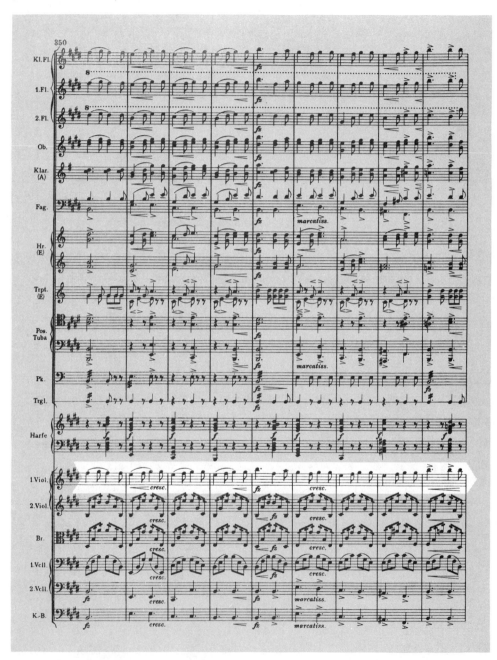

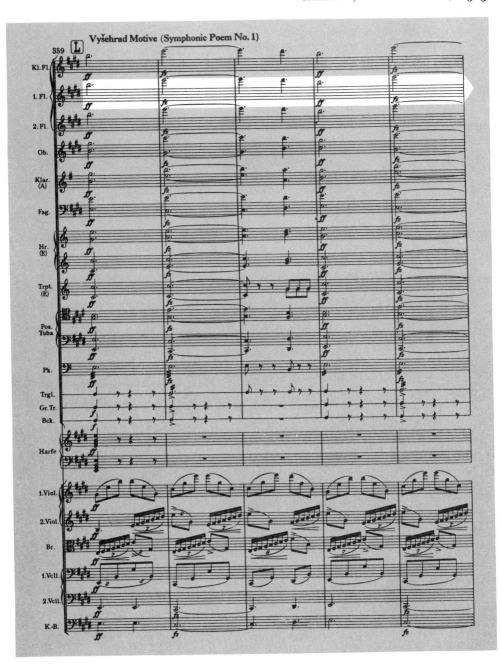

Vyšehrad Motive (Symphonic Poem No. 1)

36. JOHANNES BRAHMS (1833-1896),
Fourth movement from *Symphony No. 2 in D major* (1877)

37. TCHAIKOVSKY, Excerpts from *The Nutcracker* (1892)
March

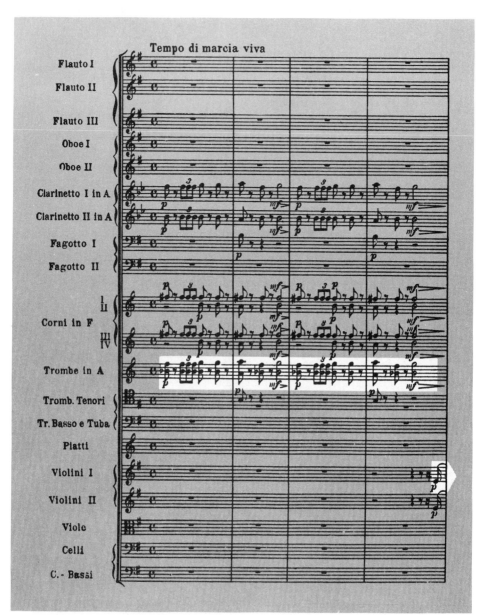

Fl.
Ob.
Cl.
Fg.
Cor. (F)
Trbe. (A)
Tbni. Tuba
Mit Paukenschlägel.
Piat.
Vl.
Vle.
Celli
C.-B.

Arabian Dance

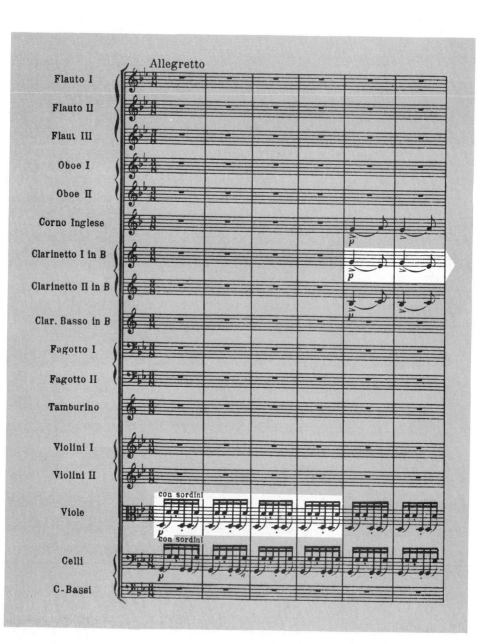

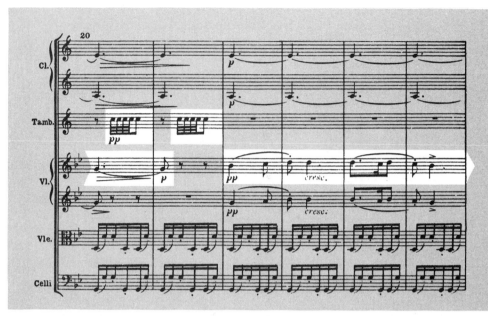

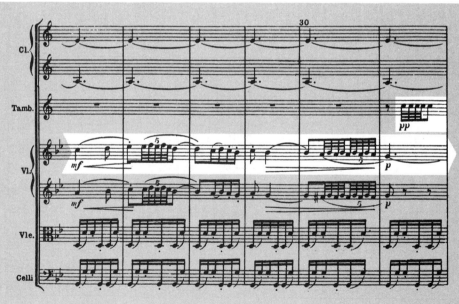

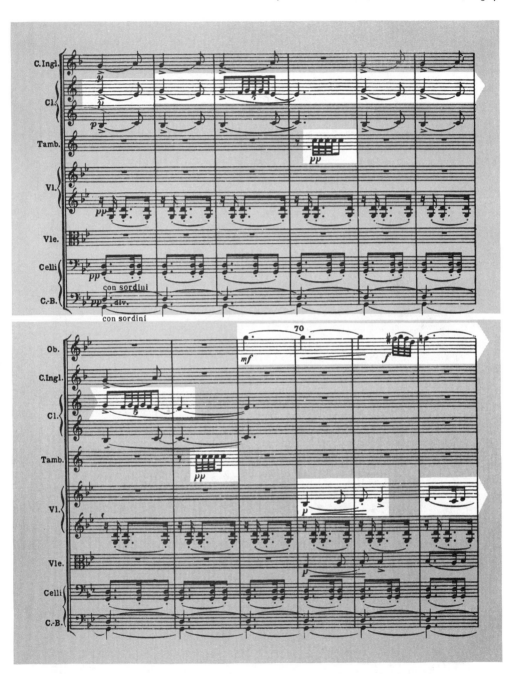

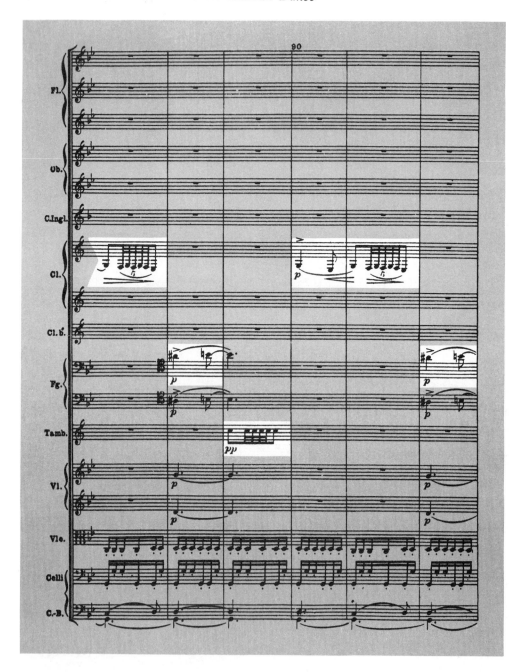

Dance of the Toy Flutes

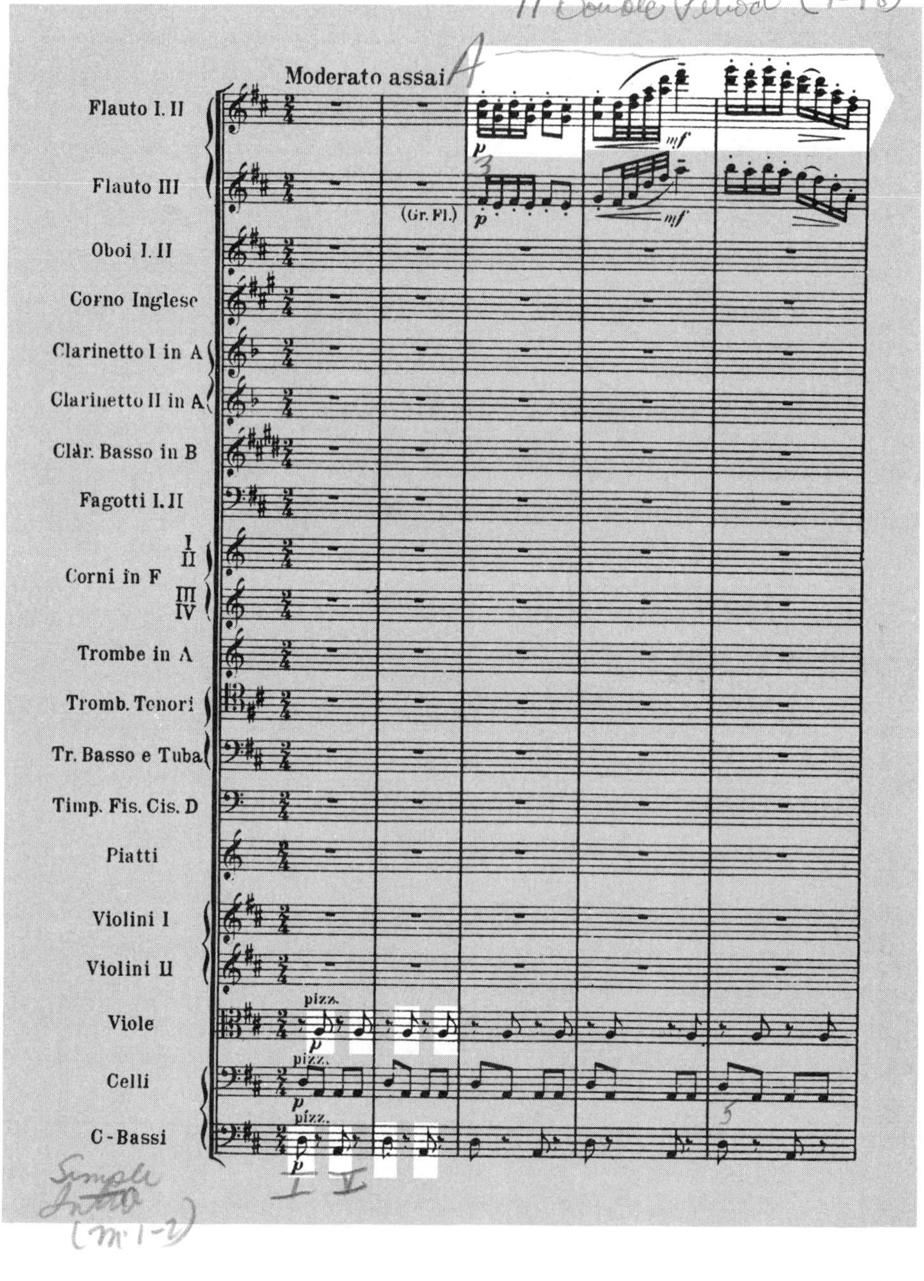

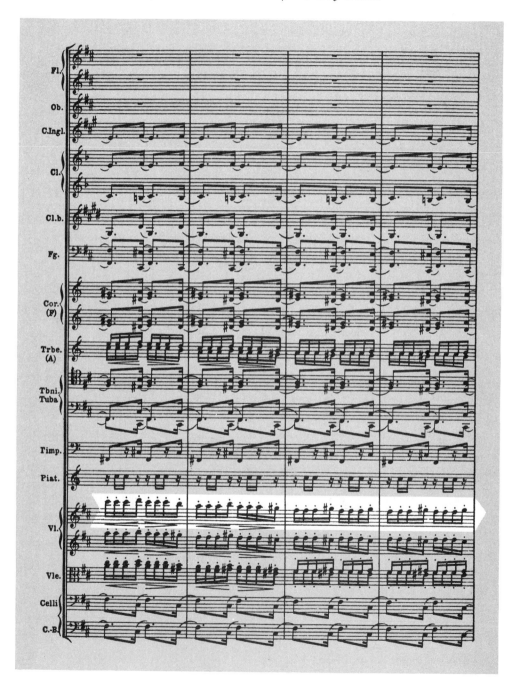

38. TCHAIKOVSKY, *Symphony No. 6 in B minor (Pathétique)* (1893)

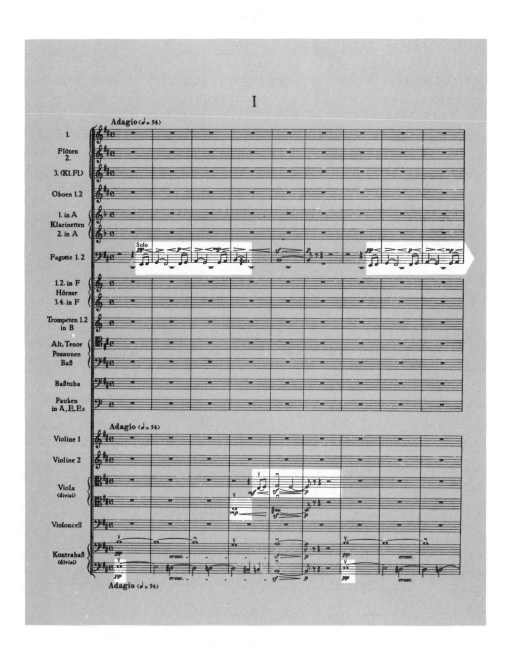

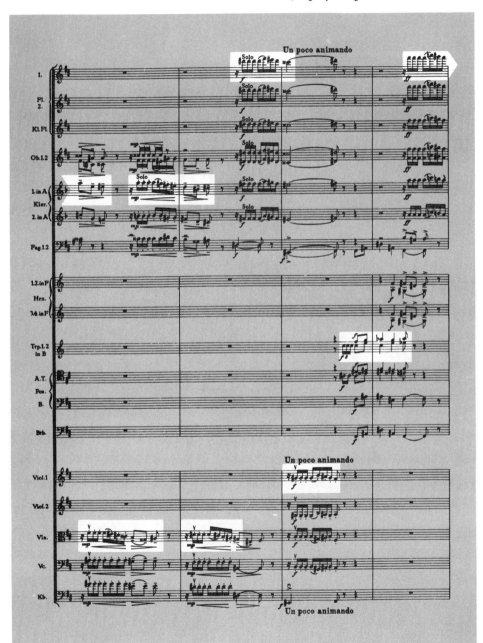

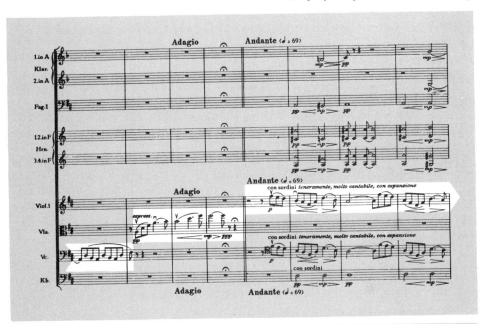

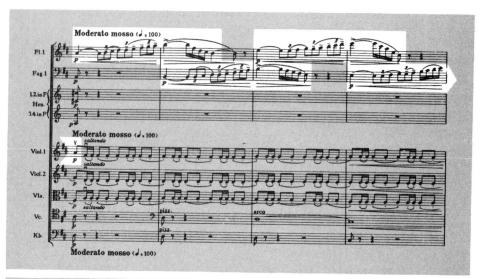

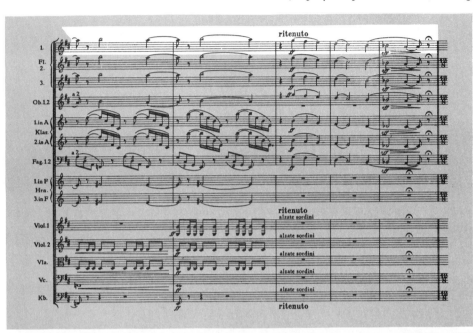

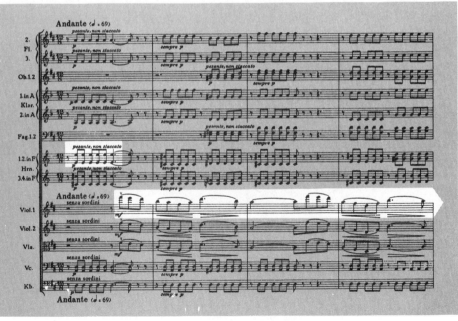

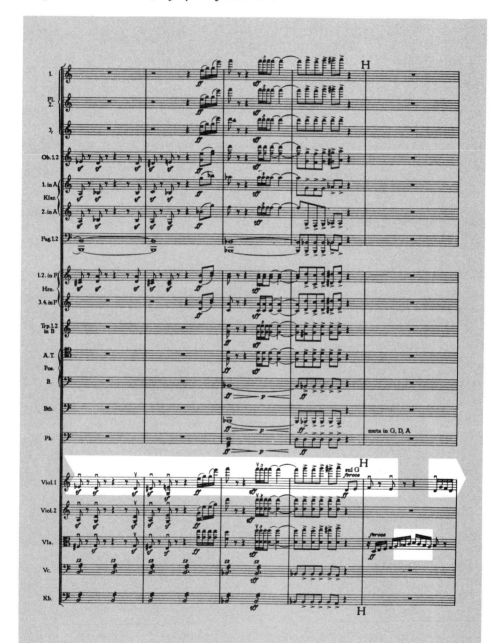

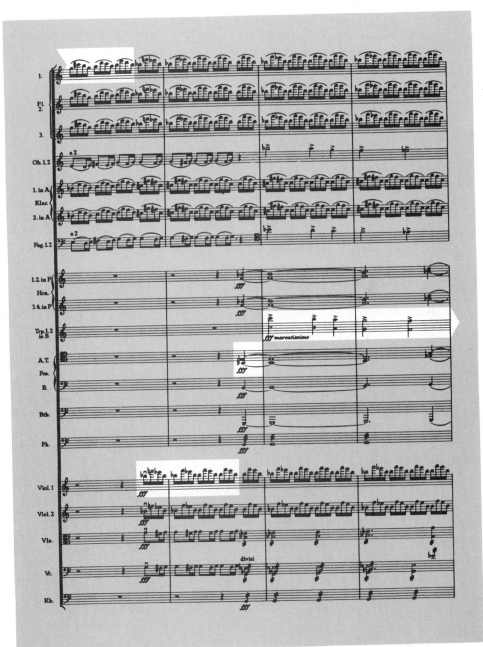

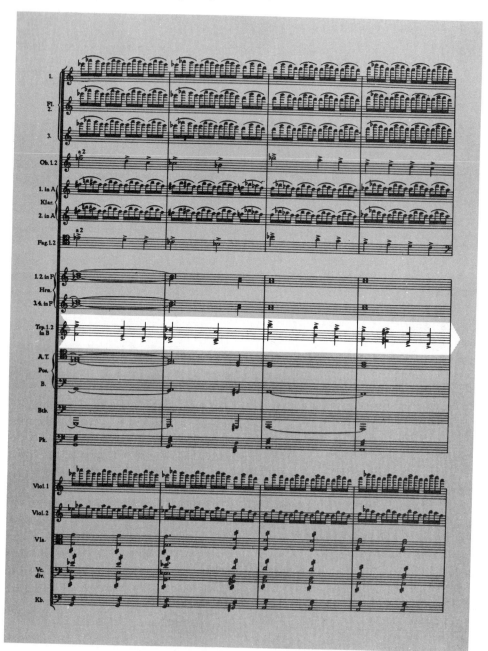

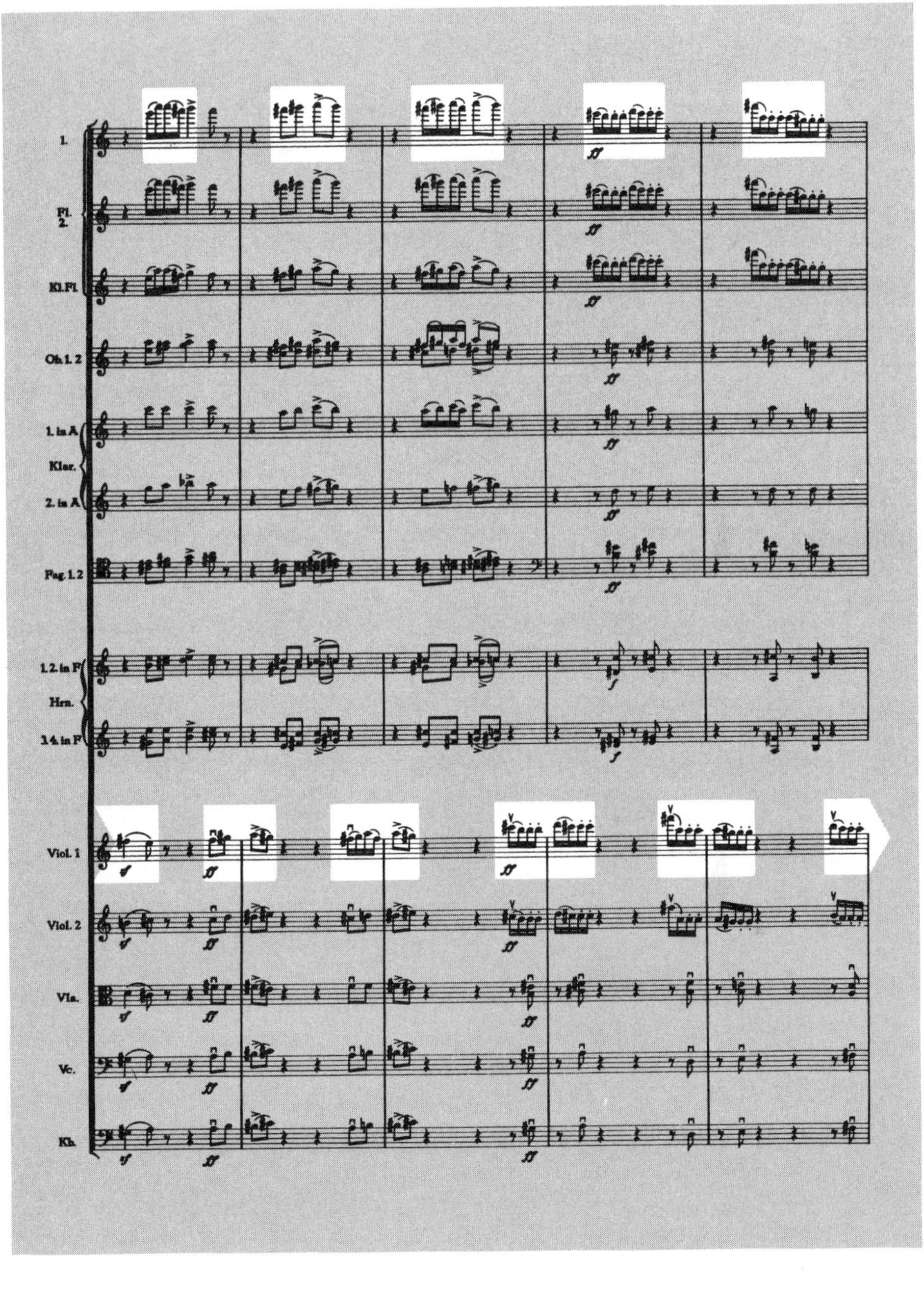
1.
Fl.
2.
Kl.Fl.
Ob. 1. 2
1. in A
Klar.
2. in A
Fag. 1. 2
1. 2. in F
Hrn.
3. 4. in F
Viol. 1
Viol. 2
Vla.
Vc.
Kb.

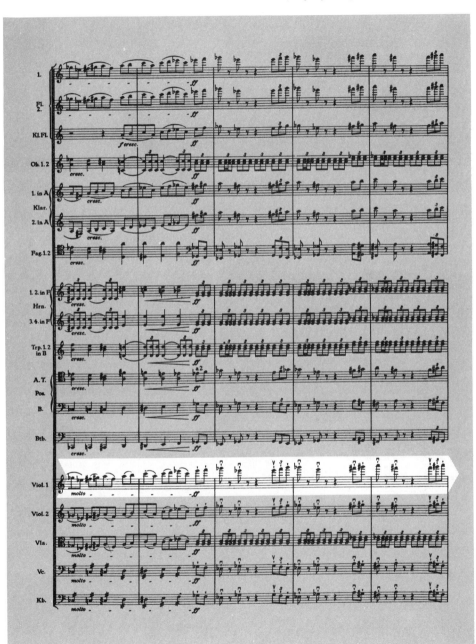

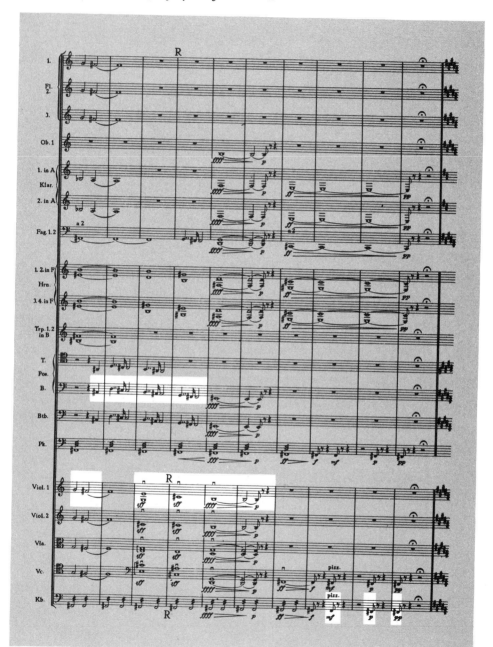

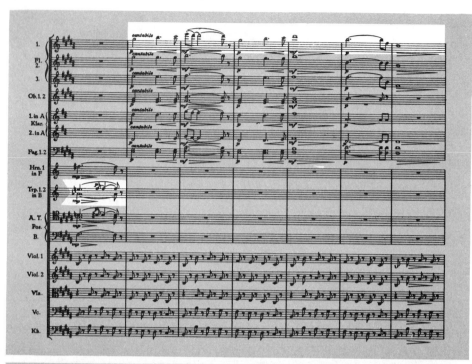

II

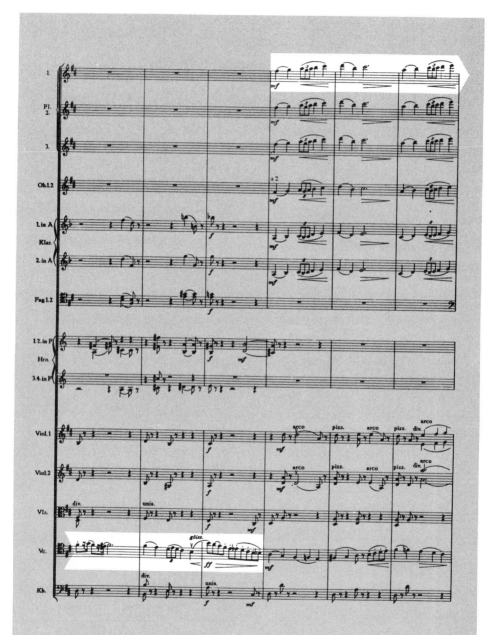

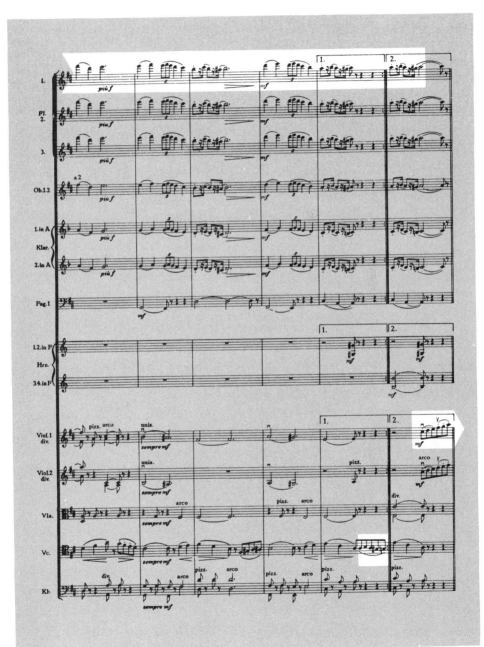

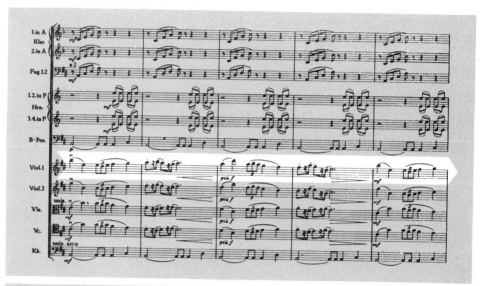

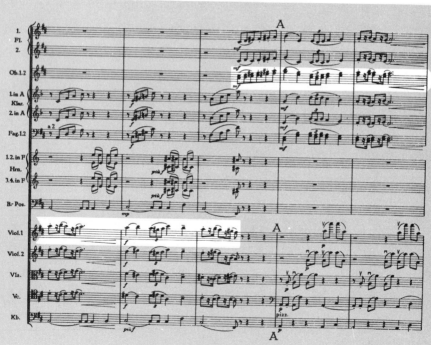

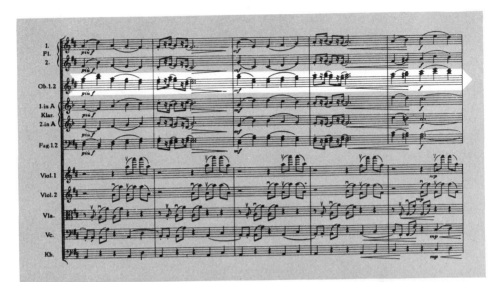

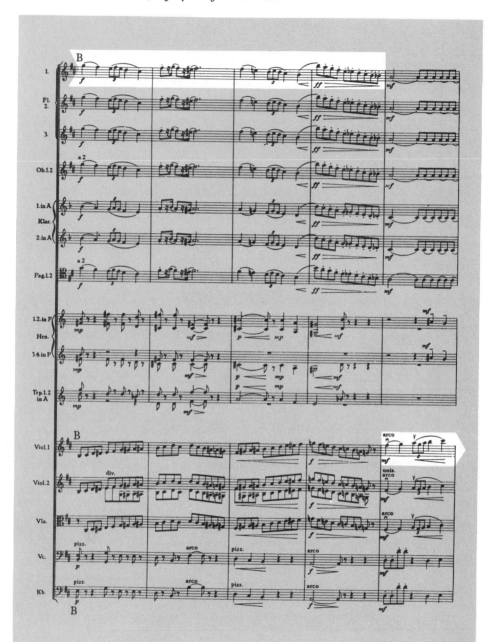

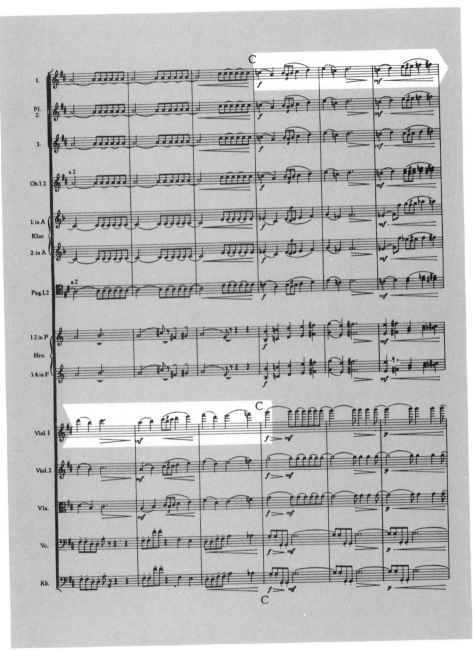

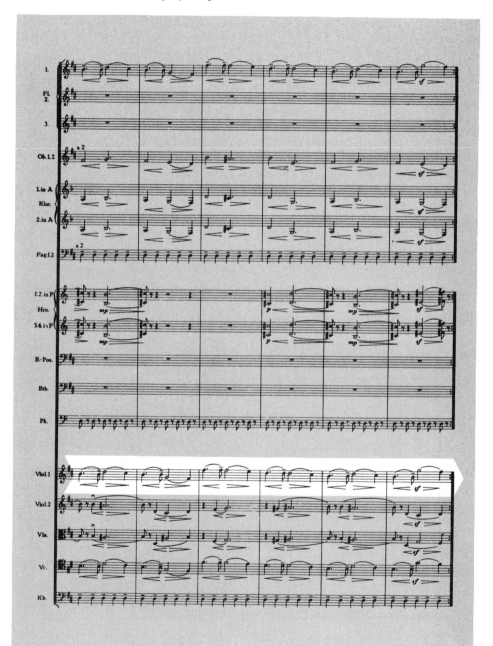

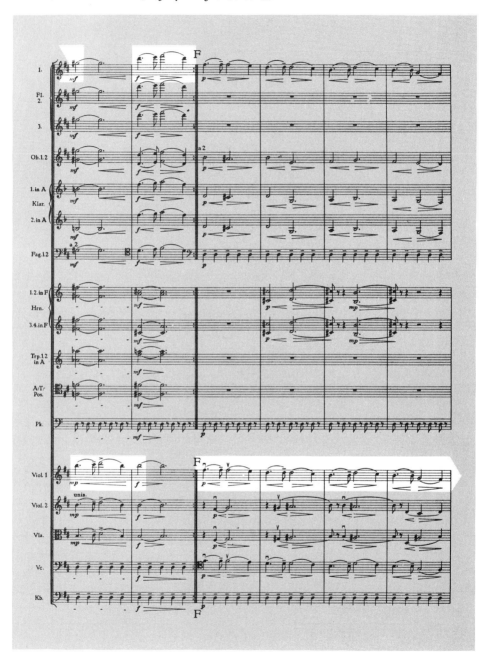

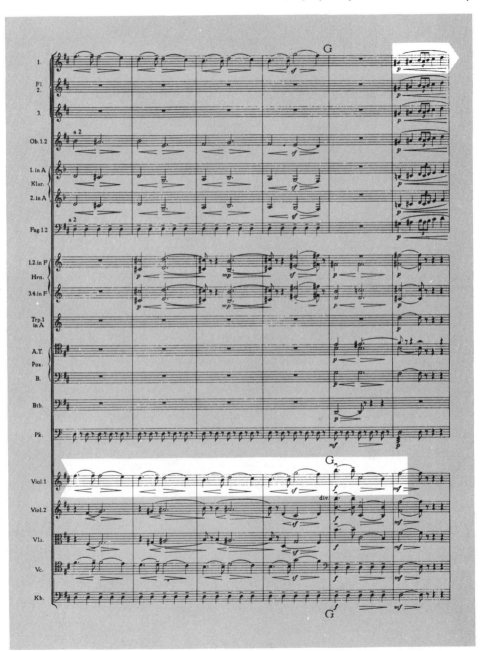

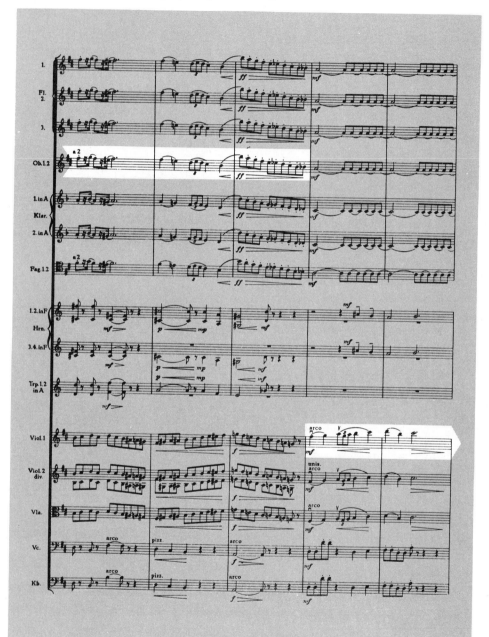

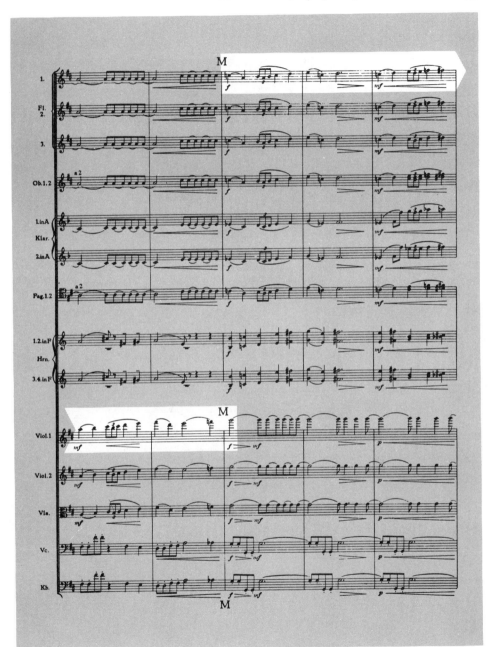

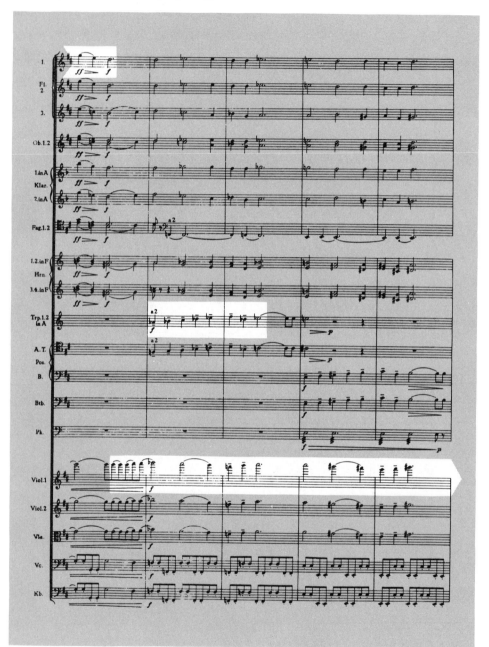

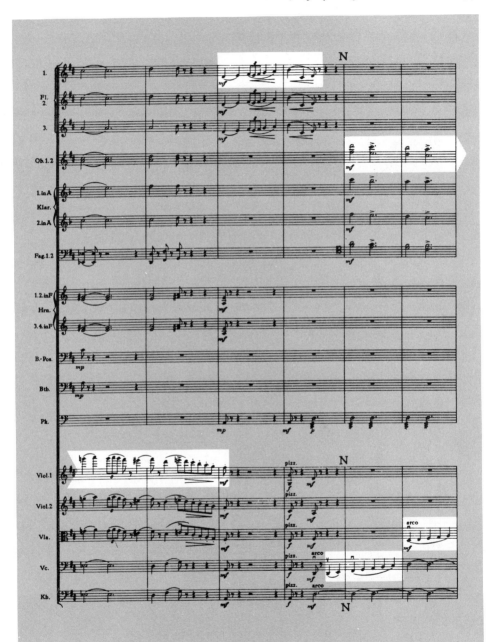

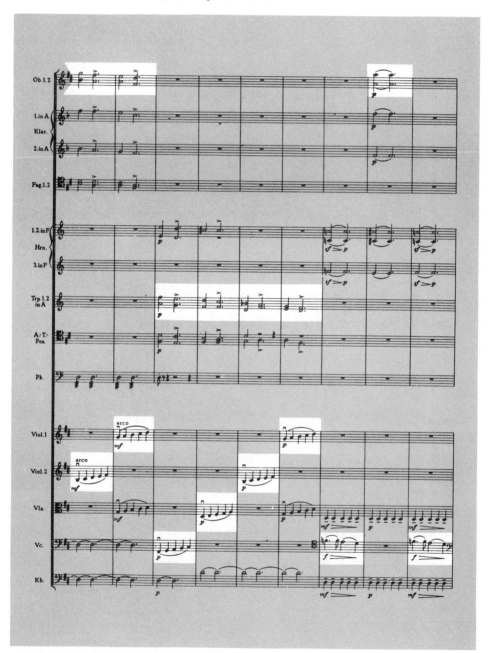

III
Allegro molto vivace (♩. = 152)
1.
Flöten
2.
Kleine Flöte
Oboen 1.2
1. in A
Klarinetten
2. in A
Fagotte 1.2
1.2. in F
Hörner
3.4. in F
Trompeten 1.2 in A
Alt, Tenor
Posaunen
Baß
Baßtuba
Pauken in Fis, G, H
Gr. Trommel u. Becken
Allegro molto vivace (♩. = 152)
Violine 1 divisi
Violine 2 divisi
Viola divisi
Violoncell divisi
Kontrabaß divisi
Allegro molto vivace (♩. = 152)

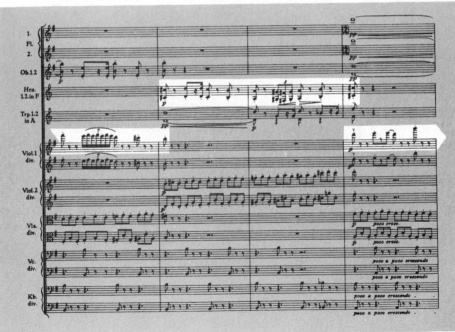

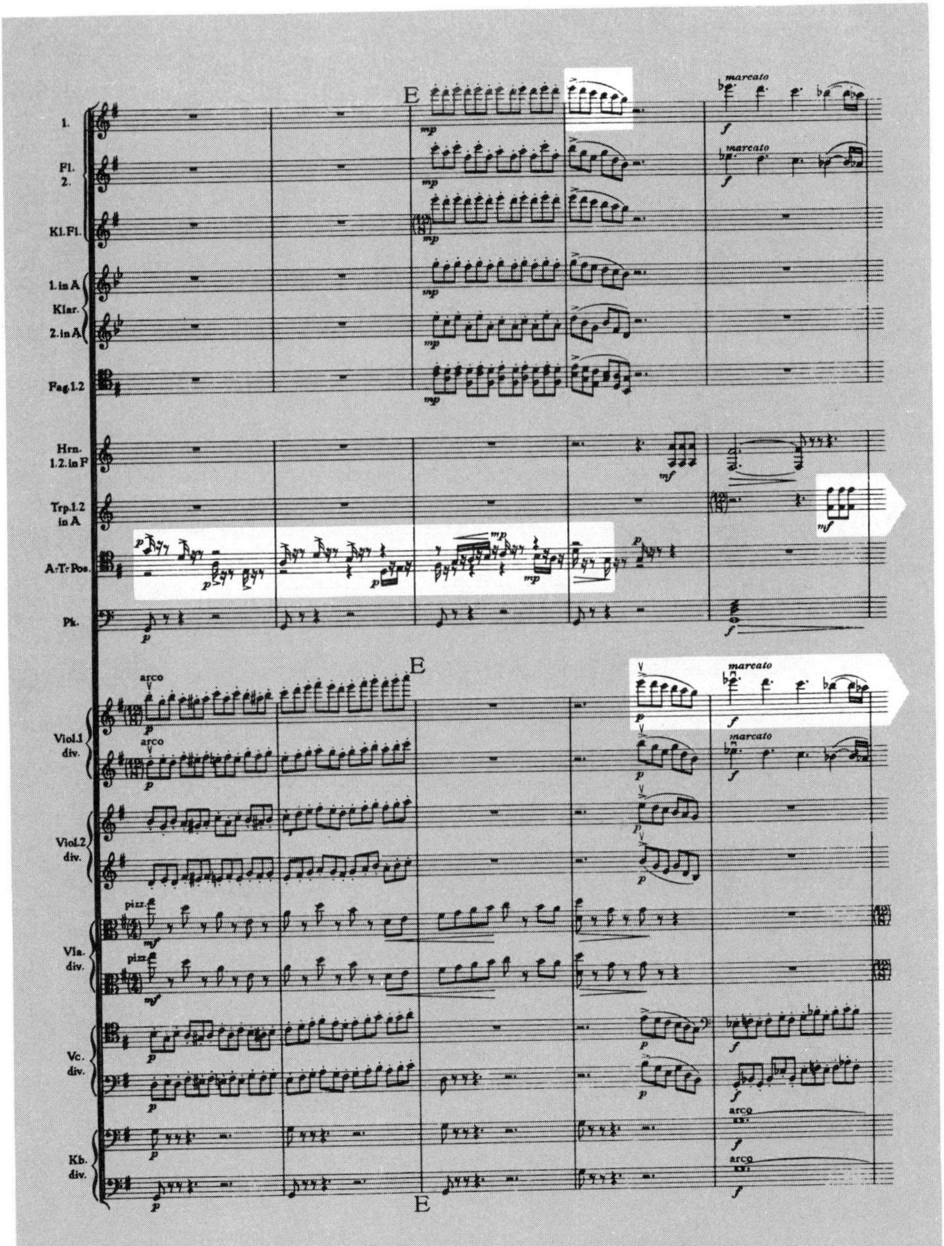
E
Fl. 1. 2.
Kl. Fl.
Klar. 1. in A 2. in A
Fag. 1.2
Hrn. 1.2. in F
Trp. 1.2 in A
A. T. Pos.
Pk.
Viol. 1 div.
Viol. 2 div.
Vla. div.
Vc. div.
Kb. div.
arco
pizz.
marcato
mp
mf
p
f

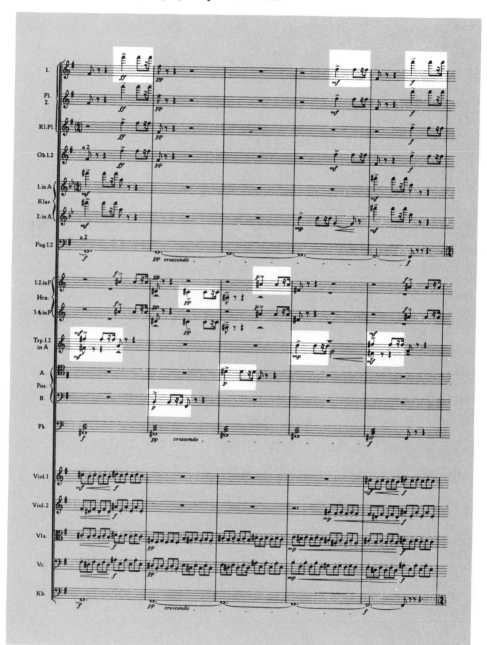

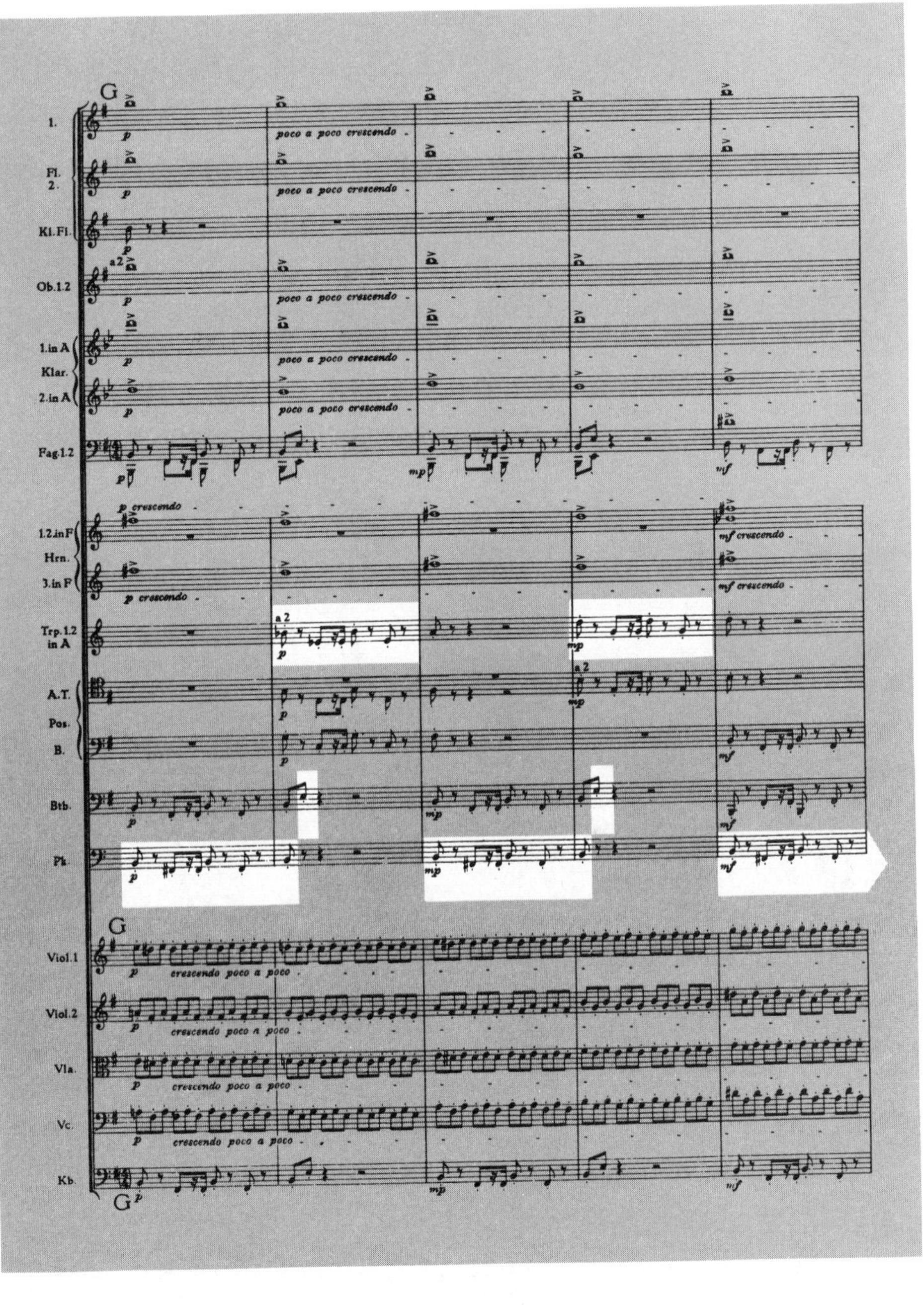
G
Fl. 1.
Fl. 2.
Kl. Fl.
Ob. 1.2
a 2
Klar. 1. in A
Klar. 2. in A
Fag. 1.2
Hrn. 1.2. in F
Hrn. 3. in F
Trp. 1.2 in A
Pos. A.T.
Pos. B.
Btb.
Pk.
Viol. 1
Viol. 2
Vla.
Vc.
Kb.
poco a poco crescendo
p crescendo
mf crescendo
crescendo poco a poco

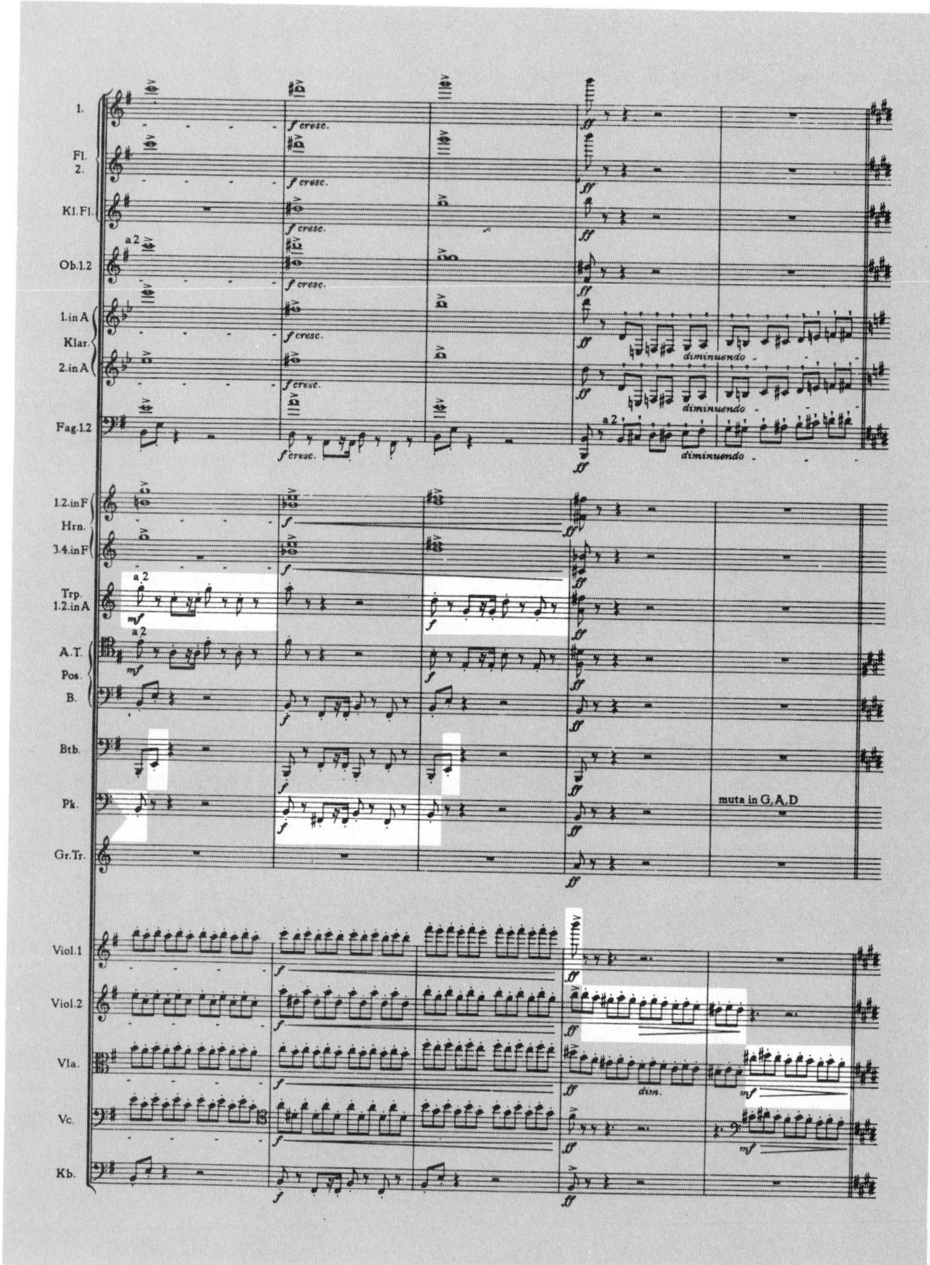
1.
Fl.
2.
Kl.Fl.
Ob.1.2
1.in A
Klar.
2.in A
Fag.1.2
1.2.in F
Hrn.
3.4.in F
Trp.
1.2.in A
A.T.
Pos.
B.
Btb.
Pk.
Gr.Tr.
Viol.1
Viol.2
Vla.
Vc.
Kb.
a 2
f cresc.
ff
diminuendo
mf
f
muta in G,A,D
dim.

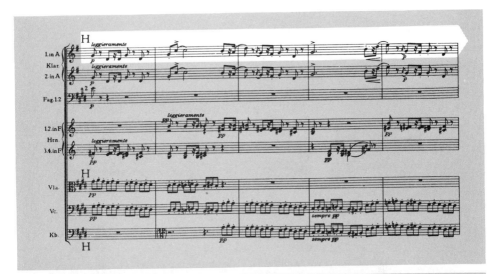

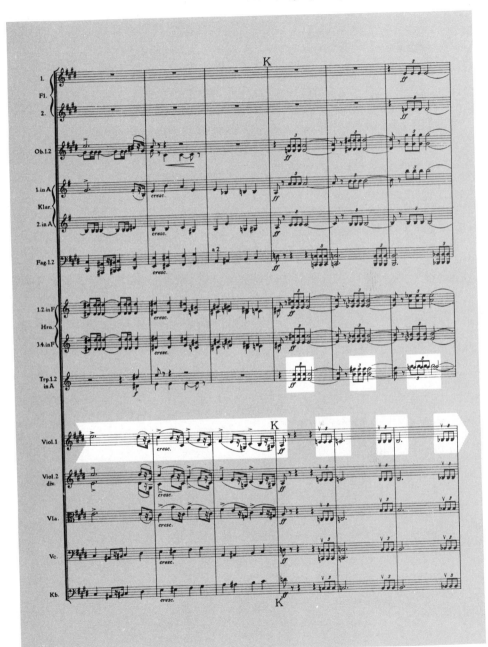

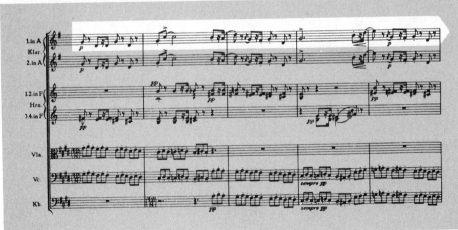

M
1. Fl. 2.
Ob.1.2
1.in A Klar. 2.in A
Fag.1.2
1.2.in F Hrn. 3.4.in F
Viol.1
Viol.2
Vla.
Vc.
Kb.
sempre p
a2
mp
mf
ff
f
pp
p
M
M

1. Fl. 2.
1.in A Klar. 2.in A
Fag.1.2
1.2.in F Hrn. 3.4.in F
Viol.1
Viol.2
Vla.
Vc.
Kb.
p
pp
un poco cresc.

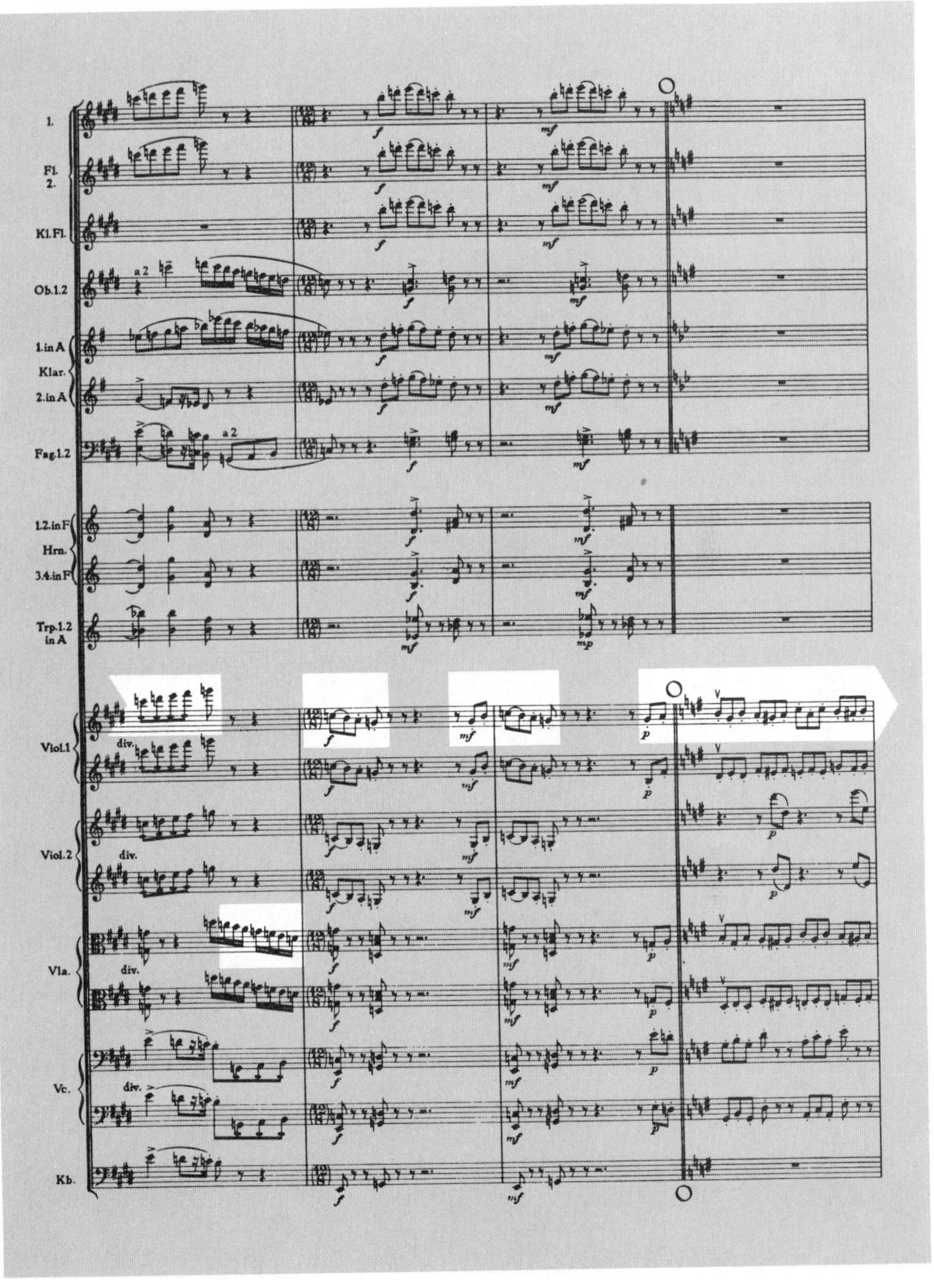
1.
Fl.
2.
Kl.Fl.
Ob.1.2
a2
1.in A
Klar.
2.in A
Fag.1.2
1.2.in F
Hrn.
3.4.in F
Trp.1.2
in A
Viol.1
div.
Viol.2
Vla.
Vc.
Kb.

1.
Fl.
2.
Ob.1.2
1.in A
Klar.
2.in A
Fag.1.2
Hrn.1.2 in A
Viol.1 div.
Viol.2 div.
pizz.
arco
Vla. div.
Vc. div.
div.
Kb.

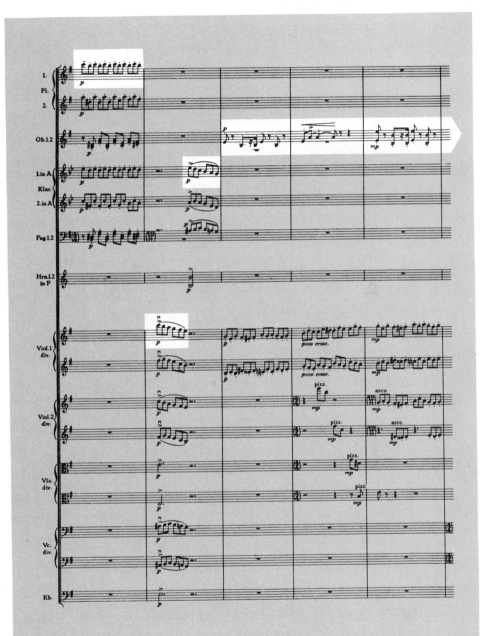

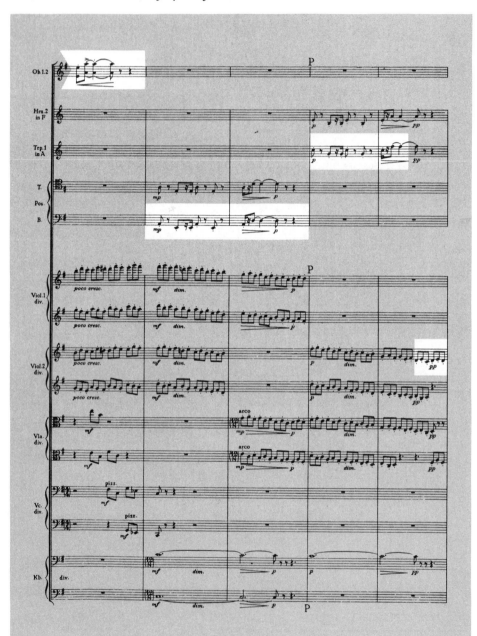

1. in A
Klar.
2. in A
Fag. 1.2
1.2. in F
Hrn.
4. in F
Viol. 1
div.
pizz.
Viol. 2
div.
Vla.
div.
Vc.
div.
arco
pizz.
Kb.
div.
diminuendo
pizz.

1.
Fl.
2.
Kl.Fl.
1.in A
Klar.
2.in A
Fag.1.2
A-T-Pos.
Pk.
Viol.1
div.
Viol.2
div.
Vla.
div.
Vc.
div.
Kb.
div.
arco
pizz.
p
mf

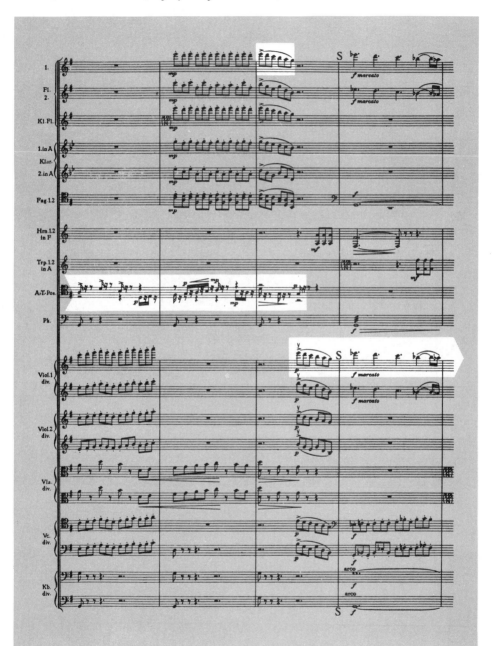

Fl. 1. 2.
Kl. Fl.
Ob. 1. 2
Klar. 1. in A 2. in A
Fag. 1. 2
Hrn. 1. 2. in F 3. 4. in F
Trp. 1. 2 in A
Pos. A. T. B.
Btb.
Pk.
Viol. 1
Viol. 2
div.
Vla.
Vc.
Kb.
leggieramente
a 2
p poco a poco cresc.
poco a poco

W
1.
Fl.
2.
Kl. Fl.
Ob. 1.2
1. in A
Klar.
2. in A
a 2
Fag. 1.2
1.2. in F
Hrn.
3.4. in F
Trp. 1.2 in A
A. T.
Pos.
B.
Btb.
Pk.
Viol. 1
Viol. 2
Vla.
Vc.
Kb.

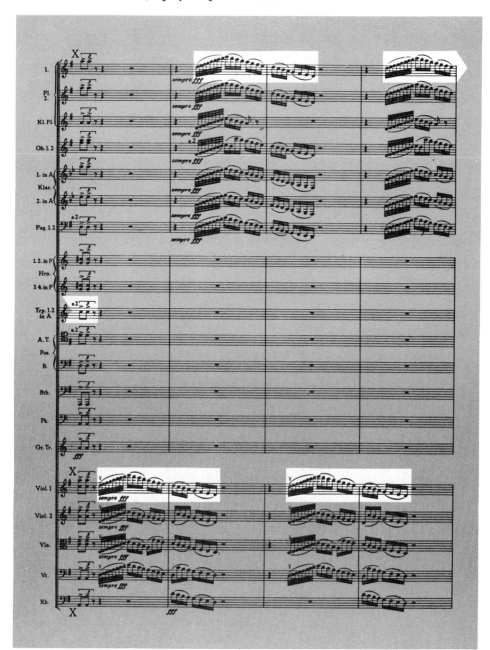

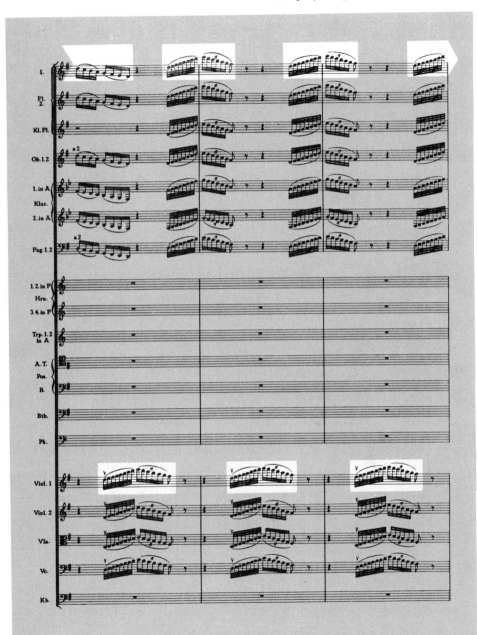

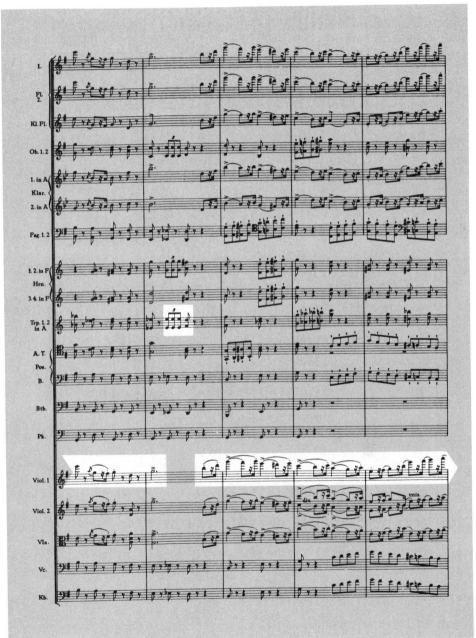

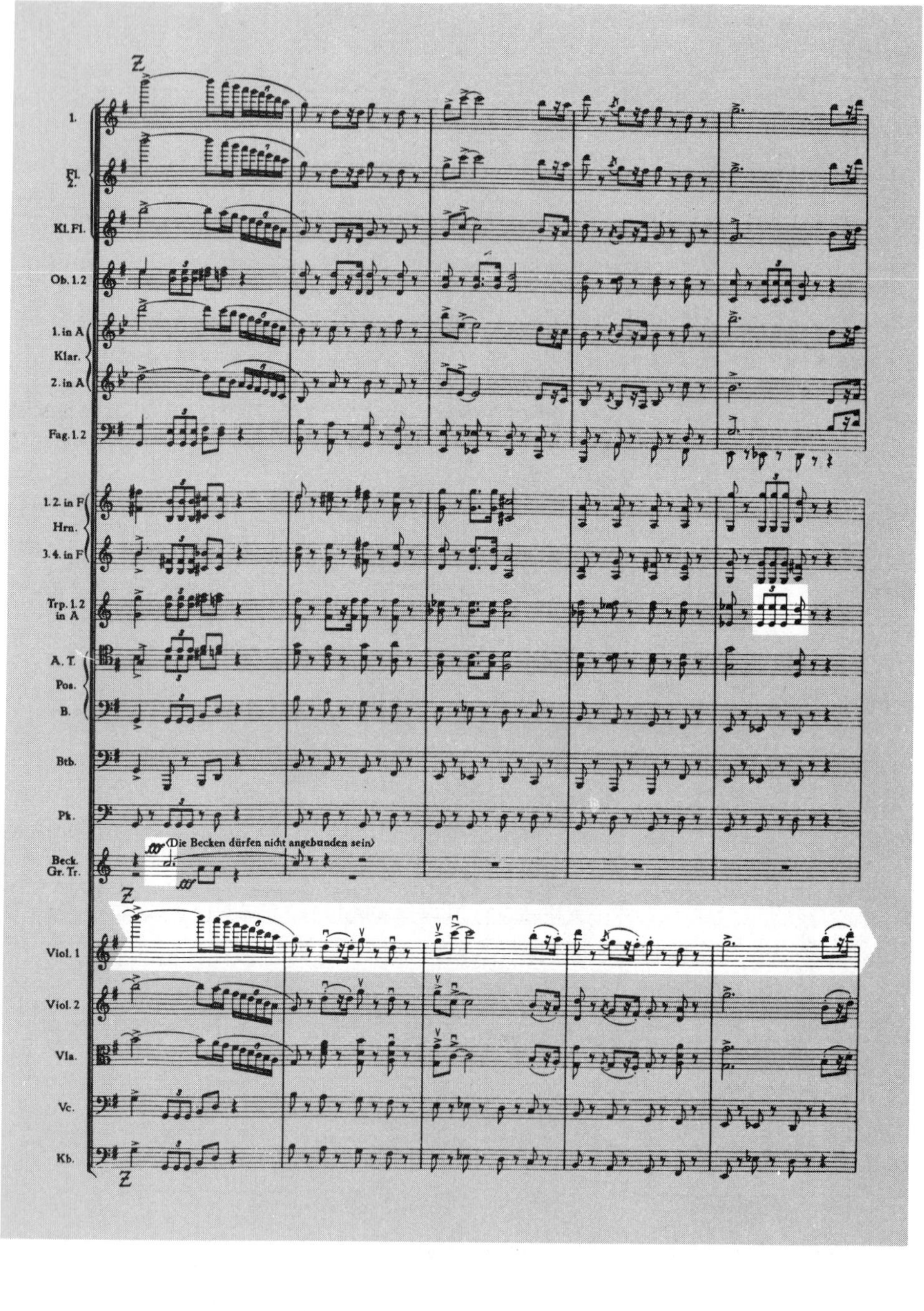
Z
1.
Fl.
2.
Kl. Fl.
Ob. 1.2
1. in A
Klar.
2. in A
Fag. 1.2
1. 2. in F
Hrn.
3. 4. in F
Trp. 1.2
in A
A. T.
Pos.
B.
Btb.
Pk.
(Die Becken dürfen nicht angebunden sein)
Beck.
Gr. Tr.
Viol. 1
Viol. 2
Vla.
Vc.
Kb.

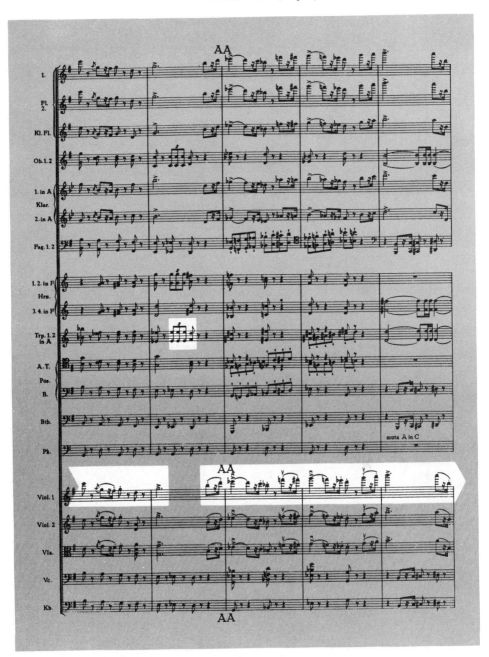

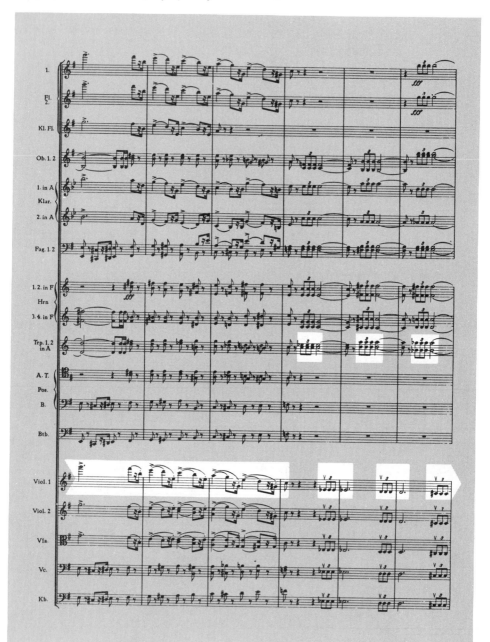

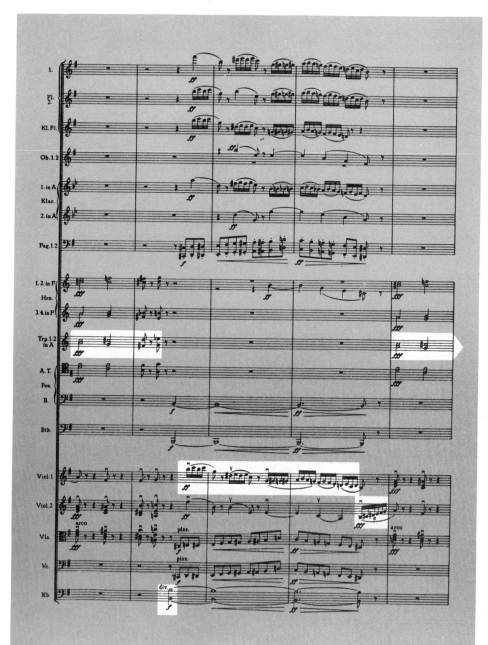

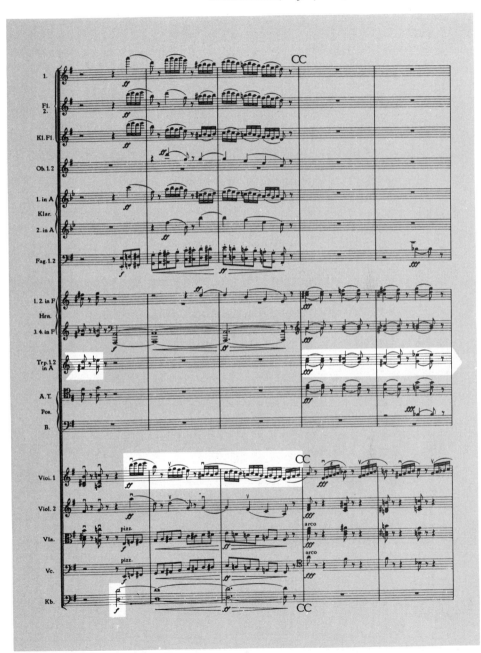

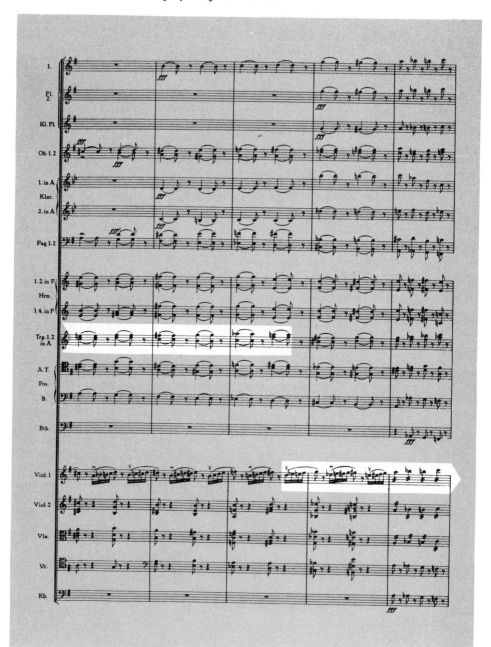

DD
1.
Fl.
2.
Kl. Fl.
Ob. 1. 2
1. in A
Klar.
2. in A
Fag. 1. 2
a 2
marcato assai
1. 2. in F
Hrn.
3. 4. in F
Trp. 1. 2 in A
A. T.
Pos.
B.
Btb.
Pk.
Gr. Tr.
Viol. 1
Viol. 2
Vla.
Vc.
Kb.

EE
1.
Fl.
2.
Kl. Fl.
Ob. 1.2
1. in A
Klar.
2. in A
Fag. 1.2
1. 2. in F
Hrn.
3. 4. in F
a 2
Trp. 1.2 in A
A. T.
Pos.
B.
Btb.
Pk.
Beck.
Gr. Tr.
Viol. 1
Viol. 2
Vla.
Vc.
Kb.
fff

1.
Fl.
2.
Kl. Fl.
Ob. 1. 2
1. in A
Klar.
2. in A
Fag. 1. 2
1. 2. in F
Hrn.
3. 4. in F
Trp. 1. 2
in A
A. T.
Pos.
B.
Btb.
Pk.
Viol. 1
Viol. 2
div.
unis.
Vla.
Vc.
Kb.

FF
Fl. 1. 2.
Kl. Fl.
Ob. 1. 2
Klar. 1. in A 2. in A
Fag. 1. 2
Hrn. 1. 2. in F 3. 4. in F
Trp. 1. 2 in A
Pos. A. T. B.
Btb.
Pk.
Beck. Gr. Tr.
fff
fff
FF
Viol. 1
Viol. 2
Vla.
Vc.
Kb.
FF

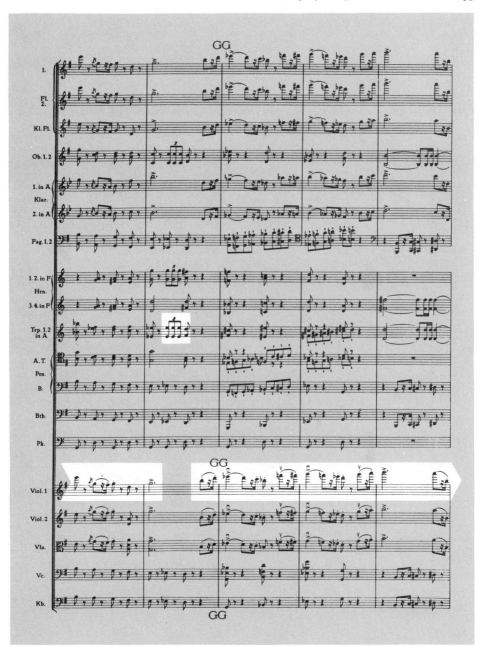

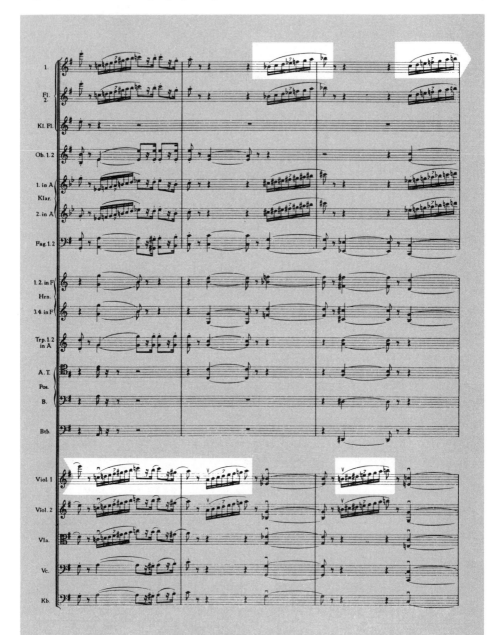

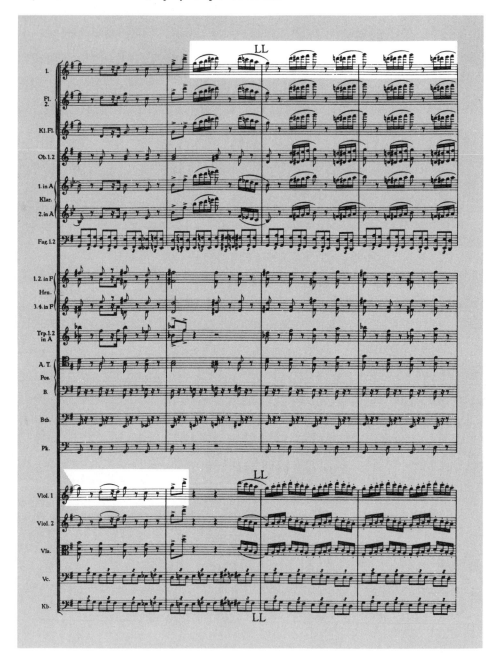

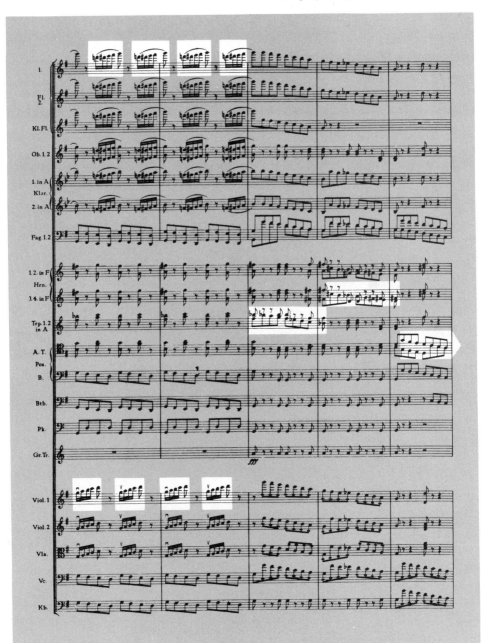

1.
Fl.
2.
Kl. Fl.
Ob. 1.2
1. in A
Klar.
2. in A
Fag. 1.2
a 2
1. 2. in F
Hrn.
3.4. in F
Trp. 1.2 in A
A. T.
Pos.
B.
Btb.
Pk.
Gr. Tr.
fff
Viol. 1
Viol. 2
Vla.
Vc.
Kb.

IV. Finale

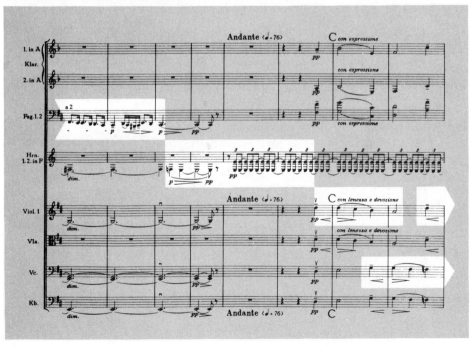

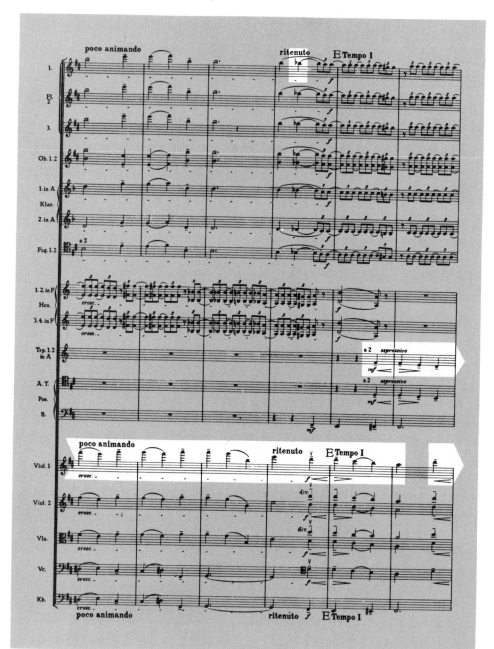

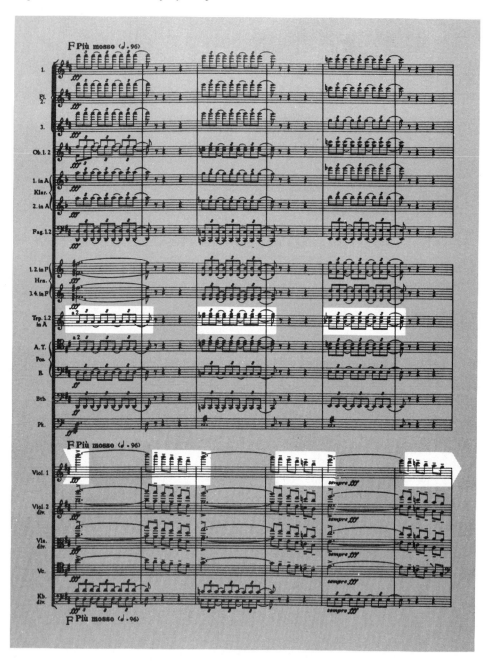

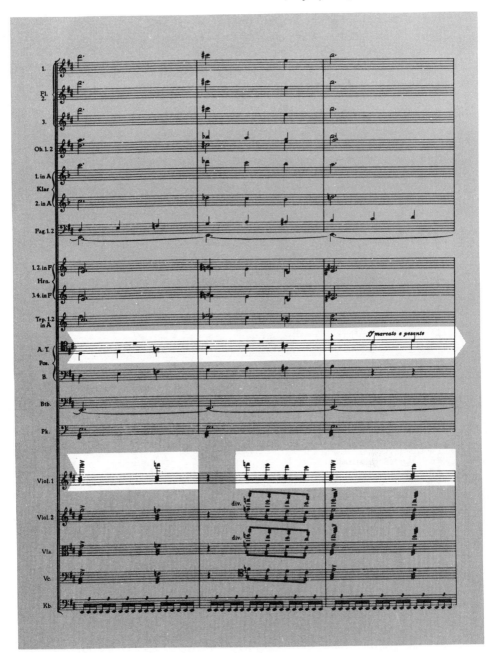

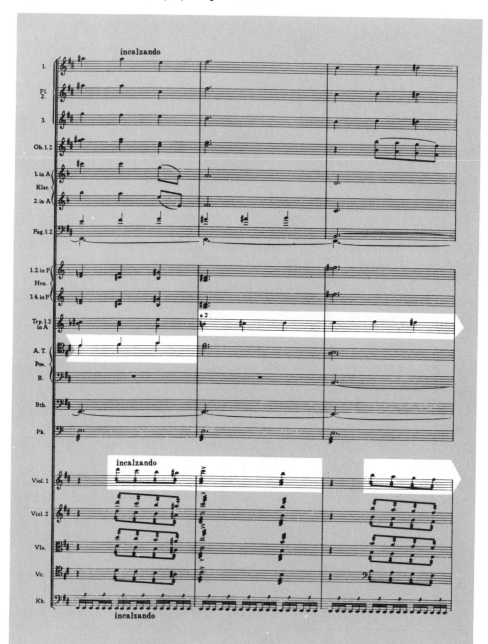

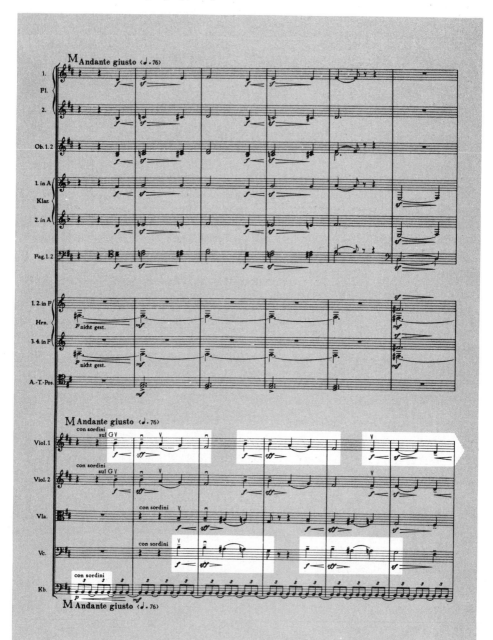

39. GUSTAV MAHLER (1860-1911),
Fourth movement from *Symphony No. 4* (1900)

NB Singstimme mit kindlich heiterem Ausdruck; durchaus ohne Parodie!
Il canto con espressione infantile e serena, sempre senza parodia!

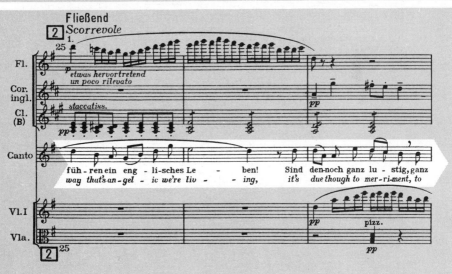

*) Hier muß dieses Tempo bewegter genommen werden, als an den korrespondierenden Stellen im ersten
*) *Questo tempo deve essere portato più mosso che nel primo movimento*   Satze

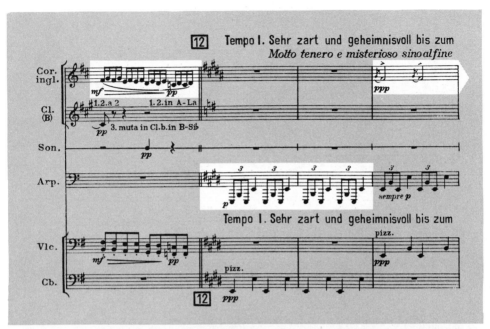

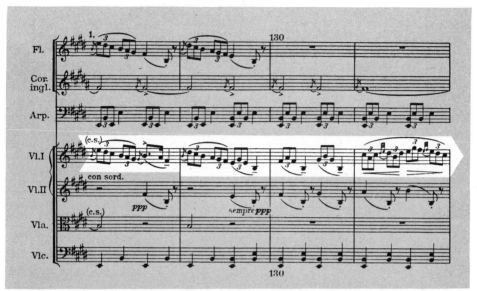

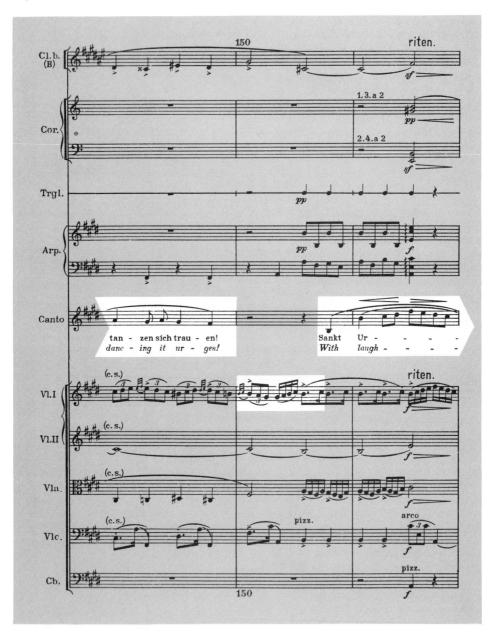

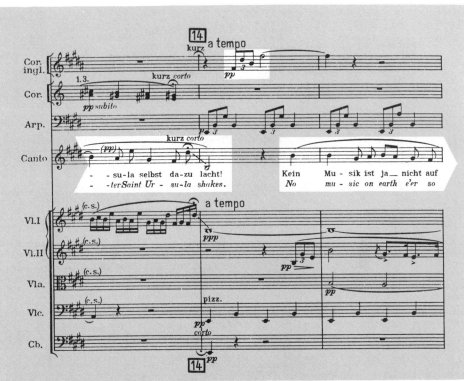

40. CLAUDE DEBUSSY (1862-1918),
Prelude to "The Afternoon of a Faun" (1894)

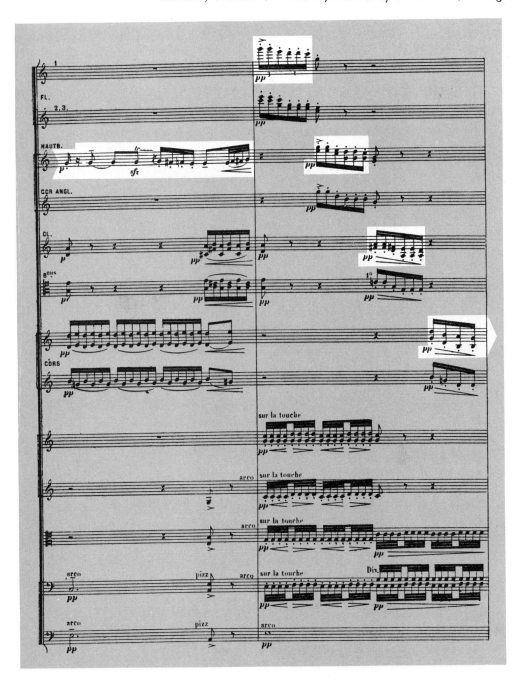

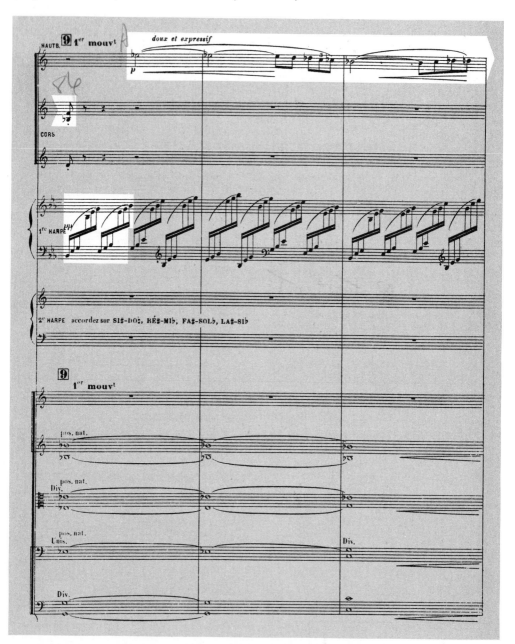

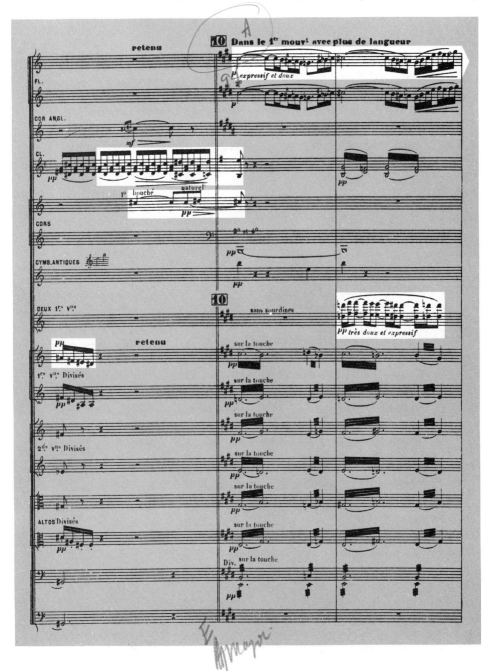

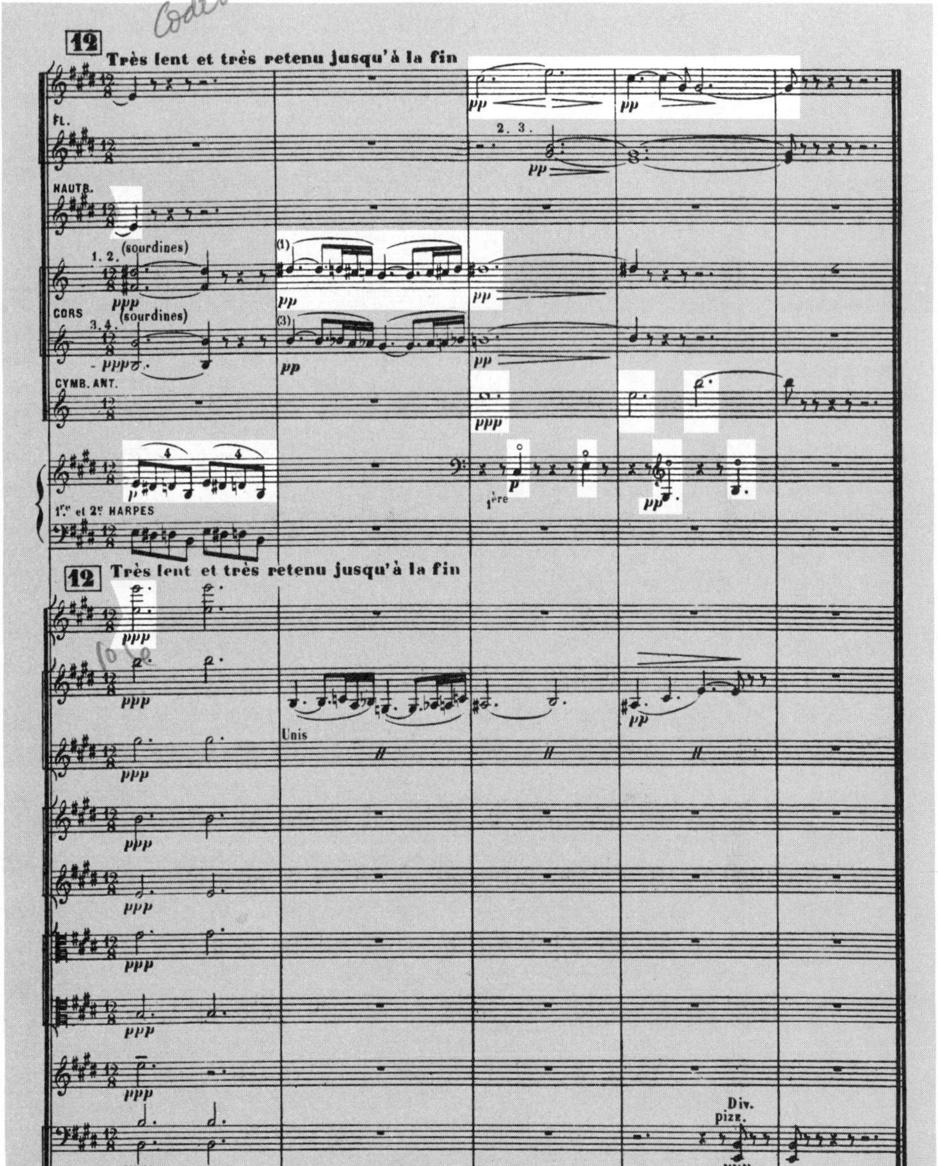
12
Très lent et très retenu jusqu'à la fin
FL.
2. 3.
HAUTB.
1. 2.
(sourdines)
CORS
3. 4.
(sourdines)
CYMB. ANT.
1ère
1re et 2e HARPES
12
Très lent et très retenu jusqu'à la fin
Unis
Div.
pizz.
pizz.

41. ARNOLD SCHOENBERG (1874-1951),
Excerpts from *Five Pieces for Orchestra*, Op. 16 (1909, REV. 1949)

Vorgefühle

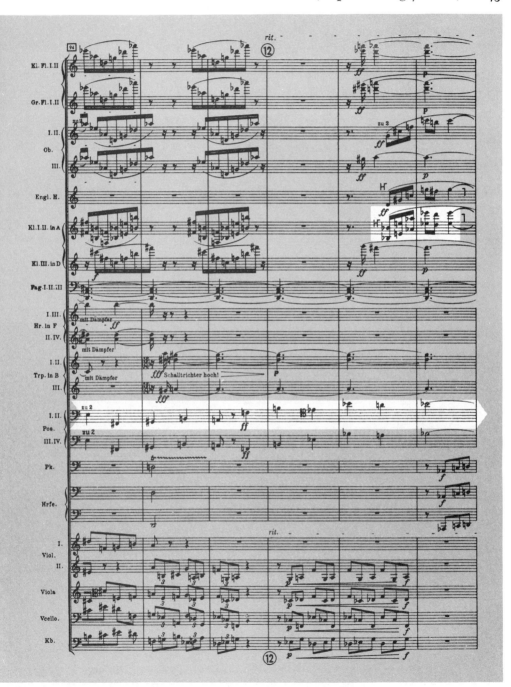

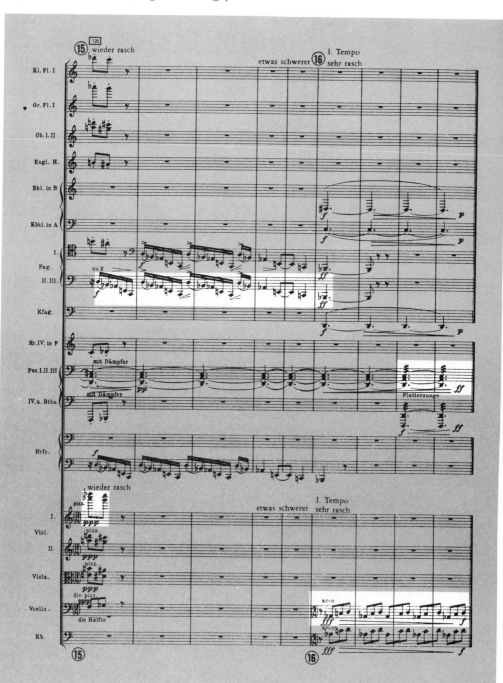

Vergangenes

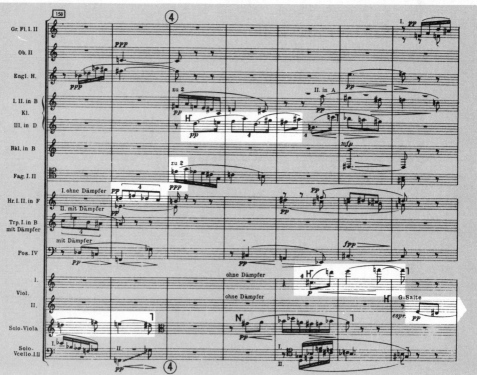

42. CHARLES IVES (1874-1954), *Putnam's Camp, Redding, Connecticut,* from *Three Places in New England* (1903-1914)

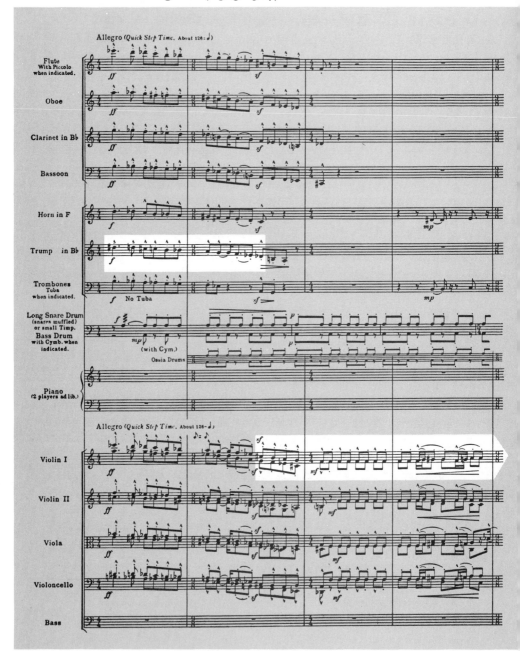

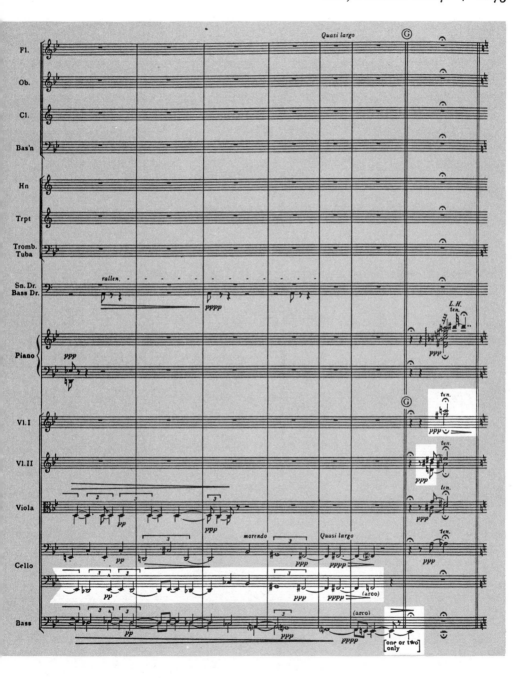

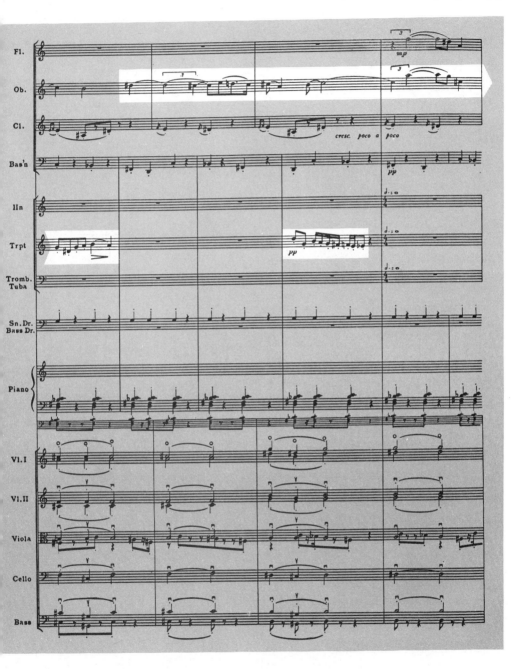

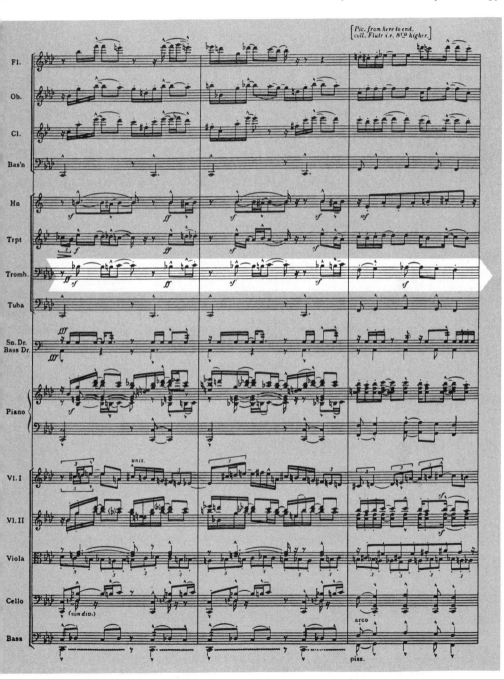

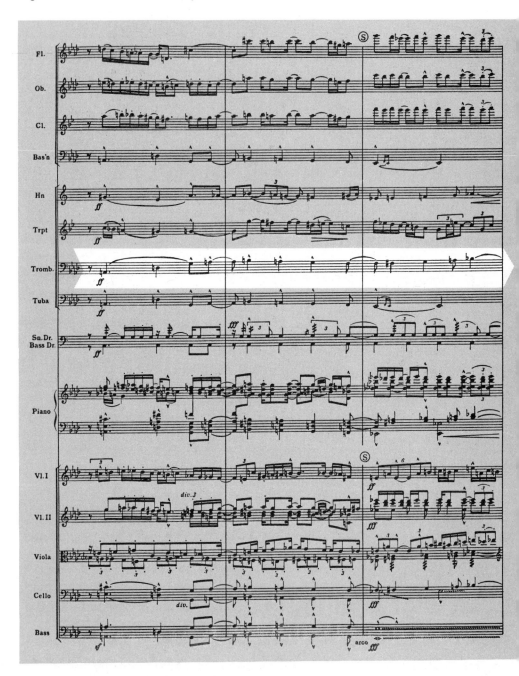

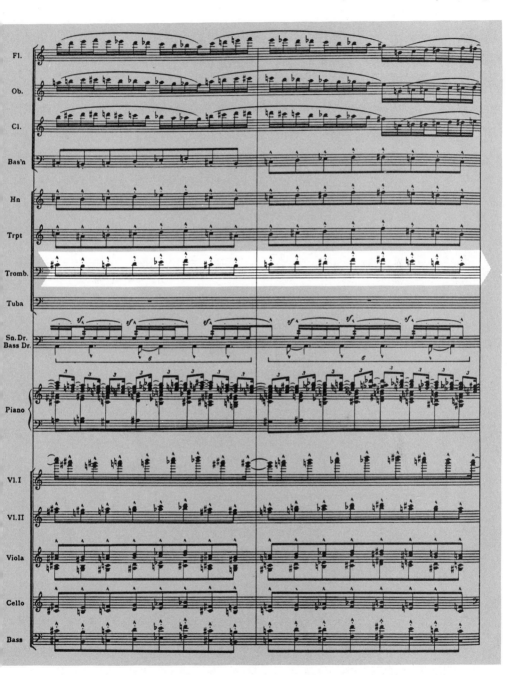

43. BÉLA BARTÓK (1881-1945),
First movement from *Concerto for Orchestra* (1943)

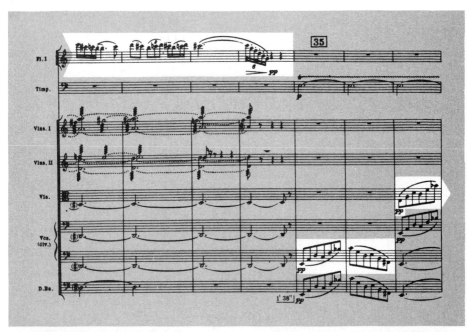

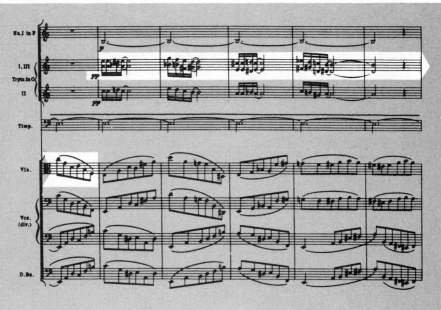

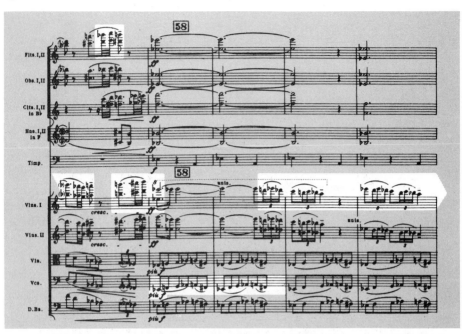

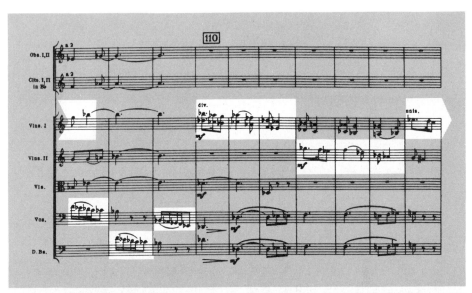

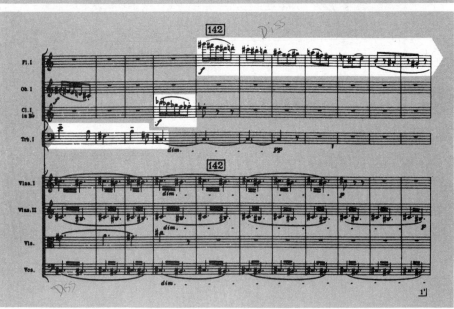

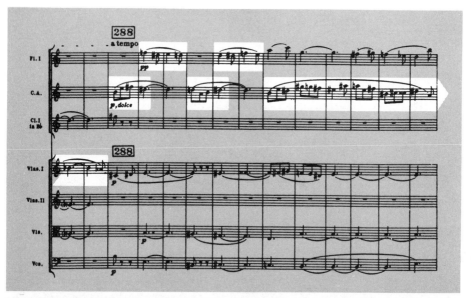

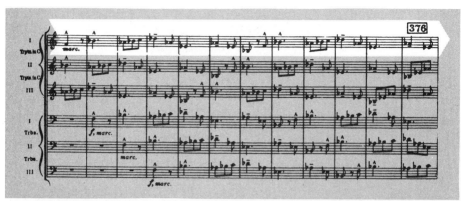

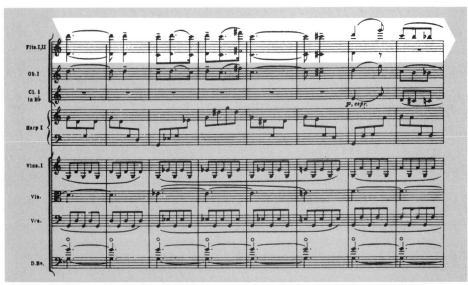

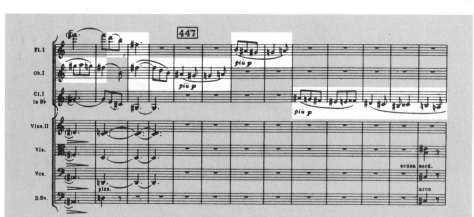

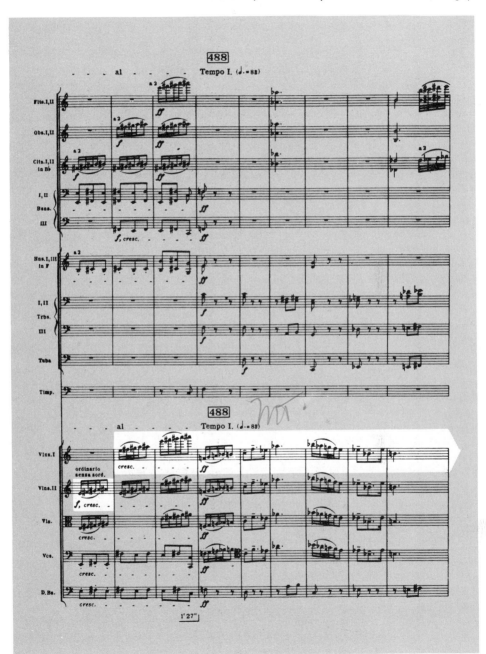

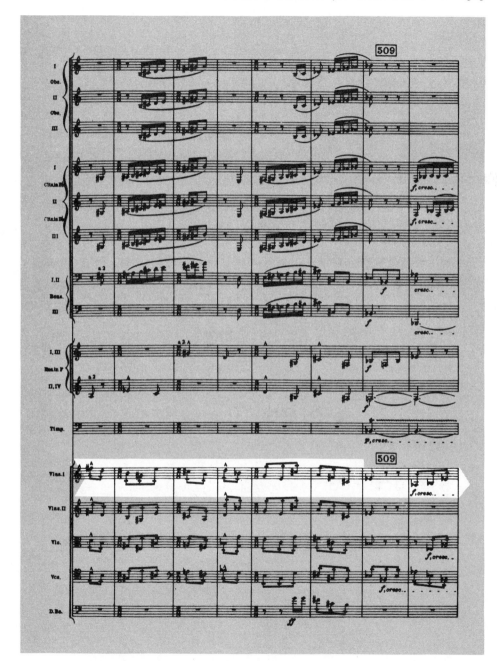

Duration of 1st movement appox. 9'48"

44. IGOR STRAVINSKY (1882-1971), Excerpts from *The Rite of Spring* (1913)

Opening scene

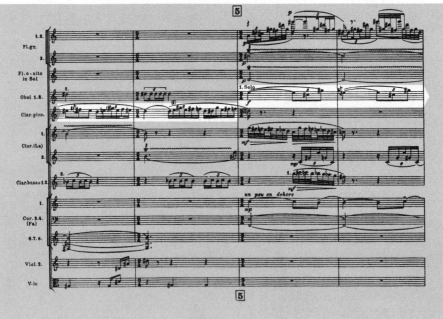

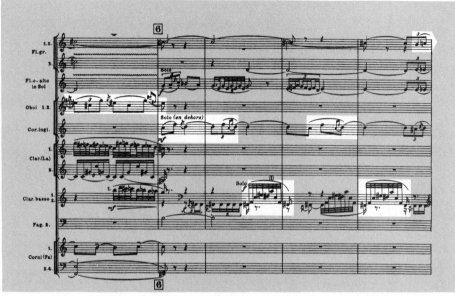

Augurs of Spring—Dances of the Youths and Maidens

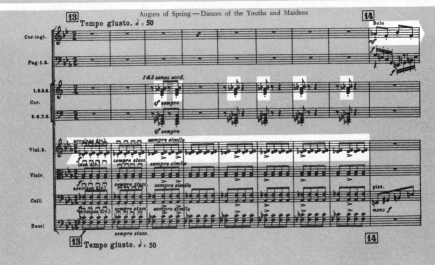

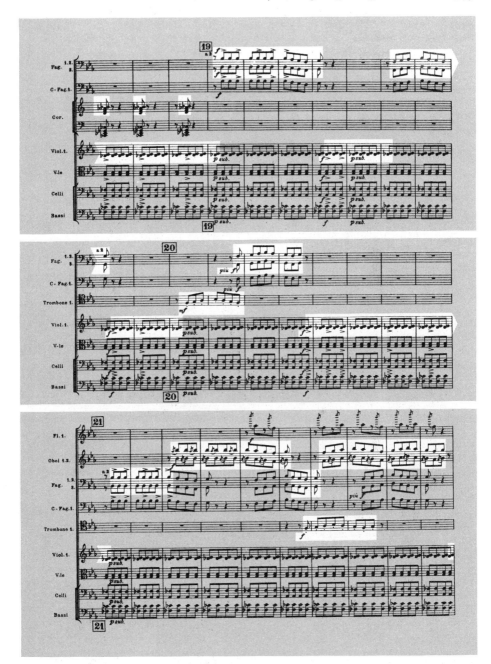

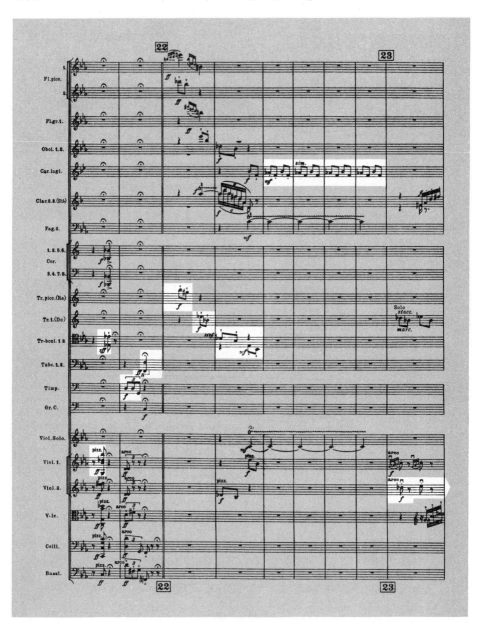

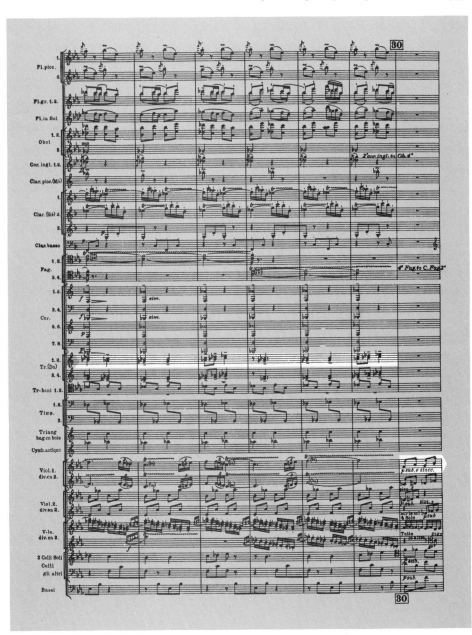

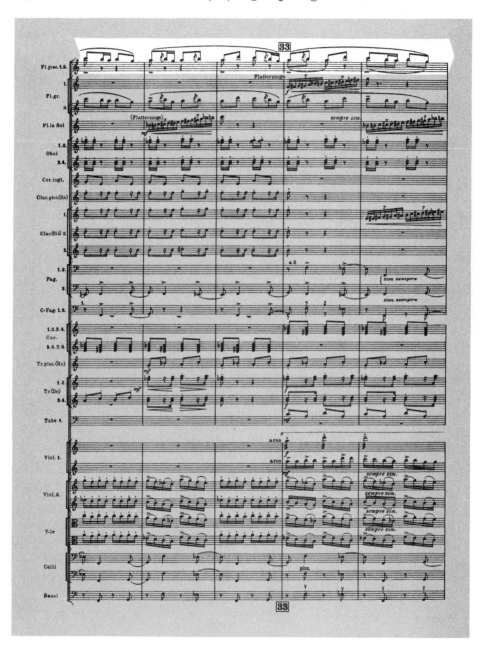

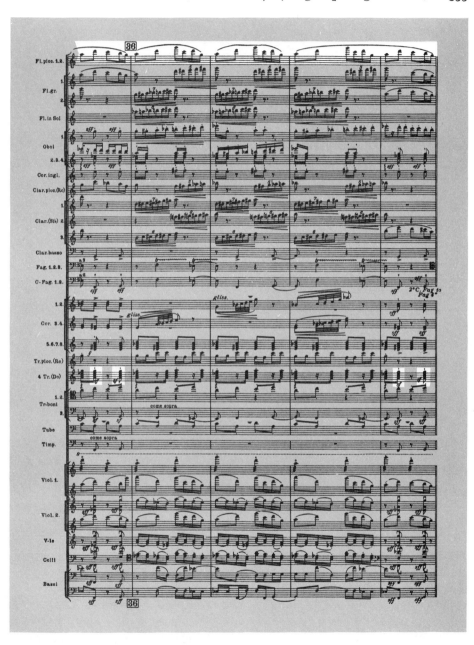

Ritual of Abduction

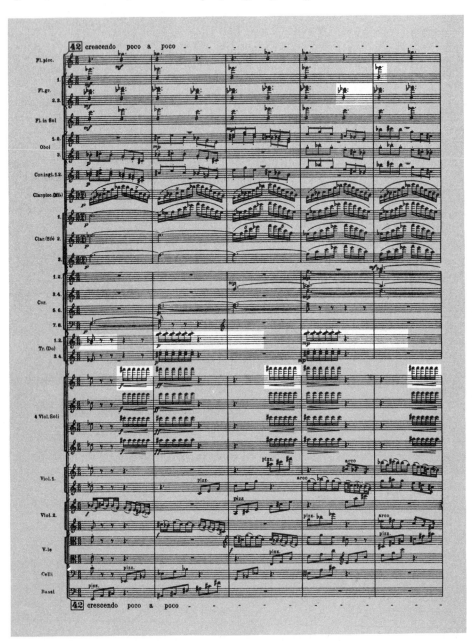

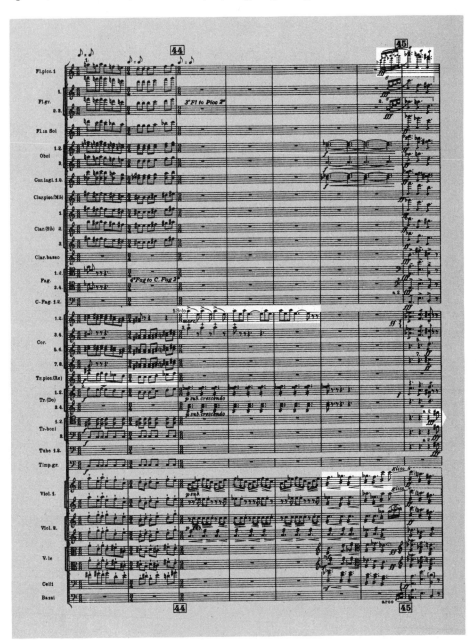

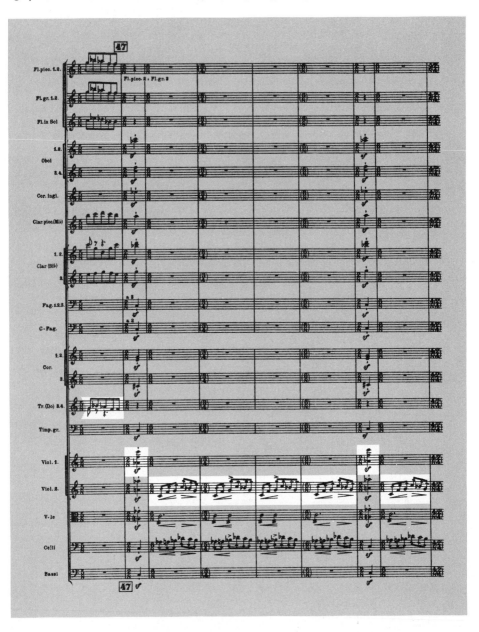

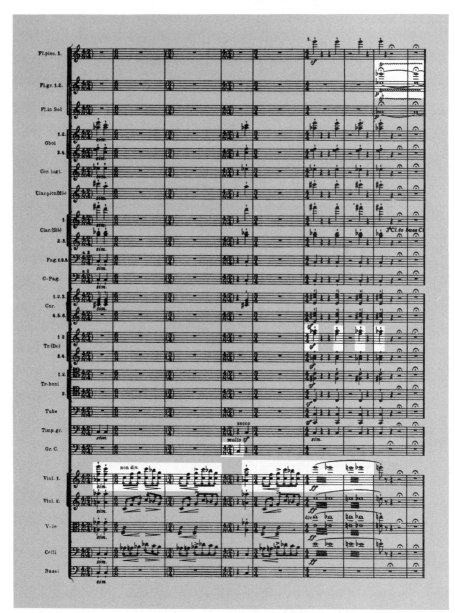

45. STRAVINSKY, First movement from *Symphony of Psalms* (1930)

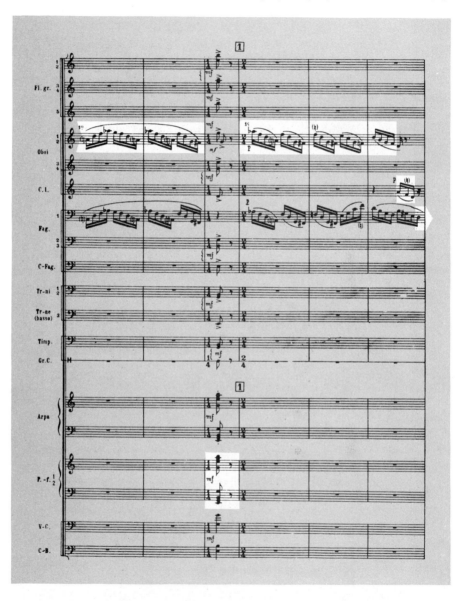

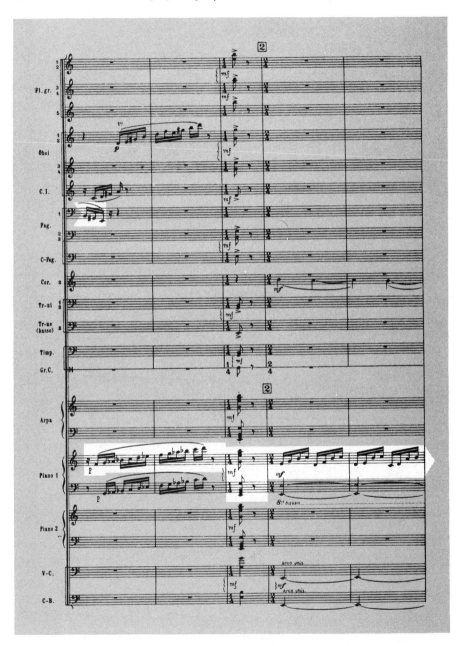

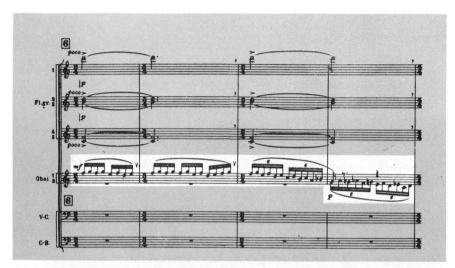

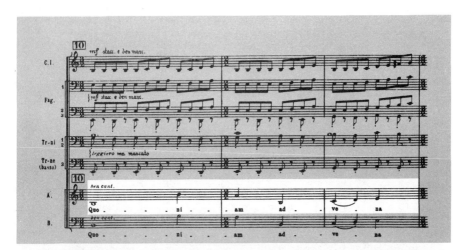

Translation

Hear my prayer, O Lord, and give ear unto my cry; hold not Thy peace at my tears; for I am a stranger with Thee, and sojourner, as all my fathers were. O spare me, that I may recover strength: before I go hence, and be no more.

PSALM 39 (KING JAMES VERSION),
VERSES 12-13

46. ANTON WEBERN (1883-1945),
Pieces for Orchestra, Opus 10, Nos. 3 and 4 (1913)

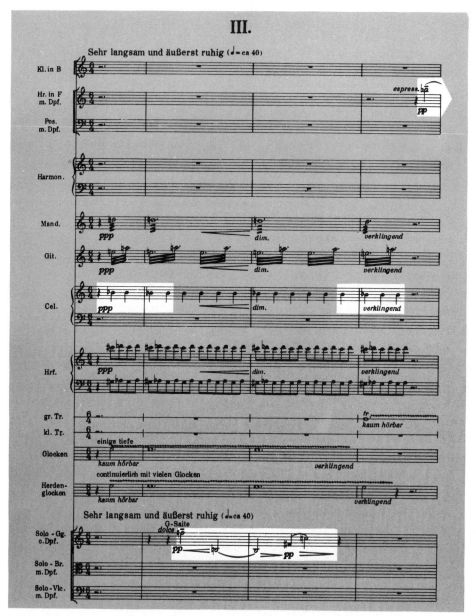

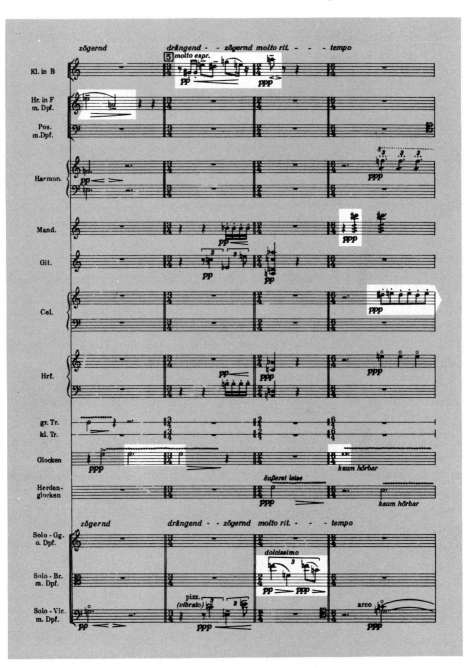

IV.

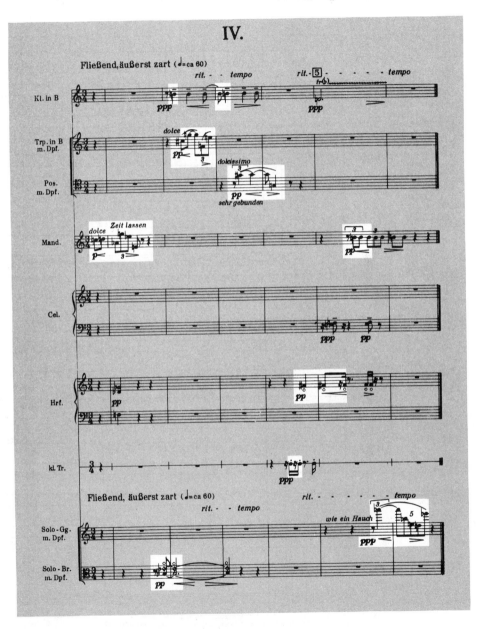

47. EDGARD VARÈSE (1883-1965), *Ionisation* (1931)

48. ALBAN BERG (1885-1935),
Act III, Scenes 4 and 5, from *Wozzeck* (1918-1921)

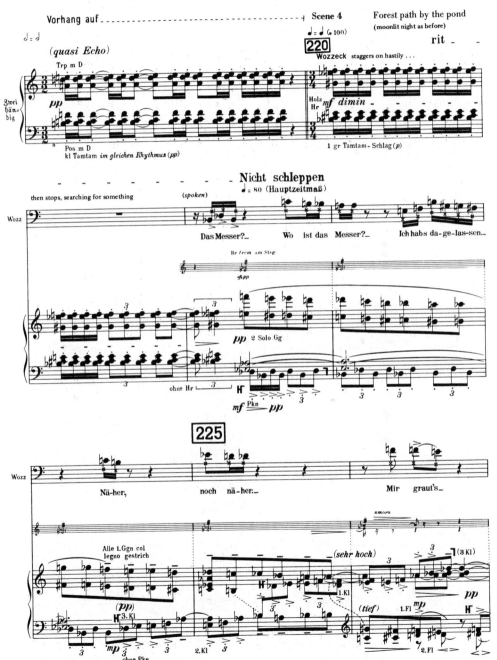

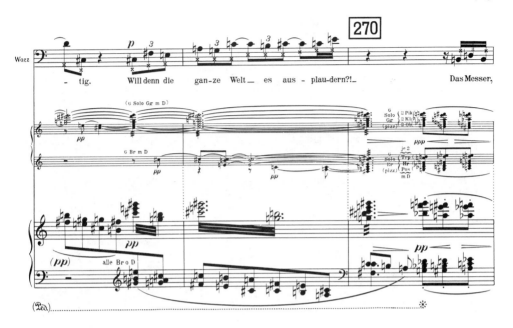

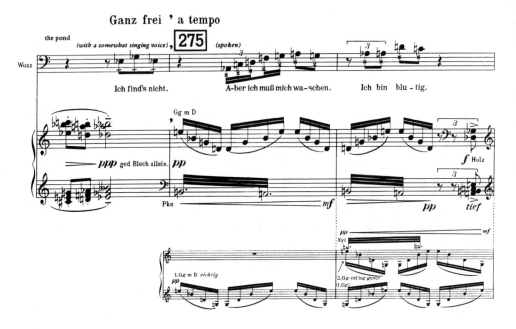

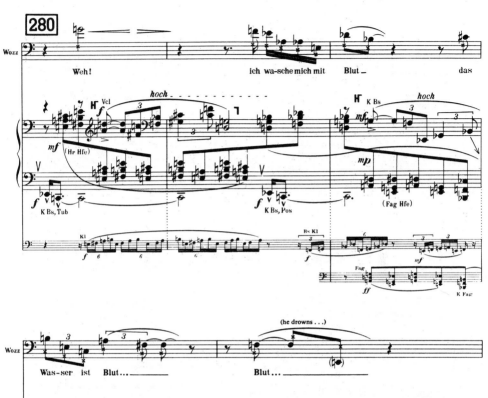

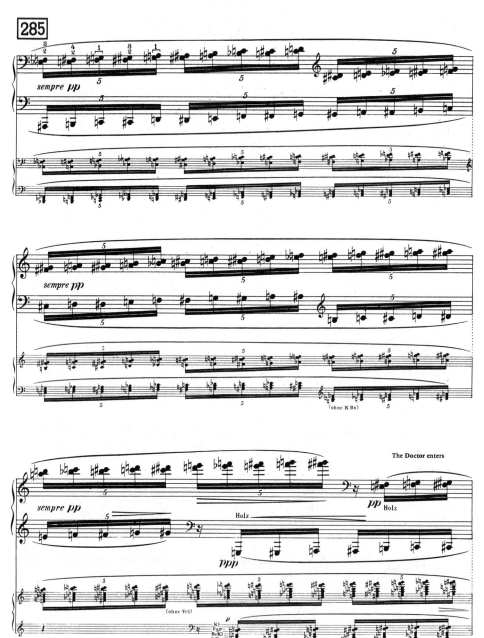

The **Captain** follows the Doctor (speaks)

sempre *pp*

The **Doctor** (stands still): *p* Hören Sie? Dort!

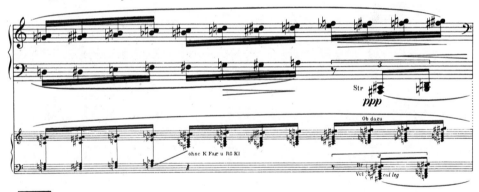

290 Hauptmann: *p* Jesus! Das war ein Ton. (also stands still)

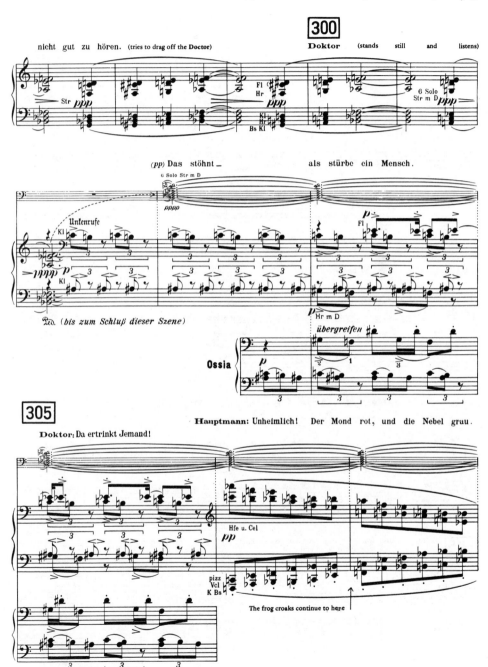

5th (last) Scene   In front of Marie's house (bright morning, sunshine)

Translation

SCENE FOUR
Invention on a Chord of Six Notes
Path in the wood by the pond. Moonlight, as before.
(Wozzeck stumbles hurriedly in, then stops, looking around for something.)
WOZZECK

Das Messer? Wo ist das Messer? Ich hab's dagelassen. Näher, noch näher. Mir graut's... da regt sich was. Still! Alles still und tot.	The knife? Where is the knife? I left it there. Around here somewhere. I'm terrified . . . something's moving. Silence. Everything silent and dead.

(shouting)

Mörder! Mörder!	Murderer! Murderer!

(whispering again)

Ha! Da ruft's. Nein, ich selbst.	Ah! Someone called, No. it was only me.

(still looking, he staggers a few steps further and stumbles against the corpse)

Marie! Marie! Was hast Du für eine rote Schnur um den Hals? Hast Dir das rote Halsband verdient, wie die Ohrringlein, mit Deiner Sünde! Was hängen Dir die schwarzen Haare so wild? Mörder! Mörder! Sie werden nach mir suchen. Das Messer verrät mich!	Marie! Marie! What's that red cord around your neck! Was the red necklace payment for your sins, like the ear-rings? Why's your dark hair so wild about you? Murderer! Murderer! They will come and look for me. The knife will betray me!

(looks for it in a frenzy)

Da, da ist's!	Here! Here it is!

(at the pond)

So! Da hinunter!	There! Sink to the bottom!

(throws the knife into the pond)

Es taucht ins dunkle Wasser wie ein Stein.	It plunges into the dark water like a stone.

(The moon appears, blood-red, from behind the clouds. Wozzeck looks up.)

Aber der Mond verrät mich, der Mond is blutig. Will denn die ganze Welt es ausplaudern? Das Messer, es liegt zu weit vorn, sie finden's beim Baden oder wenn sie nach Muscheln tauchen.	But the moon will betray me: the moon is blood-stained. Is the whole world going to incriminate me. The knife is too near the edge: they'll find it when they're swimming or diving for snails.

(wades into the pond)

Ich find's nicht. Aber ich muss mich waschen. Ich bin blutig. Da ein Fleck—und noch einer. Weh! Weh! Ich wasche mich mit Blut—das Wasser ist Blut...Blut...	I can't find it. But I must wash myself. There's blood on me. There's a spot here—and there's another. Oh, God! I am washing myself in blood—the water is blood . . . blood . . .

(drowns)
(The doctor appears, followed by the captain.)
CAPTAIN

Halt!	Wait!

DOCTOR *(stops)*

Hören Sie? Dort!	Can you hear? There!

CAPTAIN

Jesus! Das war ein Ton!   Jesus! What a ghastly sound!

(*stops as well*)

DOCTOR (*pointing to the pond*)

Ja, dort!   Yes, there!

CAPTAIN

Es ist das Wasser im Teich. Das Wasser ruft.   It's the water in the pond. The water is calling.
Es ist schon lange Niemand ertrunken.   It's been a long time since anyone drowned.
Kommen Sie Doktor!   Come away, Doctor.
Es ist nicht gut zu hören.   It's not good for us to be hearing it.

(*tries to drag the doctor away*)

DOCTOR (*resisting, and continuing to listen*)

Das stöhnt, als stürbe ein Mensch.   There's a groan, as though someone were
Da ertrinkt Jemand!   dying. Somebody's drowning!

CAPTAIN

Unheimlich! Der mond rot, und die Nebel   It's eerie! The moon is red, and the mist is
grau.   grey.
Hören Sie?...   Can you hear? . . .
Jetzt wieder das Ächzen.   That moaning again.

DOCTOR

Stiller,...jetzt ganz still.   It's getting quieter . . . now it's stopped
                                               altogether.

CAPTAIN

Kommen Sie! Kommen Sie schnell!   Come! Come quickly!

(*He rushes off, pulling the doctor along with him.*)

SCENE CHANGE
INVENTION ON A KEY (D minor)
SCENE FIVE
Invention on a Quaver Rhythm
In front of Marie's door. Morning. Bright sunshine.
(*Children are noisily at play. Marie's child is riding a hobby-horse.*)

CHILDREN

Ringel, Ringel, Rosenkranz. Ringelreih'n,   Ring-a-ring-a-roses,
Ringel, Ringel, Rosenkranz, Ring...   A pocket full of . . .

(*Their song and game is interrupted by other children bursting in.*)

ONE OF THE NEWCOMERS

Du, Käthe! Die Marie!   Hey, Katie! Have you heard about Marie?

SECOND CHILD

Was ist?   What's happened?

FIRST CHILD

Weisst' es nit? Sie sind schon Alle'naus.   Don't you know? They've all gone out there.

THIRD CHILD (*to Marie's little boy*)

Du! D'ein' Mutter ist tot!   Hey! Your mother's dead!

MARIE'S SON (*still riding*)

Hopp, hopp! Hopp, hopp! Hopp, hopp!   Hop hop! Hop hop! Hop hop!

SECOND CHILD

Wo ist sie denn?   Where is she then?

FIRST CHILD

Drauss' liegt sie, am Weg, neben dem Teich.   She's lying out there, on the path near the
                                                pond.

THIRD CHILD

Kommt, anschaun!   Come and have a look!

(*All the children run off.*)

MARIE'S SON (*continuing to ride*)

Hopp, hopp! Hopp, hopp! Hopp, hopp!   Hop hop! Hop hop! Hop hop!

(*He hesitates for a moment and then rides after the other children.*)

END OF THE OPERA

LIBRETTO BY ALBAN BERG AFTER GEORG BÜCHNER'S PLAY *Woyzeck*

SARAH E. SOULSBY

49. GEORGE GERSHWIN (1898-1937), *Rhapsody in Blue* (1924)

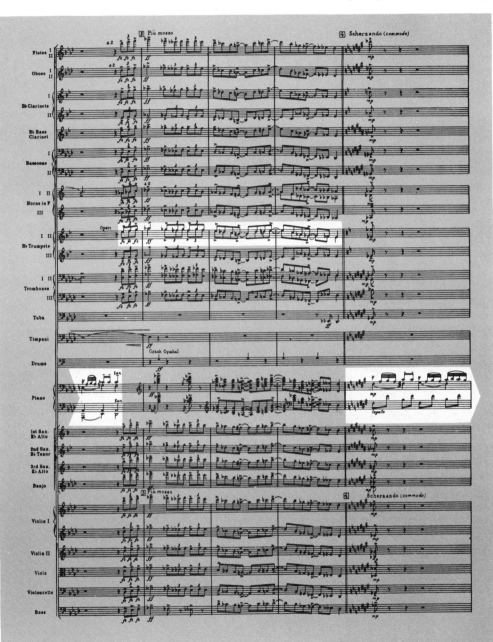

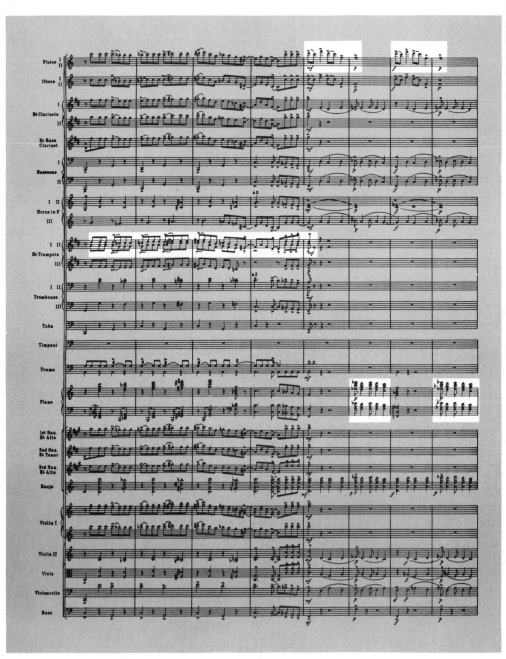

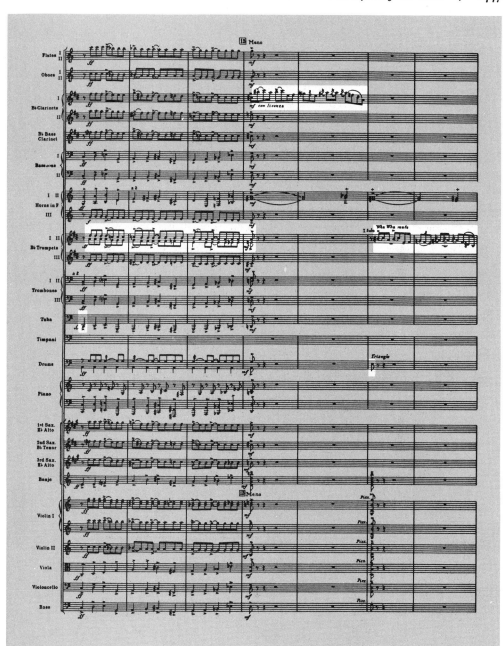

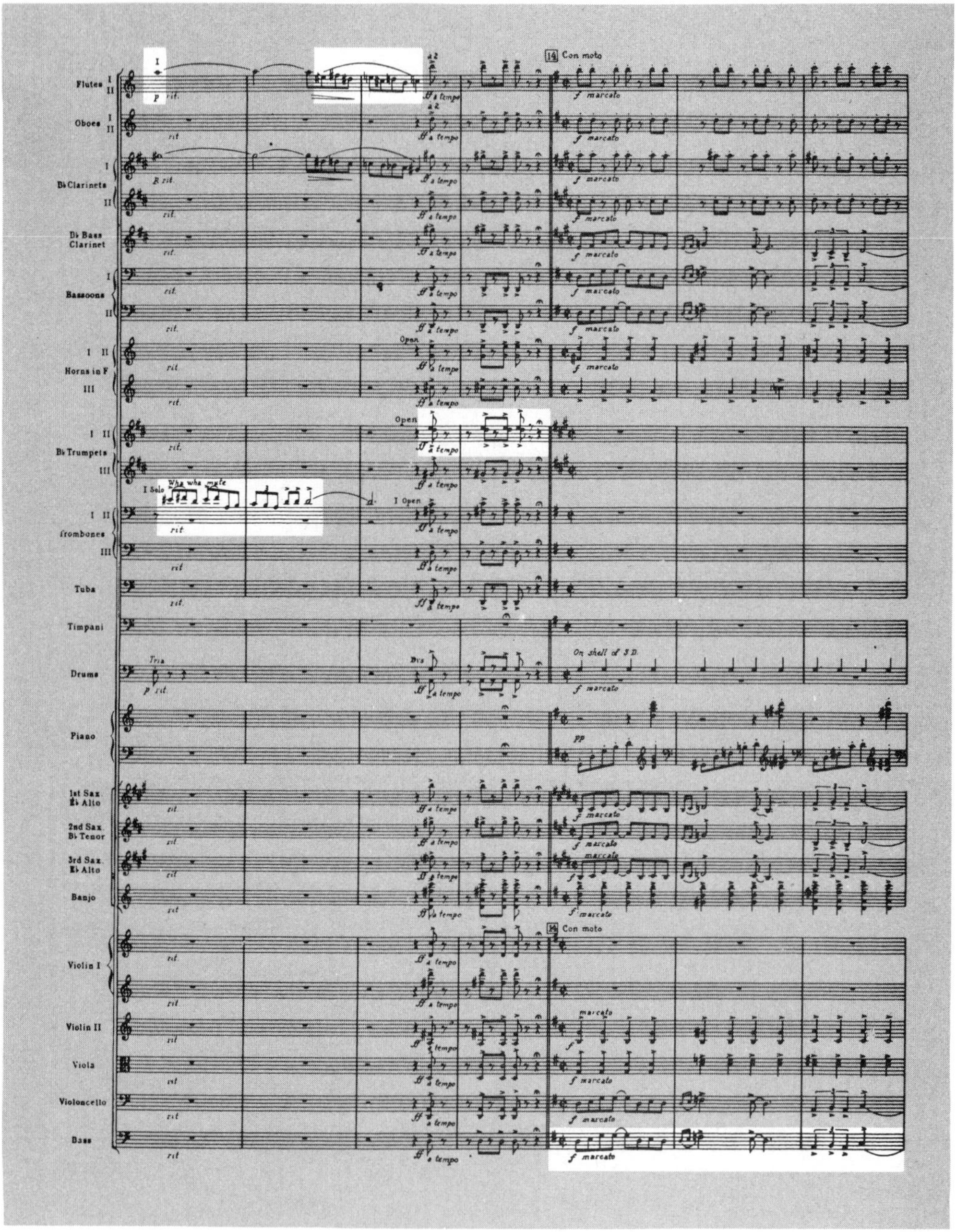
14 Con moto
Flutes I II
Oboes I II
B♭ Clarinets I II
B♭ Bass Clarinet
Bassoons I II
Horns in F I II III
B♭ Trumpets I II III
Trombones I II III
Tuba
Timpani
Drums
Piano
1st Sax. E♭ Alto
2nd Sax. B♭ Tenor
3rd Sax. E♭ Alto
Banjo
Violin I
Violin II
Viola
Violoncello
Bass
rit.
a tempo
f marcato
Open
I Open
I Solo
Wha wha mute
On shell of S.D.
Tria

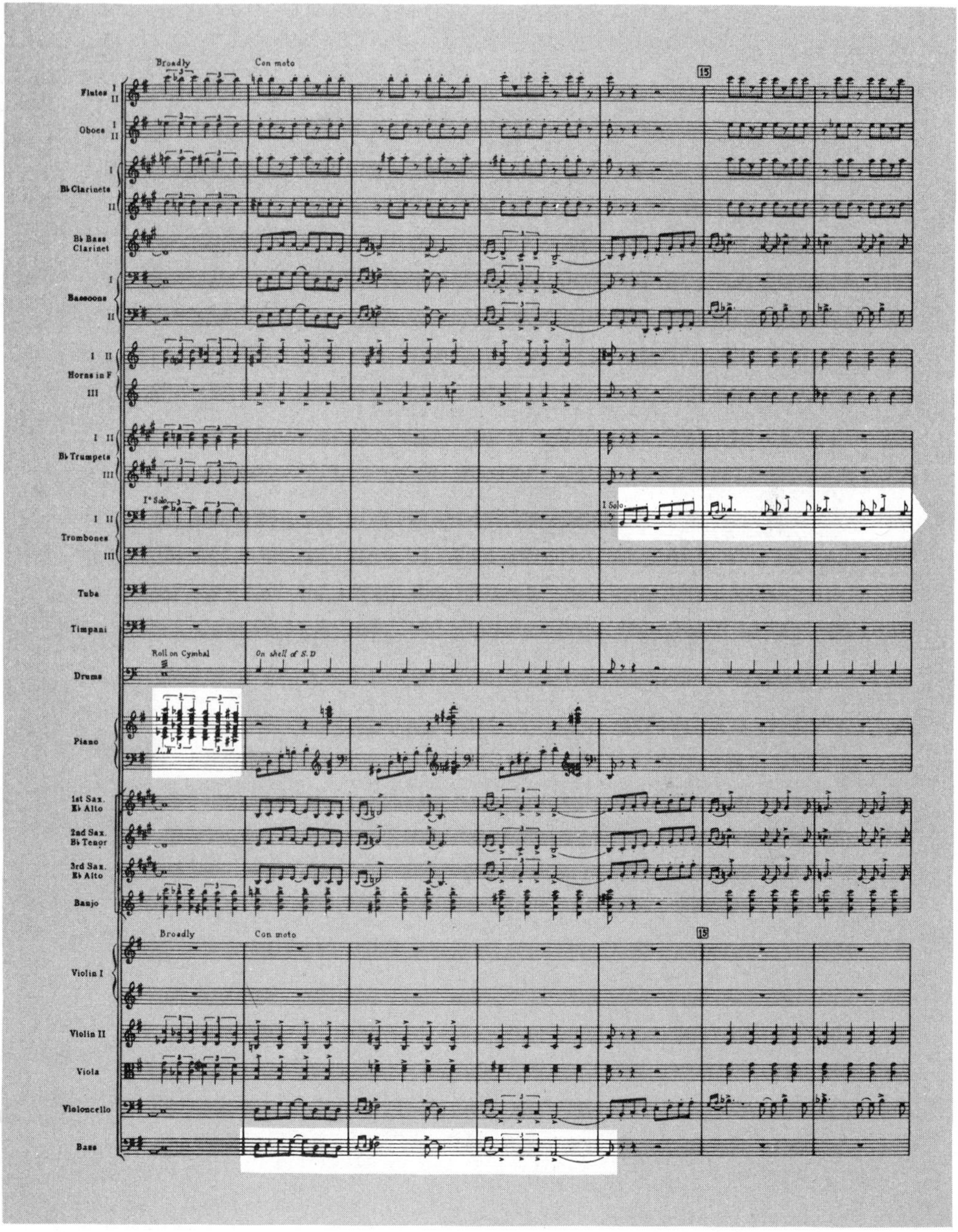

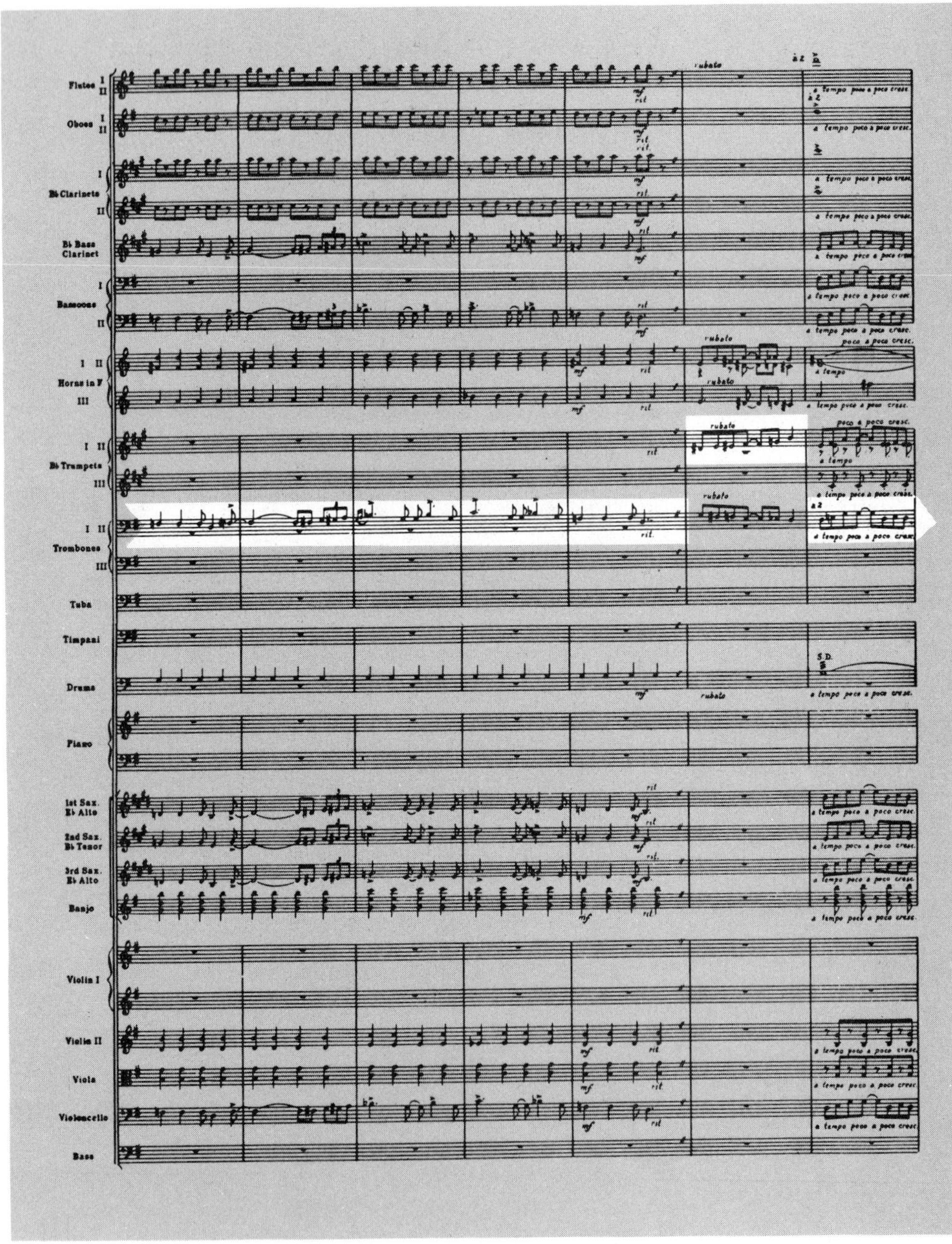

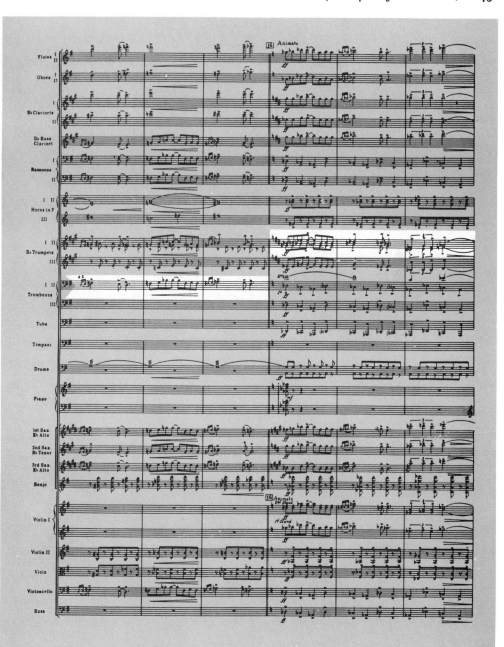

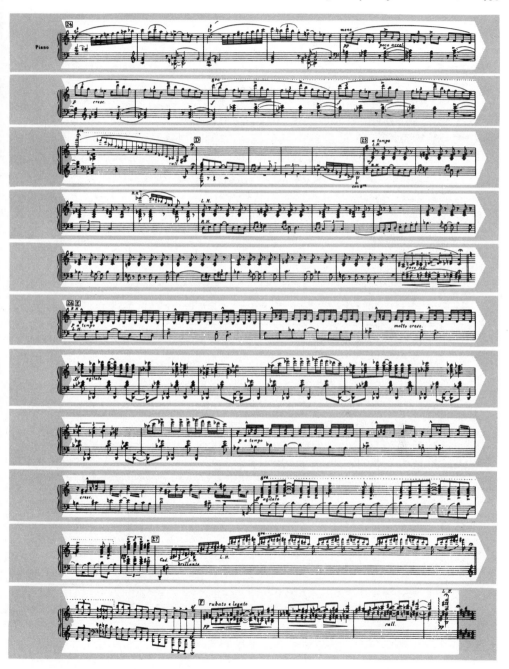

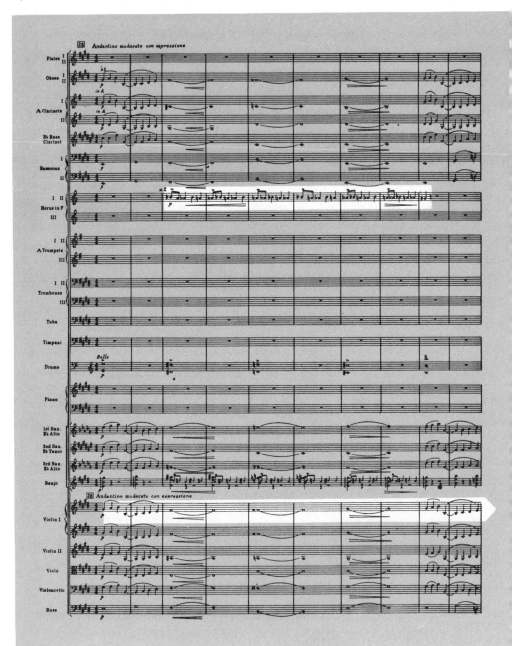

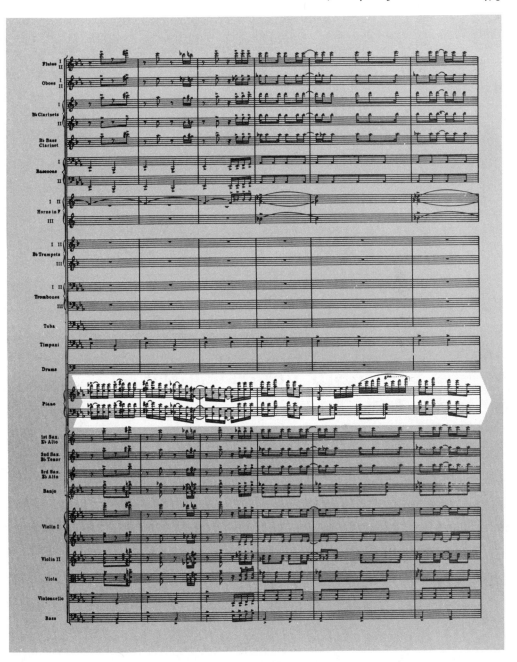

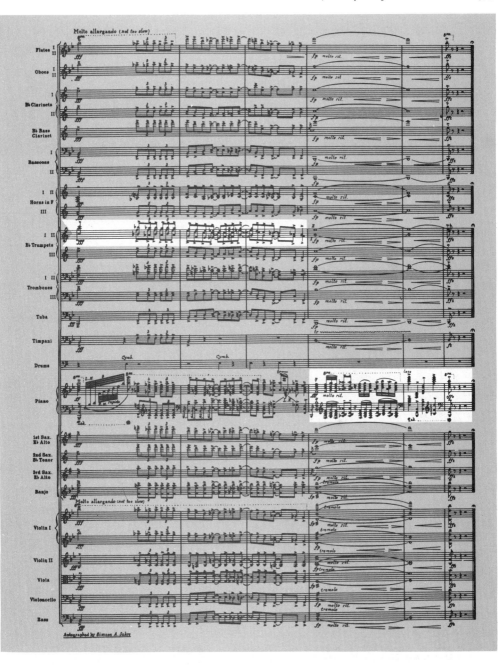

50. AARON COPLAND (b. 1900), *Hoe-Down* from *Rodeo* (1942)

Picc.
a2
Flts. I & II
a2
Oboes I & II
C.A.
a2
Clts. I & II in B♭
Bass Clt. in B♭
Bsns I & II
I & II
Hns. in F
III & IV
I
Tpts. in B♭
II & III
Trombs. I & II
B.Tromb. & Tuba
Timp
Tria.
Vln. I
Vln. II
Vla.
'Cello
Bass

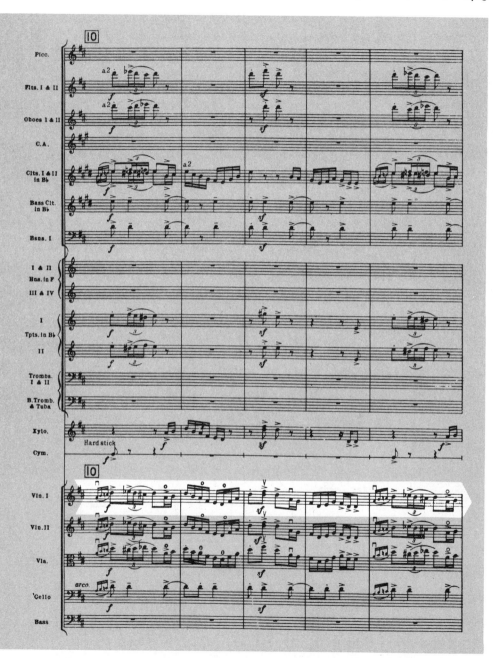

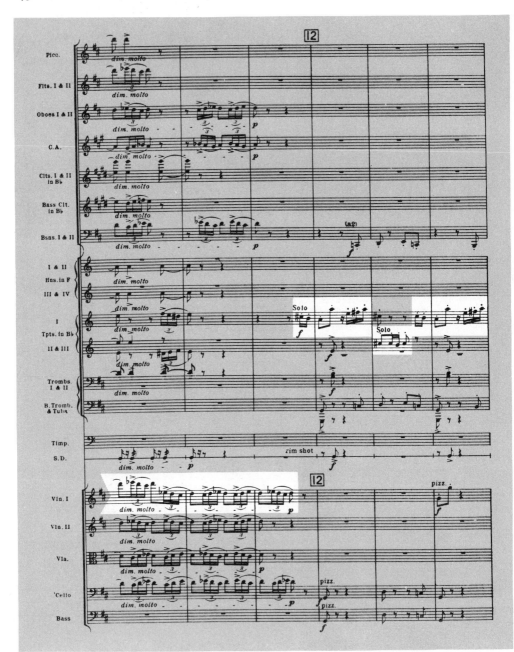

20
Picc.
Flts. I & II
a2
Oboes I & II
a2
C.A.
Clts. I & II in B♭
a2
Bass Clt. in B♭
Bsns. I & II
I & II
Hns. in F
III & IV
I
Tpts. in B♭
II & III
Trombs. I & II
B. Tromb. & Tuba
a 2
Timp.
Tri.
20
Vln. I
Vln. II
Vla.
'Cello
pizz.
Bass
pizz.

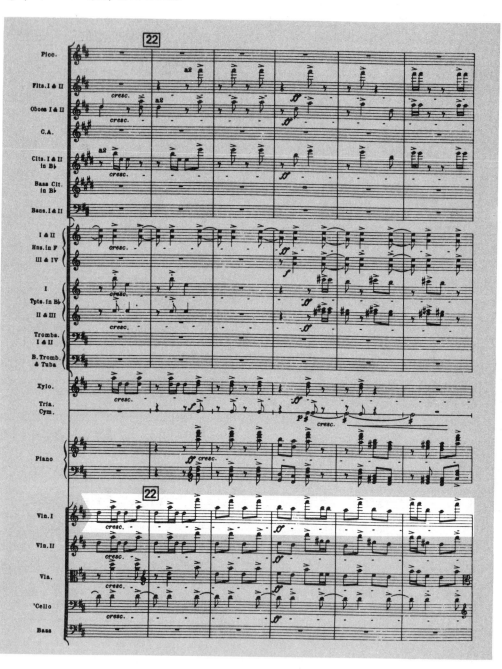

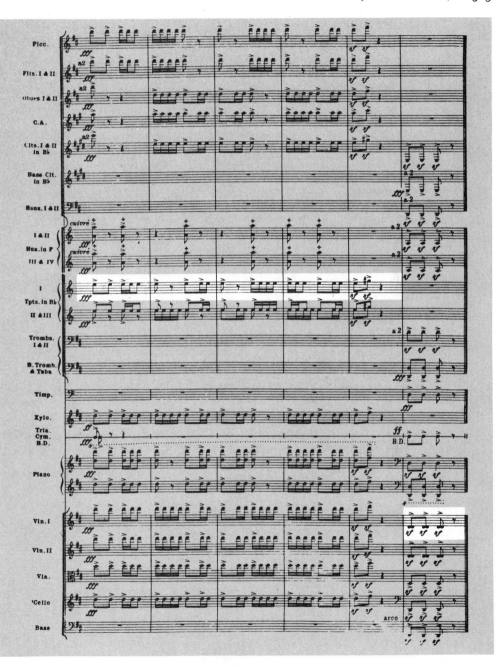

51. RUTH CRAWFORD (1901-1953),
Fourth movement from *String Quartet 1931*

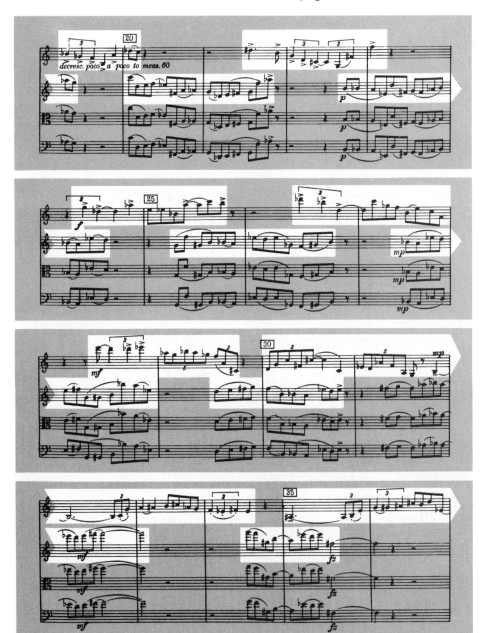

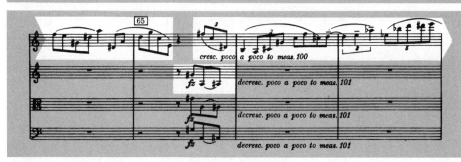

52. ELLIOTT CARTER (b. 1908), Etudes 4, 5, and 8 from *Eight Etudes and a Fantasy for Woodwind Quartet* (1950)

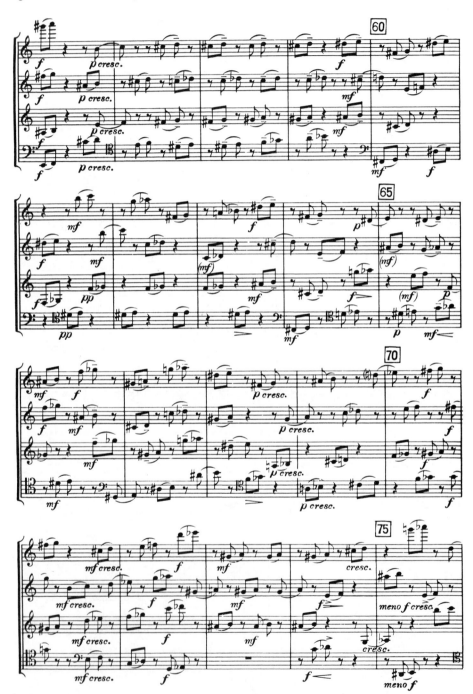

V

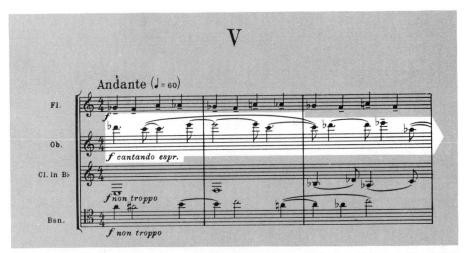

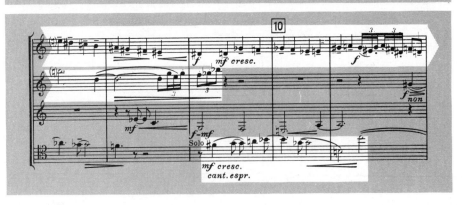

VIII

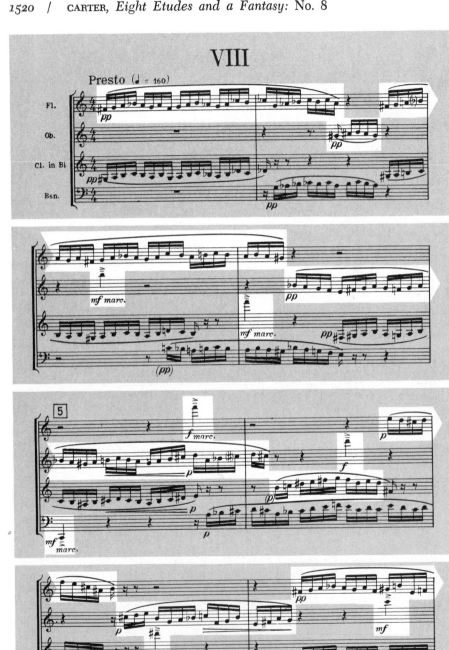

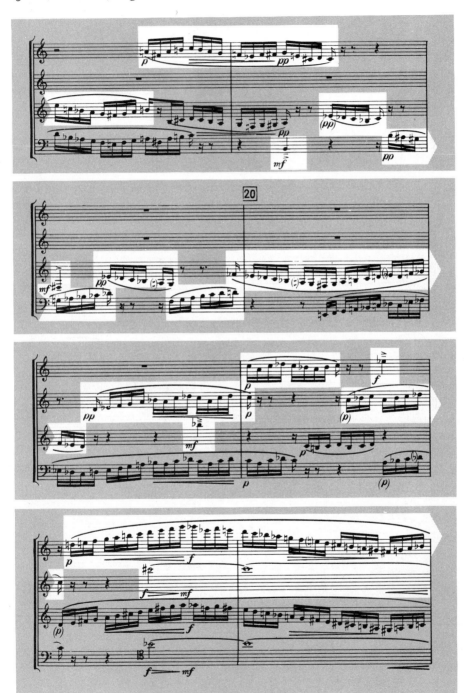

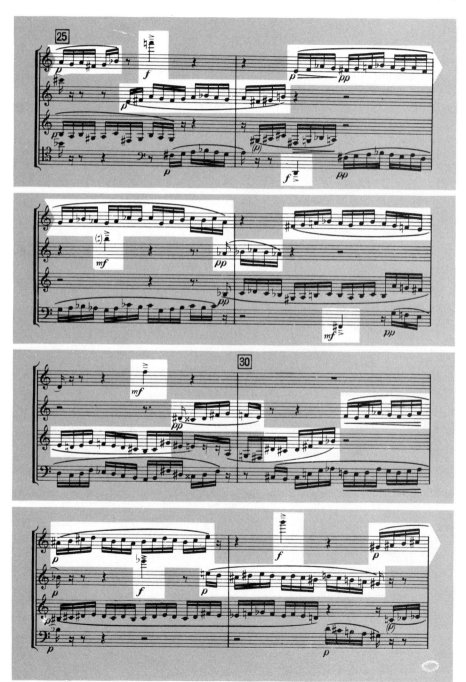

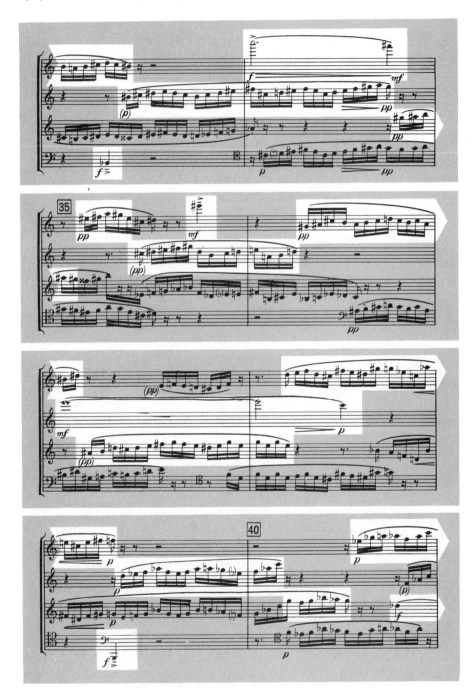

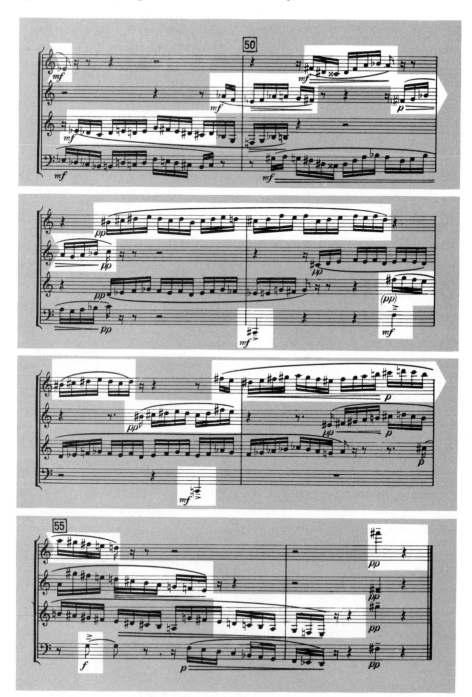

GEORGE CRUMB (b. 1929),
El niño busca su voz from *Ancient Voices of Children* (1970)

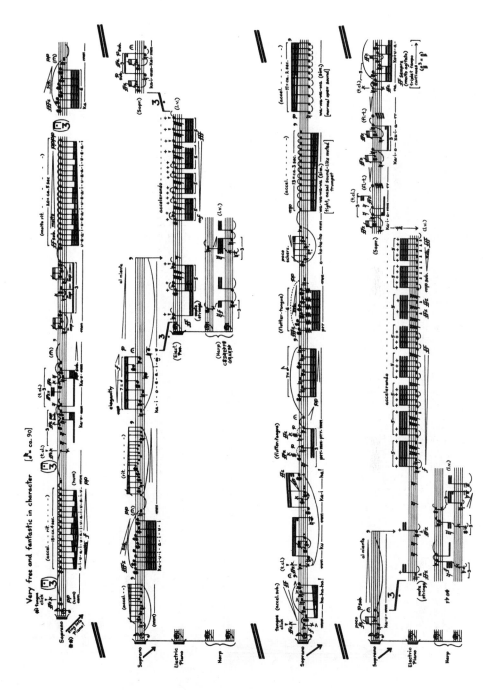

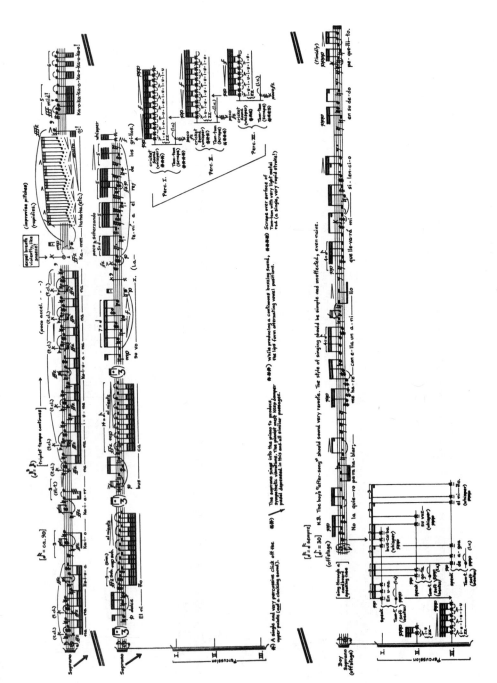

Translation

El niño busca su voz.
(La tenía el rey de los grillos.)
En una gota de agua
buscaba su voz el niño.

No la quiero para hablar;
me haré con ella un anillo
que llevará mi silencio
en su dedo pequeñito.

The little boy was looking for his voice.
(The king of the crickets had it.)
In a drop of water
the little boy was looking for his voice.

I do not want it for speaking with;
I will make a ring of it
so that he may wear my silence
on his little finger.

TEXT BY FEDERICO GARCÍA LORCA;
TRANSLATION BY W. S. MERWIN

54. MARIO DAVIDOVSKY (b. 1934), Synchronisms No. 1 for Flute and Electronic Sounds (1963)

Start this part, right after electronic cue ♯ 3, is finished.

⊕ = Air + Percussion

+ = Percussion only.

55. PHILIP GLASS (b. 1937), *Floe* from *Glassworks* (1981)

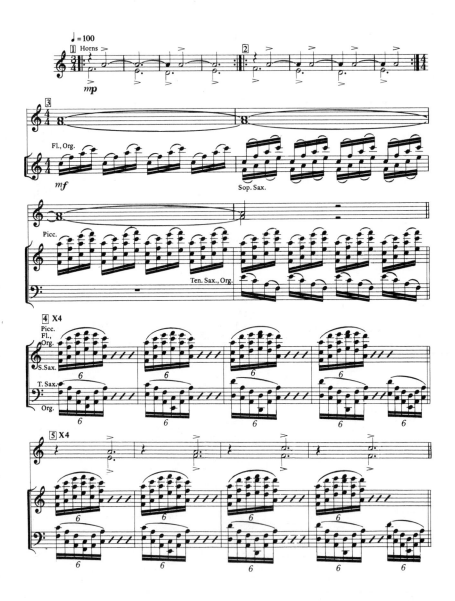

Appendix A

Reading an Orchestral Score

CLEFS

The music for some instruments is written in clefs other than the familiar treble and bass. In the following example, middle C is shown in the four clefs used in orchestral scores:

The *alto clef* is primarily used in viola parts. The *tenor clef* is employed for cello, bassoon, and trombone parts when these instruments play in a high register.

TRANSPOSING INSTRUMENTS

The music for some instruments is customarily written at a pitch different from their actual sound. The following list, with examples, shows the main transposing instruments and the degree of transposition. (In some modern works—such as the Schoenberg example included in this anthology —all instruments are written at their sounding pitch.)

Instrument	*Transposition*	*Written Note*	*Actual Sound*
Piccolo Celesta	sound an octave higher than written		
Trumpet in F	sound a fourth higher than written		
Trumpet in E	sound a major third higher than written		

Instrument	Transposition	Written Note	Actual Sound
Clarinet in Eb Trumpet in Eb	sound a minor third higher than written		
Trumpet in D Clarinet in D	sound a major second higher than written		
Clarinet in Bb Trumpet in Bb Cornet in Bb Horn in Bb alto	sound a major second lower than written		
Clarinet in A Trumpet in A Cornet in A	sound a minor third lower than written		
Horn in G Alto flute	sound a fourth lower than written		
English horn Horn in F	sound a fifth lower than written		
Horn in E	sound a minor sixth lower than written		
Horn in Eb	sound a major sixth lower than written		
Horn in D	sound a minor seventh lower than written		
Contrabassoon Horn in C Double bass	sound an octave lower than written		
Bass clarinet in Bb (written in treble clef)	sound a major ninth lower than written		
(written in bass clef)	sound a major second lower than written		
Bass clarinet in A (written in treble clef)	sound a minor tenth lower than written		
(written in bass clef)	sound a minor third lower than written		

Appendix B

Instrumental Names and Abbreviations

The following tables set forth the English, Italian, German, and French names used for the various musical instruments in these scores, and their respective abbreviations. A table of the foreign-language names for scale degrees and modes is also provided.

WOODWINDS

English	Italian	German	French
Piccolo (Picc.)	Flauto piccolo (Fl. Picc.)	Kleine Flöte (Kl. Fl.)	Petite flûte
Flute (Fl.)	Flauto (Fl.); Flauto grande (Fl. gr.)	Grosse Flöte (Fl. gr.)	Flûte (Fl.)
Alto flute	Flauto contralto (fl.c-alto)	Altflöte	Flûte en sol
Oboe (Ob.)	Oboe (Ob.)	Hoboe (Hb.); Oboe (Ob.)	Hautbois (Hb.)
English horn (E. H.)	Corno inglese (C. or Cor. ingl., C.i.)	Englisches Horn (E. H.)	Cor anglais (C. A.)
Sopranino clarinet	Clarinetto piccolo (clar. picc.)		
Clarinet (C., Cl., Clt., Clar.)	Clarinetto (Cl. Clar.)	Klarinette (Kl.)	Clarinette (Cl.)
Bass clarinet (B. Cl.)	Clarinetto basso (Cl. b., Cl. basso, Clar. basso)	Bass Klarinette (Bkl.)	Clarinette basse (Cl. bs.)
Bassoon (Bsn., Bssn.)	Fagotto (Fag., Fg.)	Fagott (Fag., Fg.)	Basson (Bssn.)
Contrabassoon (C. Bsn.)	Contrafagotto (Cfg., C. Fag., Cont. F.)	Kontrafagott (Kfg.)	Contrebasson (C. bssn.)

BRASS

English	Italian	German	French
French horn (Hr., Hn.)	Corno (Cor., C.)	Horn (Hr.) [*pl.* Hörner (Hrn.)]	Cor; Cor à pistons
Trumpet (Tpt., Trpt., Trp., Tr.)	Tromba (Tr.)	Trompete (Tr., Trp.)	Trompette (Tr.)
Trumpet in D	Tromba piccola (Tr. picc.)		
Cornet	Cornetta	Kornett	Cornet à pistons (C. à p., Pist.)
Trombone (Tr., Tbe., Trb., Trm., Trbe.)	Trombone [*pl.* Tromboni (Tbni., Trni.)]	Posaune.(Ps., Pos.)	Trombone (Tr.)
Tuba (Tb.)	Tuba (Tb, Tbaι)	Tuba (Tb.) [*also* Basstuba (Btb.)]	Tuba (Tb.)

PERCUSSION

English	Italian	German	French
Percussion (Perc.)	Percussione	Schlagzeug (Schlag.)	Batterie (Batt.)
Kettledrums (K. D.)	Timpani (Timp., Tp.)	Pauken (Pk.)	Timbales (Timb.)
Snare drum (S. D.)	Tamburo piccolo (Tamb. picc.) Tamburo militare (Tamb. milit.)	Kleine Trommel (Kl. Tr.)	Caisse claire (C. cl.), Caisse roulante Tambour militaire (Tamb. milit.)
Bass drum (B. drum)	Gran cassa (Gr. Cassa, Gr. C., G. C.)	Grosse Trommel (Gr. Tr.)	Grosse caisse (Gr. c.)
Cymbals (Cym., Cymb.)	Piatti (P., Ptti., Piat.)	Becken (Beck.)	Cymbales (Cym.)
Tam-Tam (Tam-T.)			
Tambourine (Tamb.)	Tamburino (Tamb.)	Schellentrommel, Tamburin	Tambour de Basque (T. de B., Tamb. de Basque)

Triangle (Trgl., Tri.)	Triangolo (Trgl.)	Triangel	Triangle (Triang.)
Glockenspiel (Glocken.)	Campanelli (Cmp.)	Glockenspiel	Carillon
Bells (Chimes)	Campane (Cmp.)	Glocken	Cloches
Antique Cymbals	Crotali Piatti antichi	Antiken Zimbeln	Cymbales antiques
Sleigh Bells	Sonagli (Son.)	Schellen	Grelots
Xylophone (Xyl.)	Xilofono	Xylophon	Xylophone
Cowbells		Herdenglocken	
Crash cymbal			Grande cymbale chinoise
Siren			Sirène
Lion's roar			Tambour à corde
Slapstick			Fouet
Wood blocks			Blocs chinois

STRINGS

English	Italian	German	French
Violin (V., Vl., Vln, Vi.)	Violino (V., Vl., Vln.)	Violine (V., Vl., Vln.) Geige (Gg.)	Violon (V., Vl., Vln.)
Viola (Va., Vl., *pl.* Vas.)	Viola (Va., Vla.) *pl.* Viole (Vle.)	Bratsche (Br.)	Alto (A.)
Violoncello, Cello (Vcl., Vc.)	Violoncello (Vc., Vlc., Vcllo.)	Violoncelì (Vc., Vlc.)	Violoncelle (Vc.)
Double bass (D. Bs.)	Contrabasso (Cb., C. B.) *pl.* Contrabassi or Bassi (C. Bassi, Bi.)	Kontrabass (Kb.)	Contrebasse (C. B.)

OTHER INSTRUMENTS

English	Italian	German	French
Harp (Hp., Hrp.)	Arpa (A., Arp.)	Harfe (Hrf.)	Harpe (Hp.)
Piano	Pianoforte (P.-f., Pft.)	Klavier	Piano
Celesta (Cel.)			
Harpsichord	Cembalo	Cembalo	Clavecin
Harmonium (Harmon.)			
Organ (Org.)	Organo	Orgel	Orgue
Guitar		Gitarre (Git.)	
Mandoline (Mand.)			

Names of Scale Degrees and Modes

SCALE DEGREES

English	Italian	German	French
C	do	C	ut
C-sharp	do diesis	Cis	ut dièse
D-flat	re bemolle	Des	ré bémol
D	re	D	ré
D-sharp	re diesis	Dis	ré dièse
E-flat	mi bemolle	Es	mi bémol
E	mi	E	mi
E-sharp	mi diesis	Eis	mi dièse
F-flat	fa bemolle	Fes	fa bémol
F	fa	F	fa
F-sharp	fa diesis	Fis	fa dièse
G-flat	sol bemolle	Ges	sol bémol
G	sol	G	sol
G-sharp	sol diesis	Gis	sol dièse
A-flat	la bemolle	As	la bémol
A	la	A	la
A-sharp	la diesis	Ais	la dièse
B-flat	si bemolle	B	si bémol
B	si	H	si
B-sharp	si diesis	His	si dièse
C-flat	do bemolle	Ces	ut bémol

MODES

major	maggiore	dur	majeur
minor	minore	moll	mineur

Note on Baroque Instruments

In the Baroque works, certain older instruments, not used in the modern orchestra, were required by the composers; the following list defines these terms.

Continuo (Con.) A method of indicating an accompanying part by the bass notes only, together with figures designating the chords to be played above them. In general practice, the chords are played on a harpsichord or organ, while a viola da gamba or cello doubles the bass notes.

and a bass lute (as continuo instruments).

Corno. Although this term usually designates the French horn, in the Bach Cantata No. 140 it refers to the *cornett,* or *zink*—a wooden trumpet without valves.

Taille (Tail.). In the Bach Cantata No. 140, this term indicates a tenor oboe or English horn.

Violino piccolo. A small violin, tuned a fourth higher than the standard violin.

Violone (V.). A string instrument intermediate in size between the cello and the double bass. (In modern performances, the double bass is commonly substituted.)

Appendix C

Glossary of Musical Terms Used in the Scores

The following glossary is not intended to be a complete dictionary of musical terms, nor is knowledge of all these terms necessary to follow the scores in this book. However, as the listener gains experience in following scores, he will find it useful and interesting to understand the composer's directions with regard to tempo, dynamics, and methods of performance.

In most cases, compound terms have been broken down in the glossary and defined separately, as they often recur in varying combinations. A few common foreign-language particles are included in addition to the musical terms. Note that names and abbreviations for instruments and for scale degrees will be found in Appendix B.

a. The phrases *a 2, a 3* (etc.) indicate that the part is to be played in unison by 2, 3 (etc.) players; when a simple number (1., 2., etc.) is placed over a part, it indicates that only the first (second, etc.) player in that group should play.

aber. But.

accelerando. Growing faster.

accentué. Accented.

accompagnato (accomp.). In a continuo part, this indicates that the chord-playing instrument resumes (cf. *tasto solo*).

accordez. Tune the instrument as specified.

adagio. Slow, leisurely.

ad libitum (ad lib.). An indication giving the performer liberty to: (1) vary from strict tempo; (2) include or omit the part of some voice or instrument; (3) include a cadenza of his own invention.

affettuoso. With emotion.

affrettando (affrett.). Hastening a little.

agitato. Agitated, excited.

agitazione. Agitation.

allargando (allarg.). Growing broader.

alle, alles. All, every, each.

allegretto. A moderately fast tempo (between allegro and andante).

allegro. A rapid tempo (between allegretto and presto).

allein. Alone, solo.

allmählich. Gradually (*allmählich gleichmässig fliessend werden,* gradually becoming even-flowing again).

al niente. Reduce to nothing.

alto, altus (A.). The deeper of the two main divisions of women's (or boys') voices.

alzate. Indication to remove mutes.

am Steg. On the bridge (of a string instrument).

ancora. Again.

andante. A moderately slow tempo (between adagio and allegretto).

andantino. A moderately slow tempo.

an dem Griffbrett (a.d.G.). Played on the fingerboard.

Anfang. Beginning.

anima. Spirit, animation.

animando. With increasing animation.

animato, animé. Animated.

anschwellend. Crescendo.

a piacere. The execution of the passage is left to the performer's discretion.

à plat. Laid flat.

appassionato. Impassioned.

arco. Played with the bow.

arditamente. Boldly.

armonioso. Harmoniously.

arpeggiando, arpeggiato (arpeg.). Played in harp style, i.e. the notes of the chord played in quick succession rather than simultaneously.

arrêt. Stop.

assai. Very.

a tempo. At the (basic) tempo.

attacca. Begin what follows without pausing.

attaque sèche. Sharp attack.

auf dem. On the (as in *auf dem G,* on the G string).

Ausdruck. Expression.

ausdrucksvoll. With expression.

äusserst. Extreme, utmost.

bachetti. Drumsticks (*bachetti di tamburo militare,* snare-drum sticks; *bachetti di spugna,* sponge-headed drumsticks).

baguettes. Drumsticks (*baguettes de bois, baguettes timbales de bois,* wooden drumsticks or kettledrum sticks; *baguettes d'éponge,* sponge-headed drumsticks; *baguettes mi-dures,* semi-hard drumsticks; *baguettes dures,* hard drumsticks; *baguettes timbales en feutre,* felt-headed kettledrum sticks).

bass, basso, bassus (B.). The lowest male voice.

battuto coll' arco. Struck with the bow.

beaucoup. Many, much.

Becken. Cymbals.

bedeutung bewegter. With significantly more movement.

beide Hände. With both hands.

belebend. With increasing animation.

belebt. Animated.

ben. Very.

ben accordato. Well tuned.

bestimmt. Energetic.

bewegt. Agitated.

bewegter. More agitated.

bien. Very.

bis zum Schluss dieser Szene. To the end of this scene.

Blech. Brass instruments.

Bogen (Bog.). Played with the bow.

bouché. Muted.

bravura. Boldness.

breit. Broadly.

breiter. More broadly.

brillante. Brilliant.

brio. Spirit, vivacity.

cadenza. An extended passage for solo instrument in free, improvisatory style.

calando. Diminishing in volume and speed.

calma, calmo. Calm, calmly.

cantabile (cant.). In a singing style.

cantando. In a singing manner.

canto. Voice (as in *col canto,* a direction for the accompaniment to follow the solo part in tempo and expression).

cantus. An older designation for the highest part in a vocal work.

capella. Choir, chorus.

cédez. Go a little slower.

changez. Change (usually an instruction to re-tune a string or an instrument).

circa (ca.). About, approximately.

clair. High.

col, colla, coll'. With the.

come prima, come sopra. As at first; as previously.

comodo. Comfortable, easy.

con. With.

corda. String; for example, *seconda (2a) corda* is the second string (the A string on the violin).

coro. Chorus.

coulisse. Wings (of a theater).

court. Short, staccato.

crescendo (cresc.). An increase in volume.

cuivré. Played with a harsh, blaring tone.

cum quatuor vocibus. With four voices.

cupo. Dark, veiled.

dabei. Thereby, therewith; at the same time.

da capo (D.C.). Repeat from the beginning.

dal segno. Repeat from the sign.

Dämpfer (Dpf.). Mutes.

dans. In.

dazu. In addition to that, for that purpose.

début. Beginning.

decrescendo (decresc., decr.). A decreasing of volume.

descendez le "la" un demi-ton plus bas. Lower the A-string a semitone.

détaché. With a broad, vigorous bow stroke, each note bowed singly.

détimbrée. With snares (of a snare drum) relaxed.

deutlich. Distinctly.

devozione. Devotion; affection, reverence.

dimenuendo, diminuer (dim., dimin.). A decreasing of volume.

distinto. Distinct, clear.

divisés, divisi (div.). Divided; indicates that the instrumental group should be divided into two parts to play the passage in question.

dolce. Sweetly and softly.

dolcemente. Sweetly.

dolcezza. Sweetness; gentleness.

dolcissimo (dolciss.). Very sweetly.

dolente. Sorrowful.

dopo. After, afterwards.

Doppelgriff. Double stop.

doppio movimento. Twice as fast.

doux. Sweetly.

drängend. Pressing on.

duplum. In older music, the part immediately above the tenor.

durée indiquée. The duration indicated.

e. And.

eilen. To hurry.

elegante. Elegant, graceful.

en animant. Becoming more animated.

enchainez. Continue to the next material without pause.

en dehors. With emphasis.

energico. Energetically.

entsprechend. Appropriate; corresponding.

ersterbend. Dying away.

erstes Tempo. At the original tempo.

espansione. Expansion, broadening.

espressione. With expression.

espressione intensa. Intense expression.

espressivo (espress., espr.). Expressively.

et. And.

etwas. Somewhat, rather.

expressif. Expressively.

fehlende Akkordtöne. Missing chord tones.

feroce. Fierce, ferocious.

fiero. Fiercely.

fine. End, close.

Flageolett (Flag.). Harmonics.

flatterzunge, flutter-tongue. A special tonguing technique for wind instruments, producing a rapid trill-like sound.

flebile. Feeble; plaintive; mournful.

fliessend. Flowing.

forte (f). Loud.

fortissimo (ff). Very loud (*fff* indicates a still louder dynamic).

forza. Force.

frei. Freely.

freihäng. Hanging freely. An indication to the percussionist to let the cymbals vibrate feely.

frottez. Rub.

früher. Earlier; former.

fuga. Fugue.

fuoco. Fire, spirit.

furioso. Furiously.

Fuss. Foot; pedal.

gajo. Gaily.

ganz. Entirely, altogether.

ganzton. Whole tone.

gedämpft (ged.). Muted.ʳ

geheimnisvoll. Mysteriously.

gesteigert. Intensified.

gestopft (chiuso). Stopping the notes of a horn; that is, the hand is placed in the bell of the horn, to produce a muffled sound.

geteilt (get.). Divided; indicates that the instrumental group should be divided into two parts to play the passage in question.

giocoso. Jocose, humorous.

giusto. Moderately.

gli altri. The others.

glissando (gliss.). Rapid scales produced by running the fingers over all the strings.

gradamente. Gradually.

grande. Large, great.

grande taille. Large size.

grandioso. Grandiose.

grave. Slow, solemn; deep, low.

grazia. Grace, charm.

grazioso. Gracefully.

grosser Auftakt. Big upbeat.

gut gehalten. Well sustained.

H. A symbol used in the music of Schoenberg, Berg, and Webern to indicate the most important voice in the texture.

Hälfte. Half.

harmonic (harm.). A flute-like sound produced on a string instrument by lightly touching the string with the finger instead of pressing it down.

Hauptzeitmass. Original tempo.

heimlich. Furtively.

hervortretend. Prominent.

hoch. High; nobly.

Holz. Woodwinds.

im gleichen Rhythmus. In the same rhythm.

immer chromatisch. Always chromatic.

immer im Tempo. Always in tempo.

incalzando. Pressing, hurrying.

in neuen Tempo. In the new tempo.

istesso tempo. Duration of beat remains unaltered despite meter change.

jeté. With a bouncing motion of the bow.

jusqu'à la fin. To the end.

kadenzieren. To cadence.

kaum hörbar. Barely audible.

klagend. Lamenting.

Klang. Sound; timbre.

kleine. Little.

kurz. Short.

laissez vibrer. Let vibrate; an indication to the player of a harp, cymbal, etc., that the sound must not be damped.

lamentoso. Plaintive, mournful.

langsam. Slow.

langsamer. Slower.

languente. Languishing.

langueur. Languor.

largamente. Broadly.

larghetto. Slightly faster than largo.

largo. A very slow tempo.

lebhaft. Lively.

leere Bühne. Empty stage.

legatissimo. A more forceful indication of *legato.*

legato. Performed without any perceptible interruption between notes.

légèrement. Lightly.

leggèro, leggiero (legg.). Light and graceful.

legno. The wood of the bow (*col legno tratto*, bowed with the wood; *col legno battuto*, tapped with the wood; *col legno gestrich*, played with the wood).

leise. Soft, low.

lent. Slowly.

lentamente. Slowly.

lento. A slow tempo (between andante and largo).

l.h. Abbreviation for "left hand."

licenza. With license.

lieblich. Lovely, sweetly.

l'istesso tempo, see *istesso tempo.*

loco. Indicates a return to the written pitch, following a passage played an octave higher or lower than written.

lontano. Far away, from a distance.

luftpause. Pause for breath.

lunga. Long, sustained.

lungo silenzio. A long pause.

lusingando. Caressing.

ma. But.

maestoso. Majestic.

manual. A keyboard played with the hands (as distinct from the pedal keyboard on an organ).

marcatissimo (marcatiss.). With very marked emphasis.

marcato (marc.). Marked, with emphasis.

marcia. March.

marqué. Marked, with emphasis.

marziale. Military, martial, march-like.

mässig. Moderate.

Melodie. Melody, tune, air.

même. Same.

meno. Less.

mezza voce. With half the voice power.

mezzo forte (mf). Moderately loud.

mezzo piano (mp). Moderately soft.

mindistens. At least.

minore. In the minor mode.

misterioso. Misterious.

mit. With.

M. M. Metronome; followed by an indication of the setting for the correct tempo.

moderato, modéré. At a moderate tempo.

modo ordinario (ordin.). In the usual way (usually cancelling an instruction to play using some special technique).

möglich. Possible.

molto. Very, much.

morendo. Dying away.

mormorato. Murmured.

mosso. Rapid.

motetus. In medieval polyphonic music, a voice part above the tenor; generally, the first additional part to be composed.

moto. Motion.

mouvement (mouvt.). Tempo.

moyenne. Medium.

muta, mutano. Change the tuning of the instrument as specified.

N. A symbol used in the music of Schoenberg, Berg, and Webern to indicate the second most important voice in the texture.

nachgebend. Becoming slower.

Nachschlag. Grace-note that follows rather than precedes the note ornamented.

nach und nach. More and more.

naturalezza. A natural, unaffected manner.

naturel. In the usual way (generally cancelling an instruction to play using some special technique).

Nebenstimme. Subordinate or accompanying part.

nicht, non. Not.

noch. Still.

non. Not.

nuances. Shadings, expression.

oberer. Upper, leading.

octava (8va). Octave; if not otherwise qualified, means the notes marked should be played an octave higher than written.

octava bassa (8va bassa). Play an octave lower than written.

ohne. Without.

ondegg'ante. Undulating movement of the bow, which produces a tremolo effect.

open. (1) In brass instruments, the opposite of muted; (2) in string instruments, refers to the unstopped string (i.e. sounding at its full length).

ordinario, ordinérement (ordin.). In the usual way (generally cancelling an instruction to play using some special technique).

ossia. An alternative (usually easier) version of a passage.

ôtez vite les sourdines. Remove the mutes quickly.

ouvert. Open.

parlante. Sung in a manner resembling speech.

parte. Part (*colla parte,* the accompaniment is to follow the soloist in tempo).

pas trop long. Not too long.

Paukenschlägel. Timpani stick.

pavillon en l'aire. An indication to the player of a wind instrument to raise the bell of the instrument upward.

pedal (ped., P.). (1) In piano music, indicates that the damper pedal should be depressed; an asterisk indicates the point of release (brackets below the music are also used to indicate pedalling); (2) on an organ, the pedals are a keyboard played with the feet.

percutée. Percussive.

perdendosi. Gradually dying away.

pesante. Heavily.

peu. Little, a little.

pianissimo (pp). Very soft (*ppp* indicates a still softer dynamic).

piano (p). Soft.

piatto. Cymbal; flat, even; plain, dull.

più. More.

pizzicato (pizz.). The string plucked with the finger.

plötzlich. Suddenly, immediately.

plus. More.

pochissimo (pochiss.). Very little, a very little.

poco. Little, a little.

poco a poco. Little by little.

pomposo. Pompous.

ponticello (pont.). The bridge (of a string instrument).

portando la voce. With a smooth sliding of the voice from one tone to the next.

position naturel (pos. nat.). In the normal position (usually cancelling an instruction to play using some special technique).

possibile. Possible.

pouce. Thumb.

pour. For.

praeludium. Prelude.

premier mouvement (1er mouvt.). At the original tempo.

prenez. Take up.

préparez le ton. Prepare the instrument to play in the key named.

presser. To press.

presto. A very quick tempo (faster than allegro).

prima. First, principal.

principale (pr.). Principal, solo.

punta d'arco. Played with the top of the bow.

quasi. Almost, as if.

quasi niente. Almost nothing, i.e. as softly as possible.

quasi trill (tr.). In the manner of a trill.

quintus. An older designation for the fifth part in a vocal work.

rallentando (rall., rallent.). Growing slower.

rapide, rapido. Quick.

rapidissimo. Very quick.

rasch. Quick.

rauschend. Rustling, roaring.

recitative (recit.). A vocal style designed to imitate and emphasize the natural inflections of speech.

retenu. Held back.

revenir au Tempo. Return to the original tempo.

richtig. Correct (*richtige Lage,* correct pitch).

rigore di tempo. Strictness of tempo.

rigueur. Precision.

rinforzando (rf, rfz, rinf.). A sudden accent on a single note or chord.

risoluto. Determined.

ritardando (rit., ritard.). Gradually slackening in speed.

ritenuto (riten.). Immediate reduction of speed.

ronde. Round dance; whole note (Fr.).

rubato. A certain elasticity and flexibility of tempo, consisting of slight accelerandos and ritardandos according to the requirements of the musical expression.

ruhig. Quietly.

rullante. Rolling.

saltando (salt.). An indication to the string player to bounce the bow off the string by playing with short, quick bow-strokes.

sans timbre. Without snares.

scena vuota. Empty stage.

scherzando (scherz.). Playful.

schleppend. Dragging.

Schluss. Cadence, conclusion.

schmachtend. Languishing.

schnell. Fast.

schneller. Faster.

schon. Already.

schwächer. Weaker; milder; fainter.

schwer. Heavy, ponderous; grave, serious.

scorrevole. Flowing, gliding.

sec, secco. Dry, simple.

seconda volta. The second time.

segue. (1) Continue to the next movement without pausing; (2) continue in the same manner.

sehr. Very.

semplicità. Simplicity.

sempre. Always, continually.

sentimento. Sentiment, feeling.

senza. Without.

sforzando, sforzato (sfz, sf). With sudden emphasis.

sfumato. Diminishing and fading away.

simile. In a similar manner.

Singstimme. Singing voice.

sino al. Up to the . . . (usually followed by a new tempo marking, or by a dotted line indicating a terminal point).

smorzando (smorz.). Dying away.

sofort. Immediately.

solo (s.). Executed by one performer.

sonator. Player (*uno sonator,* one player; *due sonatori,* two players).

sonné à la double 8va. Play the double octave.

sopra. Above; in piano music, used to indicate that one hand must pass above the other.

soprano (S.). The voice classification with the highest range.

sordino (sord.). Mute.

sostenendo, sostenuto. Sustained.

sotto voce. In an undertone, subdued, under the breath.

sourdine. Mute.

soutenu. Sustained.

spiccato. With a light bouncing motion of the bow.

spiel. Play (an instrument).

spiritoso. In a spirited manner.

staccatissimo. Very staccato.

staccato (stacc.). Detached, separated, abruptly disconnected.

Stelle. Place; passage.

stentando, stentato (stent.). Delaying, retarding.

stesso movimento. The same basic pace.

stimm-. Voice.

Streicher. Bow

stretto. In a non-fugal composition, indicates a concluding section at an increased speed.

stringendo (string.). Quickening.

subito (sub.). Suddenly, immediately.

sul. On the (as in *sul G,* on the G string).

suono. Sound, tone.

superius. In older music, the uppermost part.

sur. On.

suspendue. Suspended.

tacet. The instrument or vocal part so marked is silent.

tasto solo. In a continuo part, this indicates that only the string instrument plays; the chord-playing instrument is silent.

tempo primo (tempo I). At the original tempo.

teneramente. Tenderly, gently.

tenor, tenore (T.). The highest male voice.

tenuto (ten.). Held, sustained.

tief. Deep, low.

tornando al tempo primo. Returning to the original tempo.

touch. Fingerboard (of a string instrument).

toujours. Always, continually.

tranquillo. Quietly, calmly.

tre corda (t.c.). Release the soft (or *una corda*) pedal of the piano.

tremolo (trem). On string instruments, a quick reiteration of the same tone, produced by a rapid up-and-down movement of the bow; also a rapid alternation between two different notes.

très. Very.

trill (tr.). The rapid alternation of a given note with the diatonic second above it. In a drum part it indicates rapid alternating strokes with two drumsticks.

triplum. In medieval polyphonic music, a voice part above the tenor.

troppo. Too much.

tutta la forza. Very emphatically.

tutti. Literally, "all"; usually means all the instruments in a given category as distinct from a solo part.

übergreifen. To overlap.

übertönend. Drowning out.

una corda (u.c.). With the "soft" pedal of the piano depressed.

und. And.

unison (unis.). The same notes or melody played by several instruments at the same pitch. Often used to emphasize that a phrase is not to be divided among several players.

verhallend. Fading away.

verklingen lassen. To let die away.

verlöschend. Extinguishing.

vierhändig. Four-hand piano music.

viertel. Quarter (*Viertelnote,* quarternote; *Viertelton,* quarter tone).

vif. Lively.

vigoroso. Vigorous, strong.

vivace. Quick, lively.

vivo. Lively.

voce. Voice (as in *colla voce,* a direction for the accompaniment to follow the solo part in tempo and expression).

voilà. There.

vorbereiten. To prepare in advance.

Vorhang auf. Curtain up.

Vorhang fällt, Vorhang zu. Curtain down.

vorher. Beforehand; previously.
voriges. Preceding.

Walzertempo. In the tempo of a waltz.
weg. Away, beyond.
weich. Mellow, smooth, soft.
weiter. Further, forward.
werden. Become; grow.
wie aus der Ferne. As if from afar.
wieder. Again.
wie oben. As above, as before.
wie zu Anfang dieser Szene. As at the beginning of this scene.

wüthend. Furiously.

zart. Tenderly, delicately.
Zeitmass. Tempo.
zögernd. Slower.
zu. The phrases *zu 2, zu 3* (etc.) indicate that the part is to be played in unison by 2, 3 (etc.) players.
zurückhaltend. Slackening in speed.
zurücktreten. To withdraw.
zweihändig. With two hands.

Index of Forms and Genres

A roman numeral following a title indicates a movement within the work named.